For The Love of Jennie

A Tiny Love Story

Laura Ford

Skyward Publishing
Memphis, Tennessee

To my son Jason, my daughter Reagan,
To my mother Glenda and my father
Joe Ford. And to all my
friends who had
confidence in
me.

Skyward Publishing
P.O. Box 40209
Memphis, Tennessee 38174

Library of Congress Catalog Card Number: 95-68109
ISBN number: 1-881554-02-3

Painting of Major William Ray
by Laura Ford

Table of Contents

While attending college as the nontraditional student and single parent living with my mom and dad, I found solving the national deficit easier than finding a quiet place to study. No matter where I tried to hide, my two children or my mother would find me, so I decided to study in the quietest place I knew: the cemetery. Little did I know how leaning against that beautiful stone angel would change my life.

As I leaned against the monument Major had sculpted for his precious Jennie, I noticed his plot was marked with only an insignificant marker. It made me sad to see this generous man who had given so much to Hornersville so easily forgotten. I grew up with the stories about the famous Major Ray, or should I say, Buster Brown and Tige, and I was so impressed by them that my first published newspaper feature story was about Major Ray and Jennie.

Soon, these two little people not only became part of my life, but they became part of my dreams. That was when I knew I had to tell their story, and as I researched their lives through pictures, newspaper clippings, route books, and stories told by family and friends, I uncovered an amazing love story.

While I worked on the book, I thought my children were suffering from my lack of quality time with them. However, when the book was finished I found they, too, had grown not only to love these little people as I do, but my son in particular had also grown to understand them. He understood them so well, that he wanted to write a poem for the book. I was both impressed and touched when I read, "I Am a Little Person." My son said it all in a few short stanzas what I tried to say in three hundred pages.

Through my words, I want the world to know Major and Jennie as I know them in my heart. Theirs is truly *A Tiny Love Story.*

Laura Ford

I Am a Little Person

All that I see are knees
All that I hear are insults
I cannot reach the keys
I have to think of other ways

All that I know are topless trees
All that I feel are bottomless streams
I see giants over land and throughout the sea
I wish I were taller, but that's only in my dreams

All that I remember are the things that were mine
All that I dread is the loneliness below the waists of men
I now walk through the gates of heaven not as tiny, but as
divine
I now walk among the finest

and now live among the angels
and fear not of mortal men

by Jason Allen
Fifteen-year-old son
of the author

Acknowledgements

I would like to thank all of those who have helped by offering information through stories, photographs, and documents.

My thanks go to Fred Dahlinger, Circus World Museum and Library; Mr. and Mrs. H. J. Meadows, nephew of Jennie Ray; Mrs. Pat Fraser, niece of Major Ray; Mrs. El Marie Kirby who offered part of the missing link; Mr. and Mrs. Charles Miller, my great aunt and uncle; and Mary Sylvia Siverts, Public Relations Director at Brown Group in St. Louis.

Deep appreciation also goes to Mrs. Edna Allen, niece of Captain Shade Shields; Imogene Young, a great admirer of Major Ray's; and Bill and Marione Nolan, for the tapes and books on Hawaii; and thanks to the Hornersville, Missouri, community for their support.

Thanks to Kent Watkins for his expertise and generosity in helping prepare the illustrations, along with a special thank you to Stan Gibson, who was patient with me in producing a beautiful picture of me for the book. I want to also thank Curtis Steele, Associate Professor of Art, Arkansas State University, for his help in preparing the graphics and design for the book's dust jacket

Appreciation also goes to John B. Thomas for his knowledge of computers which saved my life—and my children's lives—more than once. Also, many thanks to my lawyer Wayne Wagner and his wife Charlotte, whom I have come to dearly love.

Special thanks also go to Shirleen Sando for her help in editing; and to my best friend, Gerri Farmer, who would not take credit for the fabulous final edit of the manuscript. Without her, the novel would not flow as smoothly, nor would it be as clean as it is.

I also wish to thank David and Billy Price Carroll who believed in me. Also, a very special word of appreciation goes to Diana Brown and Grovernel Grisham for their part in continually saying, "You can do it. Go for it."

Laura Ford

Chapter One

Memories

William Ray sits peering out the window into the black night, listening to the repetitious clatter of the train's wheels while thoughts of his past ramble through his mind. "Major" Ray, as he is called by the people in the professional circus circuit, ponders over the last several lonely years of his life, traveling from one town to another with a menagerie of what many refer to as human oddities.

Major stands thirty-six inches tall. He was born in Tennessee, but in 1870, at the age of ten, he and part of his family moved to the bootheel of Missouri. Two brothers and a sister, Martha, all many years older than he, remained in Tennessee.

Because he was so much smaller than his brothers and sisters, Major shared a strong relationship with his father who treated all of his children equally. Numerous long talks with his father as they rode from the small town of Hornersville to the family farm at Cotton Plant, helped strengthen Major's perception of the outside world. His father always told him the truth. He never tried to color the future in regard to Major's size and his ability to find gainful employment, attract a life's mate, or in any way live a normal adult life. His advice on love was to give God time because ". . . there is someone out there for everyone, even for a man thirty-six inches tall." He would just say, "Give it time, Willie. Give it time."

Now at thirty, Major has given it time, and he believes time is running out for him. Impatient and lonely, he yearns for someone to share his life. He aches for the same loving relationship his mother and father shared when he was growing up on that small farm.

"Excuse me, Sir," interrupts an older man wearing a dark blue porter's uniform. "Will you be wantin' anything else before I turn in for the night?"

"No," Major answers politely. "Thank you."

He quietly turns back to the window and the darkness that seems to reflect his life. He dreads retiring to his assigned sleeping car because of the unusually large man, a cruel adversary, who shares it with him.

"Smells like rain, don't you think?" asks Ephraim Sells, taking a seat next to the little man who stares out the window. "Major?" he says, when he receives no response. Ephraim Sells, a rather short but stout man with very little hair, owns one fourth interest in Sells Brothers Circus Menagerie, Inc.

"Excuse me?" Major replies. "I didn't hear you come up, and I didn't hear what you said."

"I noticed. You seemed to be a million miles away."

"I'm sorry. I was just sittin' here lookin' out the window and thinkin'." Major desperately tries to appear the proper gentleman through speech and action, but his limited schooling as a child, along with his country raising, hinders his efforts.

"Thinkin' about what?" Originally from Ohio, Ephraim likes Major's Southern drawl and often, in fun, imitates his speech.

"Oh, I don't know," Major answers. "I guess a lot about nothin' and a little about everthing."

"Major, you've been with us for over six years now, and you know, I don't think we've ever just sat down and gotten to know each other." Ephraim knows the children love Major, yet the little man never seems to have any truly close friends, especially since Frank Singleton left the company several years ago.

Singleton, a giant who stood over seven-feet, nine-inches tall, was Major's best friend. They were together from the beginning of Major's circus career with the Will H. Stowe showboat in 1881. About three years ago, Singleton left the circus and returned to his home in Kentucky, leaving behind a lonely Major Ray.

Sitting back in the lightly cushioned seat and looking at his watch, Ephraim notices it is half-past-ten. The train will arrive at Frankfort, Kentucky, early in the morning, and Ephraim needs the extra sleep, but Major needs a friend right now, and Ephraim intends to hear him out. (Or at least try to discover the reason for Major's deep depression).

"How did you get started in the circus business anyway? Everyone has to start somewhere!"

"When I was ten, my father took me to see a circus that came to Hornersville, a small town about three miles south of our farm in Cotton Plant. . . .or, I guesss I should say about ninety miles north of Memphis. Most people have never heard of Cotton Plant *or* Hornersville."

Ephraim sits carefully listening to the little man beside him.

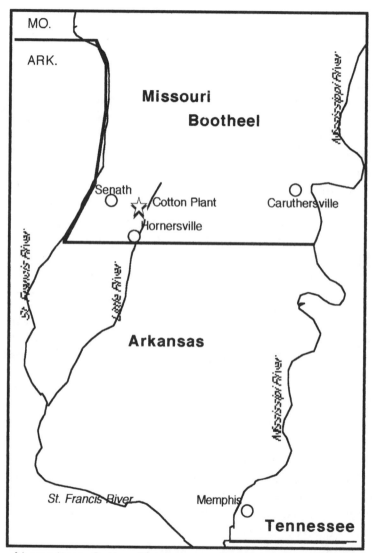

At one time, Cotton Plant was a thriving town. Now only an abandoned schoolhouse remains at its crossroads.

"While I was at the circus, I met a woman in the sideshow who was so large she could hardly move. I felt sorry for that woman, but she talked with me and helped me understand that it is not *what I am* as much as *who I am* that makes the difference. She told me I was special—not different. God made very few people like us curiosities.

"After the show when we were on our way home, I asked my pa why people were so cruel to those who were different. Pa didn't answer me right out, but while the sun was settin,' he asked if I heard the sun hit the horizon. Of course, I was waitin' to hear a noise with my ears, not listenin' for the underlyin' meanin.'"

"I gather you and your father were very close. Do you have any brothers or sisters?" Ephraim asks curiously.

"Oh, yeah. I have an older brother, John, who is the best brother a boy could have. He helped Pa more on the farm then I did, but my pa and I were still close. I have a younger sister, Sarah, who is married and lives in Holland, Missouri. I have two older brothers and a sister who live in Tennessee, but they stayed in Tennessee when we moved to Missouri. I didn't grow up with them like I did with John and Sarah. My older sister, Martha, writes to me real often."

"Are any of them as small as you?"

"No. They're normal. In fact, they're all tall and thin. I was the only one who came up with a glandular disorder or somethin' like that."

"That still doesn't tell me how you got into the circus business."

"Oh, that happened when Pa died." Sadly, he continues, "It happened in the field one evening, just before dark. I remember because Pa and I had just gotten back from Hornersville with a load of supplies to fix the fence.

He and John headed to the back field while I took some things in to Ma.

"I'll never forget holdin' Pa in my arms tryin' to hang onto his life, and I was sobbing as I watched him tryin' to hold on too. We both knew we were fightin' a losin' battle. Even then he was tryin' to help me understand a simple but beautiful truth. The sun was settin' so beautifully. Its colors of red and orange illuminated the field where we sat, and that's when Pa made me promise to take care of Ma and Sarah. Pa looked at me and said, 'Willie, the sun is settin', and if you listen close enough, you can hear it hit the horizon. Did you hear it?'

"It was then that I knew the answer to his question, and I heard the sun hit the horizon for the first time that night. I've heard it every night since." A tear rolls down Major's cheek. Swallowing hard, he continues facing the window, trying to hide his sorrow from the man sitting next to him.

Ephraim feels a lump form in his throat while he listens to Major's story. "What was the answer?"

"People look at me as bein' different, but it's up to me to show them that I can do anything I want. Nothin' can hold me back from livin' a normal life because my life is what I make it."

"You said you decided to go into show business after your father died."

"Yeah, I went to work for the Will H. Stowe Circus after I heard they were comin' to Caruthersville, a small river town about thirty miles from our farm. It was a showboat circus that traveled along the river. The Stowes were wonderful employers. They were very young and had two small children, Birdie and Willie, who were constantly into trouble."

"Didn't the Stowe Circus burn and sink just outside Memphis back in '82?" Ephraim asks, noticing a sad expression form on Major's face. "I remember reading something about that."

"Yeah." Major turns to the window again as his mind is flooded with the painful memories of losing his circus friends in the dreadful showboat fire.

Not wanting to pry any further and hearing the hurt in Major's voice, Ephraim changes the subject. "Yep, sure smells like rain."

"Yeah," Major agrees. Pulling a gold watch and chain from his pocket, he looks at the time. "It's getting late. I guess we'd better turn in for the night. Least ways, before it starts to rain."

Ephraim stands next to Major and gently places a hand on his shoulder. "If you need someone to talk to, I'm always available. Now, why don't you go on and try to get some sleep."

Together they walk to their sleeping cars. Stopping at his door, Major watches Ephraim disappear down the narrow hall to his own quarters. Then, Major reluctantly opens the door and enters the the cramped sleeping car he shares with the giant. He hopes the old ogre is asleep. He doesn't need another confrontation with him before finally settling down for another restless evening of nightmares about a burning ship and agonizing cries for help.

Chapter Two

Human Oddities

Major has worked six seasons with Sells Brothers and May 7, 1890, marks the beginning of the seventh. Traveling almost two weeks, the circus train carrying the performers and animals from Columbus, Ohio, finally arrives in Frankfort, Kentucky.

The air in the train car is cool and damp as Major wakes to the sound of rain peppering the metal roof. Although it is May, the weather seems unseasonably chilly this morning, but the lower berth Major occupies is warm and cozy. He dreads climbing from his comfortable cocoon composed of several heavy blankets and a goose down pillow. As he wipes the sleep from his weary eyes, his thoughts wander to the many years of circus performing and constant traveling that often make him want to go home; however, he is paid well and he enjoys most of the people he works with. Those he doesn't like, he avoids.

Major hears the canvas men and other roustabouts unloading the numerous tableau and cages. "Hey, grab that side!" yells one worker. "Don't let that cage slip or we'll have monkeys runnin' everywhere!" screams another.

"Well, I guess it's time to get up and look at another day," Major tells himself as his feet hit the cold floor. Many of the performers share compartments when they travel, sometimes as many as two or three to a berth. When the train arrives, tents are raised while kinkers clean and prepare for the day's performance.

Everyone looks forward to weekends because the circus is dark on Sundays, and they can stay at a hotel. Good, soft, motionless beds and a hot bath are always a welcomed sight and gratefully accepted.

Major shares his quarters with several sideshow performers who are less than desirable, and often obnoxious. Many times they carry resentment and anger because of their looks, but there are a lot of sideshow performers Major loves like he loves his own family.

"Outta my way, Squirt!" bellows a huge man moving faster through the coach than the cramped quarters allow. He purposely brushes Major aside, stepping on the little man's foot in the process.

"Ouch! Hey watch it!" squawks Major, rubbing his throbbing foot. "One of these days Robinson, you're gonna get it!"

"Yeah, and who's gonna get me? You? Ha, I've picked fleas off my dog bigger than you."

"I may be little, but remember it was the flea that practically wiped out a whole city with the black plague. You'd just better watch it," Major tells the circus giant who shares the stage with him.

Major misses the days when another circus giant was his most trusted friend and companion. Colonel W.O. Robinson, the giant who continually embarrasses and threatens him, is one of many giants who has replaced Singleton during the past three years, but Robinson is—by far—the worst.

Robinson's large seven-foot, seven-inch frame towers over Major, but Major never backs down from him. The giant's constant conceited attitude often offends many performers who come near him. His dark complexion and suave manner make him irresistible to women, but it also accentuates his poor and excessive egotistical self-centeredness.

"Come on, Major!" Ephraim Sells orders. "Time is money!" Ephraim strikes the side of the train car with his hand. Startled by the noise, Major jumps slightly.

"I'm comin'," Major yells, and, grabbing his bag, joins the others who wait outside the train. The steps leading from the train are steep, so he places his bag beside him, sits on the edge, and like a child, scoots down them one at a time.

The rain has stopped and Henrietta Moritz waits at the bottom of the steps with her umbrella at her side. Major conquers the last step, rises to his feet, and looks Henrietta in the eye.

Henrietta stands about thirty-seven and one-half-inches tall. Her hair reminds Major of corn silk, and her eyes are almost as blue as his. She is a nice companion for Major, but their relationship is strictly platonic. There is no romance; only love between friends. Henrietta joined Sells Brothers a year ago.

"Are you ready?" Henrietta asks shyly.

"Yeah, I'm ready. Let me help you with your bag." Major picks up the bag at her feet and struggles to carry the two pieces of luggage to the sideshow tableau where tents, clothing, and props are stored. Major and Henrietta desperately try to miss stepping in the large mud puddles surrounding them.

"Oh, ain't they cute?" Robinson teases, pointing to the little couple walking across the circus lot.

"Don't pay any attention to him, Henrietta. He may be big, but he's short on brains and manners." She giggles and continues walking faster to avoid a confrontation with the giant, who seems to constantly hover over them.

"What did you say, Squirt?" Robinson asks, following close behind them.

"I said you were short on brains. Along with being dumb, are you deaf too?" Major yells. Henrietta grows more uncomfortable, fearing the giant's anger and what he might do to Major.

Major runs around the corner of the sideshow tableau. The giant follows close behind. Major avoids slipping in the mud and manages to stay a few steps in front of his pursuer. Major suddenly spots Dick, the huge elephant and main attraction for Sells Brothers, being watered only a few feet away from him. When Major first joined the troupe, Dick was one of the first to greet him, and the two quickly became friends. Instead of a boy and his dog, it was a man and his elephant.

"Hey, Dick!" Major yells. The huge pachyderm turns to look at him. Somehow Dick and Major understand each other.

"All right! You've had it this time, Squirt!" Robinson roars, grabbing at the little man standing near the great elephant.

"*Now*, Dick!" Major shouts. The huge animal lets out a loud, high pitched roar and sprays a trunk of cold water over the threatening giant. Robinson gasps while the trunk of the elephant wraps around his waist, holding him until Dick's trainer appears.

Major runs laughing while Robinson stands swinging his arms madly about, trying to escape the elephant's tight grip. A few performers and many sideshow people stand nearby, watching the amusing performance. Various other little people, hired as clowns by Sells Brothers, bend over hysterical with laughter and applaud the act that deserves a standing ovation. Waving to the huge, drenching wet man, Major walks back to the sideshow tableau, yelling over his shoulder, "Remember the black plague!"

"It's about time someone put that man in his place!" says Lizzie Brown to her twin sister, Liddie, who stands watching the amusing incident. The two women—identical Albino twins with hair as white as cotton and eyes a strange pink—were with the show before Major joined in 1884. The only way to differentiate one from the other is that Lizzie always wears a brooch given to her by a suitor who was killed three years ago in a circus act, while Liddie, married to a kinker, wears a gold wedding band on her left hand.

"What happened Robinson? Fall in a puddle, or did it rain heavier on your side of the lot?" Liddie giggles, lightly poking her sister in the ribs.

"Major, you're lucky that man didn't catch you. You're going to have to watch your back now," Henrietta says, feeling another drop of rain fall on her face.

"Oh, he don't scare me none," Major states confidently. He once more picks up the bags, and he and Henrietta proceed toward the sideshow tent.

With a team of elephants ready to stretch the ropes and raise the massive canvas in place, the tent city appears within minutes. Major watches as Dick, the lead elephant, roars orders to the others. The tents are up, everyone is in place, and the parade leads the townspeople down the muddy streets to the circus entrance.

The rain continues off and on throughout the day, but the crowds still come, and the audience is delighted with the performance. Business is great. When the circus closes that evening, it is time to load the train destined for Shelbyville, Kentucky.

WITH THE LAST ANIMAL LOADED AND THE LAST tableau secured, the menagerie boards the train for the seventy-eight mile trip to Shelbyville. Major sits in the seat near the window and stares aimlessly off into space. The rain stopped hours ago, and the stars shine brightly across a black sky. His mind wanders once more as he again sits alone, reevaluating his fast-paced, but lonely life.

"Pa?" Major whispers softly, speaking to his father's spirit as he often does. "You said there's someone for everyone. You said love would come and that I would just have to wait patiently for it. Well, I have waited, and I'm still lonely. When will I meet her, Pa? When?" A star streaks across the sky as if a sign from Heaven.

"Did you make a wish?" asks Lizzie, standing next to him.

"What?" he says startled, not realizing what she asked.

"You always make wishes on falling stars, and if you believe hard enough, you'll get your wish."

"Yeah, I saw it, and He already knows what my wish is."

"You sound awfully depressed Major. What is it?" she questions sympathetically and sits beside him. The seat that faces them is empty and most who see the two people talking realize it is a private conversation and find another place to sit.

Lizzie is wise and understanding. She and Major often sit for hours talking about a variety of things from love to politics, (the last subject usually taboo for women, but Lizzie is a good listener and Major enjoys it.)

"Do you still miss him?" Major nods toward the beautiful brooch she wears on her collar.

"All the time," she answers sadly. "Do you have someone you miss?"

"Yeah, I think so."

"What do you mean, you *think* so?" She is slightly confused by his answer.

"She's somewhere, but I don't know who or where she is," he says, watching the moon reflect off Lizzie's cotton white hair. "Me and Pa used to talk a lot. One of the things we talked about was love and marriage. Pa always said that there was a lovin' companion for everyone, even for me, but I'd have to wait for her. Then, one day she would just be there."

"Sounds like your pa was a pretty wise man."

"Yeah. He was."

While Lizzie and Major talk, they fail to notice Liddie, who strolls into the dimly lit passenger car and sits in the empty seat directly behind them. Always interested in gossip, her ears are forever open for some kind of news, good or bad, that she can spread. Unlike her twin sister who is kind and generous, Liddie is persnickety and carries a grudge against everyone, including Major.

"How about Henrietta? She's your size. You two are good friends and seem perfect for one another," Lizzie asks, still unaware of her sister's presence and eavesdropping mindset.

"Naw, Henrietta is... well, just *Henrietta.* I don't feel that kind of love for her. Do you know what I mean? I love her, but I'm not *in love with her.* Ya know?"

"Yeah, I know exactly what you mean." Lizzie thinks of the man she loved and feels deeply sorry for Major. "I want that again, myself."

"Finding her isn't all that troubles me," Major confesses. "There's something else."

"What?" Lizzie asks curiously.

"It's a secret I've kept with me for years and that could very well affect any relationship that I might have with a woman."

Liddie immediately moves a little closer, straining to hear the conversation behind her. "What *is* this secret?" she asks herself.

"I don't understand," Lizzie tells Major. "What could be so bad that it would affect the loving relationship between two people?"

"When I was younger, but not too young, . . . "

Liddie moves closer as the secret unfolds. Suddenly, the lanterns in the the car swing back and forth, casting a yellow hue through the interior of the compartment. The noisy clatter of the steel wheels on iron tracks increases to an almost deafening tone as the train travels through a long dark mountain tunnel. "What is it?" Liddie mutters to herself, aggravated as she strains harder to hear what is being said.

"Lord help!" Lizzie exclaims loudly. Her voice carries fully as the train rolls out of the dark tunnel, and the passenger car is quiet once more. "I don't blame you. I think I'd have a hard time accepting *that* myself."

"What?" Liddie swears under her breath. "Dad-burn tunnel!"

Lizzie realizes Liddie is sitting in the seat directly behind them, and quickly lowers her voice. She hopes her twin sister did not hear the conversation. "Are you *sure?*" she asks Major. "Maybe you're mistaken."

"No, I'm sure. I told you it was bad." Major holds his head in deep sadness and continues searching for advice, "What should I do?"

"I don't know," she replies. "But I do know I wouldn't want anyone to find out about it—least ways until you're ready for it to be known."

An hour passes while they continue to confide in one
another. The train rounds a sharp curve, bringing the end
cars into view. Staring out the window, Major notices a
bright sickeningly familiar glow coming from one of the
cars. Standing on the seat to get a better look, he presses
his face against the cold, hard glass.

"The train's on fire!" he cries. Panic stricken, his
thoughts roll back to a different time and place when a
huge steamer, fire rising all around, sent many friends and
loved ones to their untimely deaths.

"What is it?" Lizzie shouts. She looks out the window
and sees the end of the train glowing in the night like the
bright, orange tail of Halley's Comet.

Suddenly, the train stops, pitching the passengers forward and onto the floor like rag dolls. "It's the twenty-six
tableau!" Major hears a canvas man cry. Luckily, the car
contains only sideshow equipment, but the fire is still a
threat to the remaining cars on the track.

"Quick! Get those cars unhooked from it!" the engineer
yells. "It'll have to burn out on its own!"

Major sees men running to the end of the train.
Fighting the heat, they try desperately to separate the cars
to restrict the fire to one car only. The train lunges
forward a few more feet and, again, suddenly stops. The
tableau is pulled from the rest of the cars.

Several hours later the only thing left is the tableau's
steel frame, like the remains of an animal in the desert,
picked clean by scavengers. Major watches the elephant
trainer unload Dick and fasten chains to his harness. The
chains are then attached to the huge steel frame, and Dick
is ordered to remove the hot metal from the tracks.

"Pull, Dick! Pull!" Major hears the elephant's trainer
yell. "Pull, Dick! C'mon, pull!" The huge animal's muscles
bulge while he strains to remove the heavy frame. Major

watches as Dick finally pulls the burning car, along with the tableau, off the tracks and leaves it abandoned.

Standing near the massive elephant, Major sees the chains unfastened from his harness. Dick bows his head and gently nudges Major with his trunk. Lifting Dick's ear and scratching it, Major praises him, "Good boy, Dick! You're a good boy! You did good!"

The earth seems to shake beneath Major's feet as the elephant is led to his stall. The cars are once more connected. Finding Lizzie near the front of the train, Major says good night and retires to his sleeping car.

The train rocks endlessly like a cradle, and soon it lulls Major to sleep. During the night his dreams are not invaded by the fiery nightmares that usually overtake his subconscious mind. Instead, he is visited by a beautiful, little fairy queen. Although he cannot see her face, he senses her kindness and goodness. She brings him peace. Tranquility. Love.

Chapter Three

Wishes and Winds

Days seem to fly by as the circus travels west. The nightly visits from Major's dreamland fairy queen continue, making his life brighter, bringing hope that he will meet her in the next town. He never sees her face, but he can feel the warmth and goodness emanating from her. The bright angelic light from her little wings blind him, but he always wakes to darkness around him. Major believes his father is speaking to him through his dreams, telling him to be patient because his time for happiness is nigh.

It is dawn, June 9, and the Sells Brothers train rumbles its way loudly into Kansas City, Missouri. People crowd the station to watch the circus unload its menagerie of animals and acts. The sun rises to a beautiful morning as Major steps off the train, ready for another performance.

"Good morning!" Allen Sells calls out in a cheerful greeting to Major. Allen is next to the youngest of Ephraim's brothers. Unlike Ephraim, Allen is tall and thin. The clothes he wears are not suave and sophisticated like a circus owner, but rugged and worn because he trains horses. He looks more like a cowboy than a businessman.

"Yes, it is a good morning, indeed!" says Major, drawing a deep breath and stretching his arms. "I just believe this is gonna be a wonderful day!"

"Hey, Squirt! You're awful chipper today. What's up?" asks Robinson, stepping off the train.

"Yeah, I am, and you know what? Not even someone as hollow-headed as you can mess it up for me!" Major replies, undaunted. Smiling, he hurries to catch up with the clowns who are walking toward the fairgrounds. The fairgrounds, in most places where the circus performs, are located near the tracks, making it easy to load and unload the train.

"Wait for me!" Major yells, running to catch up with four men just ahead of him. William E. Burkee, Spader Johnson, George Kline, and Charles Bliss are clowns who work with the circus. Although they are dressed in civilian clothes, their actions provide tell-tell clues to their occupation.

"Robinson's not bothering you again is he?" asks Burkee, a skinny little fellow who lifts his arms in a boxing position as if ready to fight in a ring. "If he does, I'll . . . I'll . . . I'll . . . well, I don't know what I'll do, but I'll do something!" he says, defending Major. Slowly he lowers his thin arms, causing the others to guffaw.

"I'm sure you'd just scare the pants off him," quips Kline, a larger man, but still no match for the giant they tease about.

"You're a lot braver than me!" raves Johnson, a Dwarf, not much bigger than Major. "Weren't you afraid he would break your bones if he caught you?"

"Naw, he's no problem for me!" Major boasts, standing among the four comic musketeers.

"Oh! That's right! Since the other day, we should be calling you David!" Bliss teases. His bright orange-red hair is comical enough, and he has no need for a wig. With just a smear of white make-up, and a red nose, he becomes a true clown. "I hear you knocked him down with one shot! *Of water that is!*"

"Ahh, I couldn't have done it without Dick, my faithful pachyderm!" Major laughs. "I can handle Robinson. He's nothin' more'n a big balloon—full of hot air!"

Still laughing, the five men continue walking toward the fairgrounds, passing a troupe of Japanese gymnasts who are speaking in their native tongue. The Imperial Japanese Troupe: Tukeno, Ingowa, Yastora, Tomokichie, Unakichie, and Homokichie practice their act on the dry lot. The troupe joined Sells Brothers on May 14, while performing in Mt. Vernon, Indiana.

"Amazing," Major says. "How in the world do they jump around like that so easy?"

"I want to know how they twist their tongue to talk like that!" Bliss declares.

Major sees people running here and there, setting up tents, game tables, food carts, and banners. Performers locate costumes and practice their acts in any area large enough to accommodate them. Animals are put into larger cages so they can stretch their legs before they are fed. The circus is a place of wonder for Major, and each day he thanks God for the chance to be a part of it.

The clowns finally find their tent near the sideshow tableau and begin dressing for the big parade that will soon make its way through town. Major waves good-bye to the clowns and retires to his own tent to prepare for the day's performance. Walking in, he trips over a large rope stretched across the tent entrance, and falls face-first onto the hard ground.

"Are you all right, Major?" asks Mrs. Turpin, the Long-Haired Lady. Her hair, although tied in several knots, falls all the way to her waist. When brushed out, however, the golden strands of fine silk seem to flow on forever—down her back, and across the floor, like Rapunzel in the fairy tale. Her act includes a flock of birds which love to sit on her fingers and nest in her hair.

"Yeah, I'm fine. Just a little embarrassed, that's all," Major replies, letting the beautiful woman help him to his feet. He notices a small blue finch nestled inside her hair, as if hiding from predators. "Did you know you have a bird in your hair?" he teases.

"I know, and there's not much tellin' what else you'll find in there either." She laughs and brushes the dirt from his little trousers with the palm of her hand.

"Thanks, Mrs. Turpin. I appreciate the help."

"Have any of you seen Maggie this mornin'?" asks Ned Daniels as he enters the sideshow tent. Ned is the sideshow's Spotted Man, who is always full of news. He was born with an array of birth marks that resemble leopard spots. They are dark brown, almost black in color, spaced about two to three inches apart, and cover his entire body.

"No, I haven't seen her," Major replies. "Why, what's she done now?"

Miss Maggie Day is the Circassian, or Russian Lady, with the sideshow. A huge woman in her mid thirties, Maggie speaks with a foreign accent and insists on keeping Ephraim upset with her constant fighting with men.

"I hear she had some poor man on the ground last night before we left, beating the wale out of him because he wouldn't buy one of her pictures," Ned explains.

"I don't know what they are going to do with that woman, but she and a few others around here are really puttin' our show in a bad light," Liddie complains.

"Now, Liddie. It's not our place to pass judgement on people," Lizzie tells her twin sister, while trying to feed and groom the Demon Boy, a deaf mute. He was obtained by Sells Brothers a year ago after news spread about a man who owned a wild, demon-possessed child whom he kept caged in his barn on a farm in the Tennessee hills. Because of the boy's inability to speak or hear, he had been abused and knew no love. Sells purchased him from the farmer for twenty-five dollars and placed him in the sideshow. The child is severely retarded, but responds positively to kindness.

"I wonder who would give up a young boy like this? Come here, Boy," Major orders. He hands the child a piece of peppermint from his pocket. "All he needs is love and affection."

The boy snatches the candy from Major's hand and pops it ravishingly into his mouth. His actions are as a wild animal's, but even a wild animal, at times can be tamed. The boy knows that when he is placed inside the cage for the day's performance, he is to act like a wild, demon-possessed boy, and he does what is expected of him quite convincingly.

Major walks around the sideshow tent and catches the distinct odor of whisky a few feet away. He knows it is Captain Baldwin, the Armless Wonder.

"What are you doin' sneakin' around here, Midget?" Baldwin shouts, his speech slurring slightly while he holds a bottle of whiskey between his feet and continues taking a few more swigs.

"I'm just trying to get ready for the show," Major replies, looking at the man lying against the large tent post in a pile of hay.

Baldwin uses his nimble legs and feet to replace the arms he does not have. From birth, he never knew what it was like to have arms; therefore, he doesn't miss them. The fact that he doesn't look like other people gives the Armless Wonder an excuse to constantly drink. His obnoxious behavior and nonexistent bathing habits bother Major, so he always tries to avoid him.

"Major?" Henrietta calls from the opposite end of the tent.

"I'm comin'!" Major yells, grateful for the excuse to leave the man and his bottle alone. "I guess I'll see you around, Baldwin." Shaking his head in disgust and waving his hand as a retreating gesture, Major joins Henrietta near the end of the tent where they stand on display for the world to gawk at.

"I should've come in the back way to avoid Baldwin," Major says to himself as he approaches Henrietta, who is already on the stage.

"It's almost time for the gate to open," she announces. "We'd better get ready."

Major hears the parade nearing the lot. The sound of John Stein playing the huge calliope, with upbeat time and melody, filters through the air. From the open canvas door, Major watches as people follow the parade to the fairgrounds. They scramble to look at everything available to them, hungry to see the likes of which they've never seen before.

"Here they come! Get ready!" Major yells, climbing up the back stairs of the stage platform.

It is afternoon. The air in the tent is already stifling. Major wipes the sweat from his brow with a white hand-kerchief he takes from his pocket. Henrietta stirs the hot air with a delicate, floral lace hand fan. A soft breeze occasionally brings the smell of popcorn and roasted peanuts through the tent, offsetting the revolting stench of animals and straw that permeates the canvas.

Several hours pass, along with scores of people who stop to stare, tease, and laugh. Maturing with the circus, Major has learned how to work the crowd with quips of wit and a few dance steps.

"Hey, little guy, is that your wife?" an older man asks, curious. His gray beard hangs neatly along his chest, completely covering the white cotton shirt he wears beneath a gray suit.

"No. Is that *your* wife?" Major points to the fragile woman standing next to the old gentleman. The bonnet covering her gray hair is securely tied beneath her chin, making sure gusts of wind do not blow it off her head and expose her gentle skin to the harsh sun.

"Yes, Sir, she is, and the best darn wife a man ever had!" he answers proudly, squeezing her tightly. "Are you married?"

"No, Sir, but I hope to be one day."

"She'd make a pretty wife for you," says the farmer's wife, looking at Henrietta, who blushes. "You know it's not good for a body to be alone through life; it just wasn't the way the good Lord meant it to be."

"Yes, Ma'am. I agree with you, but I'll know when I find her, and I have a feelin' she's not far away."

"I hope not, honey," the elderly woman tells Major. Her husband places a steady hand under his wife's elbow to encourage her to exit the tent of strange characters.

"Good-bye and good luck to you, Little Man!" the farmer exclaims as he and his wife leave the sideshow tent.

The elderly couple is the last to leave before closing for an hour's break. After picking up an apple and a cold glass of lemonade, Major strolls to the backyard—an area reserved for the circus family to eat, rest, and play.

Sitting at a small table reserved for Major and several other little people in the circus, he thinks about the elderly couple who spoke so nicely to him. The way the old man held carefully to his wife's arm, making sure she didn't stumble, reminded him of his own parents. How he loved to watch his mother and father as they fussed over one another, always making sure the other was happy. Suddenly, a gust of wind blows his handkerchief from the table.

"Come back here!" Major mutters, chasing the piece of white cloth as it blows across the grounds. He follows it, grabbing and stumbling in an attempt to halt its wayward journey, until it stops under a bench outside the Big Top.

"Gotcha!" Major says aloud, picking up the handkerchief and putting it in his pocket. Looking up, he notices two little black-heeled boots hanging in mid-air. His eyes continue to follow a tiny image, silhouetted by the sun, that seems to radiate a heavenly glow. "Oh, my!" he stammers. "Oh, my!"

"Excuse me?" a frail, polite voice interrupts his curiosity.

The voice of an angel speaks to him as he discovers a beautiful little lady sitting on the bench with a Bible in her hand. Major kneels at her feet, mystified by her beauty and grace. It's *her*, and he knows it. She's the tiny fairy queen who slips into his dreams each night, comforting him and releasing him from the nightmares that have plagued him for so many years.

"It's *you*," he stammers again.

"I'm sorry, Sir. I have no idea what you're mumbling about, but would you please stand up! You're making me nervous!" She quickly looks around to see if anyone is watching.

"Oh, I'm sorry. I didn't mean to stare," Major replies apologetically. He stands and brushes the dirt from his trousers. "I'm Major William Ray, Ma'am. I work for the circus. I don't think I've ever seen you around here before. Are you new?"

"Me? Oh, no. I'm just here to see the sights with my family. They're over there looking at the animals. I just became tired and needed to sit for a while."

The young lady slips from the edge of the bench to stand only an inch taller than Major. Her dark hair, neatly tied back with a pink ribbon, hangs loosely down her back. Her bangs are cut short and delicately curl on top of her head. Her large, dark brown eyes and long eyelashes mesmerize him.

Major's stomach is but a field of butterflies, and his heart beats so loudly he fears she can hear it pounding its frantic beat through his chest. He stands unable to say a word as he beholds her incredible beauty.

The young woman, nervously clutching her Bible in her left hand and extending her right, softly says, "Hello, I'm Miss Jennie Meadows."

Chapter Four

Jennie

Major holds Jennie's hand, lightly places a kiss on her tiny wrist, bows deeply, and says, "I'm honored to make your acquaintance, Miss Meadows."

The instant their eyes meet the temperature rises. It isn't the heat from the June afternoon that puts the red glow in Jennie's cheeks, but the idolizing stare from the man she just met.

When Jennie speaks, Major hears only the voice of an angel. She is perfect from head to toe, and Major feels like the world has just been placed at his feet. He wants to know more about the miniature woman standing in front of him.

"My hand please, Mr. Ray," she insists, pulling her creamy-white hand slowly from his grasp.

"Oh! Forgive me, sweet lady. Your beauty overwhelms me and I forget my manners," he speaks poetically to the porcelain doll-like young woman standing before him.

To Major, Jennie has the face of an angel, thus he does not even notice the weakness in her left eye that causes her partial blindness. Major realizes Jennie is what his

father said he would find. She is his light at the end of the
tunnel; his salvation. Now that he's found her he knows
he must win her heart.

"Please, won't you join me?" Jennie asks, nodding
toward the bench behind her.

"Thank you. I'd like that." Offering his hand, Major
helps her onto the high wooden bench. The splinters jutting from the rough oak planks pull at her skirt as she
comfortably seats herself. Major springs himself up with
his hands and sits next to her.

A hot breeze fills the air, blowing a few loose strands of
hair across Jennie's face. She gently pulls them away and
tucks them neatly behind her ear.

Major notices the delicately painted floral pattern trail-
ing down the front of her pale pink skirt. The detailed
work of lilacs and violets reveal the handiwork of an
artistic genius.

"I can't help noticing the beautiful flowers on your
dress. Did you paint them?" he asks, trying to start a
conversation.

"Yes, I did. Thank you."

"Are you from around here?" Major asks.

"No. Well, I'm from Yates Center. That's about thirty-
five miles west. Where are you from?"

"I'm from a little town in Missouri called Cotton Plant."

"How did you find your way into the circus?" she in-
quires curiously. Jennie stares uncontrollably into Major's
pale blue eyes where she can almost see her own image
staring back.

"Before my father died, I promised to take care of my ma
and younger sister. This was the only way I could do that,
so I joined a circus nine years ago, and here I am."

"How exciting!" she exclaims and looks toward some
children who are busy playing with a large barrel ring,

chasing it as it rolls across the dusty ground, slinging the gritty soil into the air.

"Jennie?" yells a large, rugged-looking man. Major sees her father walking across the circus lot toward them. His long stride and heavy feet kick up the dry earth behind him, sending clouds of dust swirling like dirt devils.

"Jennie?" he shouts again.

"Yes, Papa. I'm here," she answers loudly.

The man's voice thunders across the lot like the roar of a huge black bear echoing through the forest. Major watches as the six-foot-four-inch, barrel-chested, large-boned he-man approaches the bench where Major sits with Jennie. He cringes at the thought of the man's overpowering hand throwing him through the heavy canvas tent behind them like a baseball hurling toward a stack of bottles.

"Who is this man, Jennie?" he asks gruffly.

"Papa, I want you to meet, Major William Ray. He works for the circus, and Papa look! He's small like *me*." Jennie's eyes light up as she introduces Major to her father. "Mr. Ray, I 'd like you to meet my papa, Layton Meadows."

"Pleased to make your acquaintance, Sir," Major says politely. "You have a beautiful daughter," he adds. He would like to impress her father, but at the same time he doesn't want to seem too forward.

"It's a pleasure, I'm sure," Layton replies, unimpressed and slightly agitated. He shakes Major's extended hand.

Major tries unsuccessfully to continue the conversation intelligently. "Your daughter says you're from Yates Center. Have you lived there long?"

"Jennie," Layton orders without answering Major's question. "The rest of the family is about ready to head for the Big Top. You need to say good-bye to Mr. Ray here and come on and join us."

"All right, Papa," she answers. "You go on and I'll be there in a minute."

"Don't keep us waitin' girl," he almost growls, unhappy with Major's presence. "We'll wait over here for you, in front of the Big Top."

"It was nice to have met you, Mr. Meadows." Major tips his hat, but Layton only grumbles as he stomps toward the entrance of the main tent.

The Kansas air is always hot and dry; however, the looks from her father as he stands waiting for his daughter create a chill so cold that even a wood furnace could not chase away.

"You better go, Miss Meadows. Your pa is growing impatient, and I don't blame him." Major stands and places his hands around Jennie's sixteen-inch waist to help her down from the bench. He is sure he will find some sign of tiny fairy or angel wings protruding from the middle of her back, but he sees none. He sees only the angelic form standing before him: soft, beautiful and as fragile as the petals on a rose.

"Please, Mr. Ray," she begs politely. "Call me, Jennie."

"Yes, Miss Jennie. And you may call me Major."

He watches her glide across the circus lot toward her father. The way her feet seem never to hit the ground, she has to be a fairy queen or an angel. But, *where are her wings?*

"I'll meet you here after the show," he calls to her. Jennie nods and disappears into the Big Top.

Major's heart pounds in his chest and he feels exhilaration the likes of which he has never known. As blood races like floodwaters through his veins, he can barely contain his happiness.

"Whoopee—Pa—*whoopee!* I found her. I *found* her, Pa! She's the one! At last, I've found her!"

ENTERING THE LARGE TENT WHICH HOUSES THE MAIN attraction, Jennie is astounded by its size. Sound from the great calliope echoes throughout the enormous canvas hall and pierces the atmosphere. Layton takes his daughter by the hand, making sure she is not lost in the throng of people filling the tent.

Jennie's mother, Julia, younger sister, Maggie, and two brothers, Harding Joel and Harold Dewitt, follow close behind. Julia holds Harold's hand tightly as she tries to keep her youngest son near her and out of trouble.

"Let's sit here," Layton says, carefully lifting Jennie onto a nearby bench. "Can you see, baby?"

"Yes, Papa," she answers, but her thoughts are not all on the circus performers who hang from the high trapeze, or the clowns whose painted faces entertain the cheering crowd.

Layton notices Jennie's inattentiveness. "Jennie, look at the beautiful horses," he says, knowing how she loves the large loping animals. "Those women sure can ride."

Lovely women attired in shiny spangled clothes ride the bare backs of strong horses outfitted with colored plumes and rhinestone harnesses. Excited, Jennie claps her tiny hands together as the equestrians perform in the center ring.

"Oh, my!" she cries, as her thoughts are pulled from the vision of the little man she met previously to the colorful costumes and amazing horses in the ring. "They are so beautiful! How I wish I could ride like that."

Layton sighs with relief when he successfully directs his daughter's thoughts to the circus. Jennie keeps her eyes on the circus acts, while her father keeps his eyes on her.

Suddenly, a troupe of clowns appear in the center ring. "Oh, Papa!" she squeals. "Clowns!" Jennie's eyes light up with excitement and total amusement as she becomes enchanted with it all.

Several little people are among the colorful group. Jennie has never seen so many individuals *like her* in one place, and her thoughts turn once more to Major who waits outside the Big Top for her. Layton notices that Jennie has grown quiet, and he begins to worry.

Jennie is enjoying the show, but she will be glad when it ends because now, meeting Major excites her more than the circus and its colorful surroundings.

IT IS EVENING AND THE SHOW IS OVER. MAJOR receives permission from Jennie's father to introduce her to the circus performers, including Dick the elephant. Dick is to Sells Brothers what Jumbo is to Barnum.

Major has never met anyone like Jennie, nor has Jennie met anyone quite like Major. Jennie is full of life, never allowing her height to hinder her want for freedom and her dreams for a normal grown-up life. Major discovers that his little fairy queen is strong in her convictions and not afraid to speak out against anyone who tries to thwart her hopes and aspirations.

The circus tents, silhouetted by the red setting sun, create a beautiful romantic backdrop for Major and Jennie as they stroll across the fairgrounds to join her parents at their wagon. The more Major and Jennie talk, the closer they become. They are kindred spirits, thrown together by an act of God and a white handkerchief.

"Miss Jennie," Major says, watching her brown hair blow in wisps across her face. Her hair falls freely from the pink ribbon that tries to tame it. "I have never known anyone like you. Although I've only known you for one short day, my heart seems to have known you for a lifetime. The moment I saw you sitting there on that bench, I knew you were the one—the one woman in my life my father assured me so many times that I would find someday."

"Wait! Slow down!" Jennie cries. "Major, I want you to know that I'm truly honored and flattered, but I don't *know* you. It's not proper for a gentleman to speak to a lady in this fashion, especially when the gentleman has just met her."

"I'm sorry if I've offended you, but Miss Jennie," Major pleads, touching her porcelain-white cheek, "I love you with all my heart, and I have loved you even before this day."

"Sir, it's not *proper* for you to speak to me in this manner. However, I would like very much to know you better," Jennie responds softly and with a smile. "Maybe you could write to me?"

"Can I?" he asks impatiently.

"I would be delighted to receive your letters." She smiles coyly. "And I will anxiously answer every single one."

"Until I see you again, Miss Jennie." Major bows deeply and places a delicate kiss on her wrist. Embarrassed, but flattered, she tries to pull her hand from his.

"I'll write to you often," Major promises, still clinging to her hand.

"Jennie!" her father says, approaching from behind, curious to see what is keeping her.

She blushes slightly and hopes her father didn't hear any of their conversation or see the light kiss Major planted on her wrist. "I'm coming, Papa. Good-bye, Major. I look forward to your letters."

Major holds on until the tips of her petite fingers pass through his own. He watches her father lift her into the wagon to join her brothers and sister. Suddenly, after realizing he has no address, Major shouts across the lot, "Where do I mail them?"

"What?" she stands and yells back. Her father pulls at the hem of her dress, trying to make her sit.

"Your letters! Where do I send them?"

"General delivery! Yates Center!" she answers loudly.

A lantern hanging on the wagon lights their way through the Kansas City streets as they begin their journey home. Major watches the light fade and darkness slowly take its place.

Chapter Five

The Secret

Major tosses and turns throughout the night while
visions of Jennie sweetly invade his dreams. Her face
glows with innocence, as her perfect figure waltzes through
his mind.

Morning finally arrives. While the circus roustabouts
and performers raise the tents, Major composes a letter to
Jennie:

Leavenworth, Ks.
June 10, 1890

My Dearest Little Jennie,

*I seat myself to write you this letter of pure
and loving words. I hope this letter finds you
and your family well and in good health, for I
am not. My heart bleeds as it pleads to see
your most kind and caring face. My hand
aches to feel the warmth of your most soft and
gentle hand.*

*I know we met only yesterday, but I have
waited an eternity to see you, to touch you, to
know you. It would please me greatly if you
would answer the letters I sit to write. We*

will travel far this day, but you will be for-
ever nearby, on my mind and in my heart. . . .
Enclosed please find route for three weeks.
                              I am yours truly,
                              Major Willie Ray
                              Sells Brothers Circus Inc.

Because the letters bring him closer to Jennie, Major
continues to write, hoping they will build the long distance
relationship he struggles so hard to keep. The train stops
in another small town during the early morning hours,
and unable to concentrate on his work, he takes pen in
hand to etch another poetic letter announcing his most
perfect and divine love for her:

                                   Bethany, Mo
              June 14, 1890
My Dear Little Jennie,
        I seat myself to write you a second time.
We have traveled long and hard and are now
in a small town in Missouri called Bethany. I
hope this letter finds you and your family
well.
        The weather is hot and sometimes most
unbearable, but with you on my mind and in
my heart the weather is tolerable. You my
dear, sweet Jennie, are like a cool drink of
water to my thirsty lips, and I only anticipate
the day when I may quench my soul with
your divine presence . . .
                              I am yours truly,
                              Major Willie Ray
                              Sells Brothers Circus Inc.

While Major travels through Missouri and into Iowa, he waits impatiently for a letter from Jennie, a letter that will verify his beliefs in her feelings toward him. Soon his ability to write to her daily becomes impossible because of his hectic schedule. With no word from Jennie, he grows weary, but never stops writing.

Tuesday, June 23, Major again sits down to compose a letter to his beautiful Jennie. The early morning air, already hot and sticky, causes a trickle of sweat to drop from his forehead to his hand, making it difficult to hold the pen. Suddenly, he hears the voice of Lewis Sells, "Major? Major, where are you? Have you seen Major?" he asks Lizzie Brown, who is standing near the opposite side of the sideshow tent.

"Yeah, he's around back, I believe," she replies.

"Major?" Lewis yells again.

"Here," Major answers. "I'm over here."

Major watches Lewis, the second oldest Sells brother, round the corner of the tent, holding a letter high in the air. His dark, well-tailored suit enhances his tall, middle-aged, athletic form. Lewis is only a few years older than Allen, but while Allen is rugged and manly, Lewis is more scholarly. As treasurer and third partner for Sells Brothers, Lewis' ability to crunch numbers and balance the books keeps him busy.

"I have a letter here for a Major William Ray. Hmm, I smell the lovely fragrance of a woman. Rose water, maybe?" Lewis grins and holds the letter close to his nose, just out of Major's reach.

"Oh, come on! Give it to me! Please?" Major pleads, growing impatient. His eyes brighten and his stomach flutters. He knows it is a letter from Jennie.

"All right, but don't take too long. The show starts in a few minutes."

"I won't be long," Major assures him. Holding the letter carefully in his hand, he notices the delicate handwriting across the front. He gently opens the precious envelope and reads . . .

> June 17, 1890
> *My Dear, Dear Major,*
> *I seat myself to answer your most welcome letter that came to my hand this grand and glorious morning. I was most pleased and delighted to read your most kind and loving words of affection toward me. I, too, have thought about you often and waited most patiently for your letter. I would be most pleased if you would continue to write, and I will answer each letter quickly and lovingly.*
> *I must tell you, Papa was not at all excited at the arrival of your letter, but Mama has quieted his words, and he now says nothing, critical or otherwise . . . .*
> *God be with you until we meet again.*
> *From your loving Jennie.*

Major's eyes brighten as he reads Jennie's letter over and over again. Placing it in his shirt pocket, close to his heart, Major sits to answer her letter:

> Lincoln, Nebraska
> June 24, 1890
> *My Dear Sweet Jennie,*
> *I seat myself to answer your most kind and welcome letter that came to my hand today. You have made me the happiest little man in the world, for I have the friendship of a*

kind and gentle woman. The weather is warm and business has been fair. On Sunday, Peter Collins, a canvas man, was drowned while bathing. It was on that same night that a magnificent electrical storm appeared in the sky, and a tornado formed and frightened most of the circus people from the hotel to the train cars. It was most horrifying, but the thought of you pulled me through the frighting evening . . . .

My dear, sweet Jennie, I know we have known each other for only a short time, but I believe that fate and God have placed us together. I wish to most honorably court you, for my heart is heavy without you by my side. I dream of nothing but you as your beautiful face appears to me each night. I wish to marry you, sweet Jennie, if you will have me . . . .

I wait patiently for your letters and your answer to come to rest in my hand.

I am yours Truly,
Major Willie Ray
Sells Brothers Circus Inc.

A month has passed since Major met and fell in love with the woman in his dreams. He continues to write Jennie once, sometimes twice a week. He writes of his undying love for her and his loneliness without her.

Their long distance romance continues, and with each letter Major receives from Jennie, he misses and wants her more and more.

July 1, 1890
My Dear, Dear Major,
I seat myself to answer your most wel-
comed letter that came to hand yesterday. I
hope this letter finds you well, as we are all
healthy.
While I was horseback riding today, my
thoughts were not on the speech I am expected
to give at the farmers picnic and parade next
week. Images of you and memories of our
conversation seemed to occupy my time. I
find myself imagining you with me at the ice
cream parlor during warm summer evenings.
Papa brought me a little white rat the
other day. He is so cute. Maggie was afraid
of him, but she soon realized he was nothing
like the field mice that run through the attic.
Harding Joel has been worried about his sick
jackrabbit, but . . .
God be with you,
Your loving Jennie

A long month and many letters later, Major again asks
Jennie to marry him. She accepts his proposal with delight, and even though he too is delighted at her accep-
tance, his secret again invades his conscience, and he
realizes that soon she must be told.

UNCOMFORTABLE IN THE CROWDED WASHROOM floor
of his sleeping coach, Major decides to sit in the dining car
to await the trains arrival in Trenton, Missouri. Gathering
his clothes around him, he carefully steps over several
gamblers who have invaded his sleeping car, along with his

berth, and heads for the door. Stretching to reach the
latch which is positioned high above his head, Major lifts
it, but the strong wind from the moving train makes it
almost impossible to move. Placing his shoulder to the
door, he gives a hard shove and opens it. Neither the noisy
roar of the engine nor the clatter of the iron wheels
awaken the sleeping gamblers inside.

The air is hot but still welcome as it blows Major's lightweight body around like a leaf in a March wind. Re-
gaining his footing on the dark, steel grid below, he
carefully reaches for the door on the opposite car.

Major is ready for a struggle to get into the dining car,
but the door swings open with surprising ease. "Come on
in, Little Man. You're gonna get blown clear off the train if
you don't stay inside," says the young black porter who is
standing on the opposite side.

The tables lining each side are adorned with white
tablecloths. Four chairs are positioned, two on each side
of the table. A few people are in the diner, although the
pre-dawn hours restrict the items being served. Coffee is
available, and Major orders a cup as he sits down next to
the window. Staring out, he sees only a moonlit
landscape stretching into the distance. The moon's
radiant light mysteriously reflects off a coyote chasing a
rabbit as the rabbit tries desperately to hide from its
predator.

Major directs his attention to the letter he holds tightly
but carefully in his hand. After reading it several times, he
places it on the table in front of him and quietly sips his
coffee. The train rocks back and forth as it travels down
the tracks. Ignoring its hard rocking motion, he
concentrates on the letter in front of him.

"Major?" Lizzie says, suddenly appearing beside him.
"Feel like company?"

"Sure, sit down and make yourself comfortable." Major points to a chair across from him.

"Another letter from Jennie?" Lizzie asks, looking at the letter on the table.

"Yeah. She said she'll marry me, Lizzie." His voice fills with sad confusion.

"That's wonderful. You wanted to marry her, didn't you?"

"Yeah, I love her with all my heart, but Lizzie, what will happen when she finds out about—*you know?*" referring to the secret locked deep inside of him that has haunted him for so long. "I know I have to tell her, but *how?*"

"She may already know," Lizzie answers. Her head drops, and she looks at the floor, trying to avoid Major's eyes.

"What do you *mean* she may already know?" he cries accusingly. "How? *I* haven't told her!"

"I know, but I think Liddie may have told Jennie's mother."

"How did Liddie know? I only told you. Did you say somethin' to her?"

"No! I didn't say anything, but she was close enough to hear that night. After the train came out of that noisy tunnel, I saw her sitting directly behind us, but I was almost sure she didn't hear anything."

"Then, what makes you think she did hear us?"

"Because she told me she thought Jennie's mother should know about it."

"Did she say she knew what it was we were talking about?" he drills, trying to discover the extent of Liddie's knowledge of their conversation. "Did she come right out and repeat our secret?"

"No, but . . ." The morning sun reflects orange against Lizzie's snow-white hair as Major looks up, staring in disbelief at what she is telling him. "Major, you need to tell Jennie before her mother or someone else does."

"I know. But *how?*" He looks out the window as if he will find the answer in the shadows of the trees or inside the dusty abandoned buildings that whiz by.

"Write her a letter. Let her know everything. Explain it all—the circus, the people, the life, your love . . . and your secret."

"I can't tell her *that* in a letter," he sighs. "What if she already knows?"

"Tell her you need to talk to her, that is, if her mother hasn't already told her. Just ask if anything was said. You'll know soon enough, and if it makes a difference and she won't marry you, then she wasn't good enough for you. But, if she says it doesn't matter . . . she'll always love you and you'll know her love is real and forever."

The train slows as it nears Trenton. The sun peers over the horizon to reveal a beautiful morning. "I'll write as soon as we get set up. Thanks, Lizzie. You're a good friend," Major says, and after placing the letter from Jennie in his inside jacket pocket, he waits for the train to stop.

MOST OF THE WORK IS DONE AND THE CANVAS CITY is in place. Major searches for a quiet spot to compose his letter to Jennie. Everywhere he goes someone seems to send him scurrying. Finally, he locates a wooden crate lying between two tents. The front of the crate has been removed and lies nearby. Pieces of straw are scattered around and about it. A couple of its thin wooden slats are cracked or broken. Major strains to turn it over so he can use the bottom as a table on which to write a letter of love to his sweetheart.

Because of the size of his hand, the pen he writes with tilts to one side, making his hand cramp as he tries to carefully and poetically, compose his letter. Major thinks about the words he will place on the paper in front of him, the significance of the information he is about to reveal and the importance of its secrecy. He begins to write:

> *(Only let your parents see this)*
>
> Trenton, Mo.
>
> *July 28, 1890*
>
> *My Dear Little Jennie,*
>
> *I seat myself to answer your most kind and ever welcome letter, which came to hand yesterday morning and found me in good health and leaves me the same. I do hope and trust this may reach you soon and find you and your parents, brothers, and sister in the best of health as well . . .*

Major stops writing for a moment. Dipping the tip of his pen into the ink well in front of him, he listens to the sounds around him. A few gamblers stand on the opposite side of the canvas tent discussing the strategy for cheating people who will visit the circus today. Repulsed by the conversation, and knowing Jennie's spiritual strength, Major decides to tell her a little about the unholy activities surrounding the business where he works. Once more, he takes pen in hand to continue:

> *There are a few things I believe you should be aware of before you position yourself at my side...*

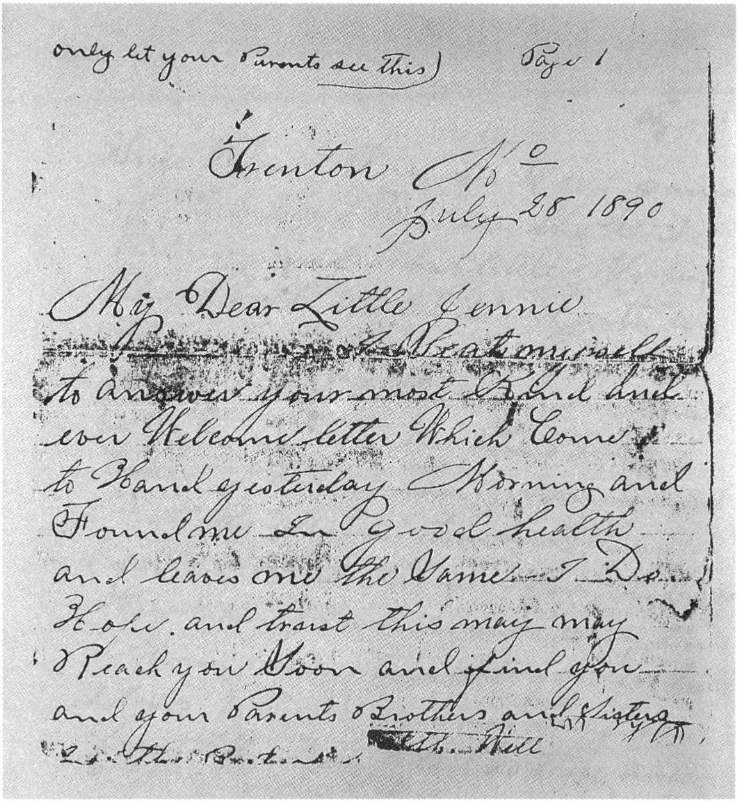

Illustration 1: Copy of the original letter Major wrote to Jennie.

Courtesy of Mr. and Mrs. Charles Miller

Suddenly, the noise from the adjacent tent becomes unbearably loud, and Major once again lays down his pen.

"Hey! You go! This *my* tent!" Major hears Maggie Day yell nearby in her deep native Russian accent.

"I'm goin', I'm goin'," a deep voice replies. The sound of objects crashing to the ground are so loud that Major wonders if he should move his writing station to a safer area.

Maggie is famous for her temper tantrums, and Major, like everyone else, is accustomed to them This one, however, is a real doozie, and he is forced to wait for the dust to settle and the war to end on the opposite side of the tent before continuing this most important letter.

"Hey, what are you doin' back here, Squirt?" Robinson's deep voice startles Major, causing the pen to waver. Several drops of ink splatter the edge of the page.

"It's no concern of yours, Robinson. Just go away and leave me alone," he yells, trying to hide the paper he was writing on.

"What's that?" the giant says, reaching for the letter lying on the small, make-shift table. "A letter to your little woman?"

"I said leave it alone!" Major screams, shoving Robinson back with his elbow.

"You know, you didn't introduce me to that little lady of yours in Kansas City. You hurt my feelin's. Now, why would you go and do a thing like that?"

"I didn't intend to introduce you to her," Major snaps. "You're not worthy of being introduced to a lady such as Jennie. Now stay away from me!"

"Major? Is something wrong back here?" Lewis Sells, overhearing the conversation between Major and

Robinson, emerges from the side of the tent to rescue the little man from the obnoxious Goliath towering over him.

"Robinson was just leaving, weren't you?" Major declares.

Sourly, Robinson turns and leaves.

"Thanks, Lewis."

"You're welcome. We'll need you in about an hour, all right?"

"Sure." Major watches Lewis disappear around the corner leaving him once more alone and able to return to his writing.

The pen in his hand once again becomes burdensome to hold, and he lays it next to the words already written on paper. Telling Jennie about his secret will be difficult, but he knows the words will come and hopes she will understand.

The heat between the two tents grows worse as the sun rises high in the sky. Looking at the handkerchief he pulls from his pocket, Major thinks of Jennie and the day he followed the handkerchief as it blew across the lot to land at her feet. Wiping the sweat from his brow, he returns the white cloth to his pocket and finishes writing his letter.

Chapter Six

The Letter

Jennie's doll-like hands work diligently on the small piece of fabric in her lap. The stitches she sews—each one the exact length as the other, fall naturally, giving perfect form to the soft piece of cloth. However, Jennie is flighty and takes spells of uninterest, many times leaving her sister or mother to finish the work she starts.

"Mama, when will Papa be home?" Jennie asks impatiently, laying the work aside to gaze out the open door.

"Land sakes child, that's the tenth time you've asked me that in the past ten minutes, and I'll tell you the same thing I told you ten minutes ago: I don't know, " answers Julia Casandra Meadows, a tall, thin, and rather fragile woman. She continually fusses over her eldest daughter who, at nineteen, stands only thirty-seven inches tall.

"She's lookin' for a letter from her boyfriend," spouts Maggie, Jennie's younger sister.

Unlike Jennie, seventeen-year-old, Maggie stands about five-feet-six-inches tall. She pulls the front of her dark hair up and allows the rest to hang loosely down her back. Maggie admires her older sister, but frequently wishes Jennie would finish her own projects. Maggie constantly teases Jennie about Major and her dream of marrying him.

"Oh, you be quiet," Jennie shouts. "You're just jealous because you don't have a man like my Major who wants to court you."

"Am not!"

"Are too! Are too!" Jennie chides.

"Oh, stop it you two! You're gonna drive me crazy with this silly bickering," Julia scolds.

The August sun's heat is felt throughout all of Kansas. The rains are few and far between, making the ground hard, and the crops poor. Nothing helps to cool the four-room bungalow that houses the family of six. Each wall has a window or a door, which allows air to circulate through the rough wood structure, but even the well-ventilated rooms cannot make the occupants comfortable. Constant high temperatures beget short tempers.

Jennie does not go back to her sewing but watches her mama work in the kitchen. Taken by the heat, Julia wipes a few beads of sweat from her forehead with her stained, white apron while she moves about the cramped room.

The cornbread, made early while the morning was cool, is wrapped in a clean cloth and tucked safely inside a basket, away from the flies and gnats that swarm everything. The steam from a pot of beans on the stove rises and disappears through a nearby window. Jennie pulls a stool to the counter and climbs up to sit and watch her mother prepare the turnip greens for supper.

"Mama? You know Major asked me to marry him, don't you?" Jennie asks softly.

"Yes." Julia Meadows speaks only the one word in reply to her daughter's question, and continues cleaning the greens.

"Well? How do you feel about it?"

"You do what you think is best for you, Jennie, but I think you need to look at the situation long and hard before you make any permanent decisions."

"What do you mean?"

"What do you want from marriage, Jennie? Can you live a life so different from your own? You know how hard it is around this little town with people who stare and tease you. Can you accept a life where you'll be placed on a stage and exhibited as a freak for the rest of your life?"

Her mother's words are hard but true. People always stare and make fun of her. Even now the women in town laugh at the thought of little Jennie Meadows getting married.

"Mama, I love Major. He is a kind and gentle man. Besides, how many men am I going to meet that are three-feet-tall?" she jokes.

"Well, it's not me you have to convince. It's your papa. You know how he feels about you, and you also know how he feels about circus people."

After washing the greens and priming the pump in the kitchen, Julia fills the pot full with water. She always wanted running water in the house, and when Layton built the place, he made sure she had it.

"Yes, Ma'am, but he has to remember that although I'm not very big, I am a grown woman." Their conversation is cut short by four-year-old Harold Dewitt, who comes running through and hides behind his mother's long skirt.

"What in the world, Harry? What have you done now?" she asks, hearing twelve-year-old Harding Joel running toward the house yelling at the top of his lungs.

"Nothin' Mama, honest." Harry says in a sweet and innocent voice.

During the summer the youngsters wear no shoes, and Harold's feet are black as pitch from running outside. His trousers are short, and show several years of wear. Wiping his runny nose along his sleeve, he cleans a white swath across his dirty face.

"Don't wipe your nose with your sleeve, Harry," his mother tells him, reaching down to clean his nose with the tail of her apron. He wriggles away, trying to make her stop.

"Harold Dewitt, so help me if I catch you, I'll clobber you good!" Joel yells, clamoring up the back porch steps, rapidly closing in on his little brother. Harding Joel is a lanky boy who stands almost as tall as his father.

"Wait a minute," Julia orders, grabbing her older son's arm with one hand and holding her younger son at arm's length with the other. "What's goin' on around here?"

"Harry let the chickens out again, and I'm havin' to round 'em up by myself 'fore Papa gets back from town," Joel yells, grabbing once more for his little brother.

"Harry, is that true? Have you been playin' in that chicken coop again?"

"Yes, Ma'am, but I didn't mean to let 'em out Ma, honest I didn't," Harry answers innocently, trying to stay out of his older brother's reach.

"All right, boys, that's enough. Harry, you go with your brother and help get those chickens corraled, and the next time I catch you in that coop I'll be the one to clobber you. Understand?" Julia shakes her finger, scolding the little boy. "Now, git!"

Both boys run out the back door calling, "Here, chick, chick, chick. Here chick, chick, chick," while they work to chase or coerce the feathered brood back into their nesting place.

It is late in the evening, but the hot summer sun still hangs high above. Jennie can hear the boys outside trying to round up the few chickens that remain loose and running free across the dirt yard.

"Is that your papa I hear?" Julia asks, hearing the wagon as it pulls close to the house.

"Papa? Papa?" Jennie calls and turns to slide down the cabinet, her feet searching for the stool below her. Julia reaches out to help her down, then watches as her daughter runs to meet her father at the front door.

"There's my little girl," Layton Meadows says, picking Jennie up and swinging her around.

"Oh, Papa, put me down! You know I'm too old for that now!" she squeals.

"Oh, I'm sorry. That's right. I forget. You're a young lady now," he apologizes, standing her safely on the floor.

"Papa, do you have the mail?" she asks, brushing the wrinkles from her dress.

"The mail? Was I supposed to pick up the mail?"

"Oh, Papa, where is it?"

"Why, the way you was acting you'd think maybe there was somethin' in here for you," he says, taking several letters from his dirty shirt pocket. Holding them up, he flips through each envelope one at a time.

"Papa!" Jennie pleads. "Is there a letter for me?"

"Well, what do you know! Here's a letter addressed to Miss Jennie Meadows. I wonder who *that's* from?"

"Now, Layton Franklin Meadows, you give that child her letter. She's been waitin' for you all day just to see if she had any mail," Julia scolds her husband.

"All right, honey. Here you go." Her papa hands her a stuffed envelope, heavy with pages.

"It's from that little man in the circus," Layton whispers to Julia, who motions for him to follow her into the kitchen and allow their daughter to read her mail privately.

Jennie flops in a chair and quickly opens the envelope containing the letter dated July 28, 1890. She notices it was written in Trenton, Missouri, and contains a lot of pages. Happily, she reads the first paragraph but suddenly grows serious as her eyes scan the words which cause her to question the man she has grown to love.

> . . . *There are 4 or 5 games of chance run in the sideshow and what little money the people would spend with us the gamblers get. Too bad for us to sit there, not make anything, see the people cheated out of their money, and not be allowed to warn them. For we know the secret of the trick. They can let a man win every time or loose every time. So you see how it is?. . .*

Being a Christian woman, Jennie questions her ability to live under the evil influence of deceit and dishonesty. And what about her darling Major? Is he like the others? If he is, can she change his ways by the divine guidance of the Lord?

> *The Circassian lady is just about as bad as they (the gamblers) are. She fights with the men and insults them if they don't buy her pictures. Mr. Lewis Sells, hoping to catch her at some of those tricks, gave her a terrible turning over. He told her the next time she done anything of the sort she would have to leave the show. Oh, I was glad she was scolded. She has behaved very well since.*

We have a very disagreeable lot of curiosities this season. I will tell you who they are; the Circassian Lady, who I have already mentioned, the Armless Man, and the Giant. The Armless Man never changes his clothes or takes a bath. There is one thing he does take. His whiskey. He gets drunk every week. Well, he drinks continuously, but only gets dead drunk once a week. We all shun him.

Then, there is the Giant. He drinks. He always wants to be making love to the ladies. Of course, they don't know his true intentions and many ladies fall into his web and are insulted. Mr. Hanner saved one lady from his clutches day before yesterday, thank God. No, I don't like him. He did not like it because I did not give him an introduction to you in Kansas City.

Jennie stops reading for a moment to think about the people Major works with and wonders what it will be like to live among them. The circus atmosphere from what she saw was wonderful, but that view was from the perspective of a young girl in the stands. Hoping for better news, Jennie continues to read Major's letter.

Mr. Ephraim Sells and wife have been away 21 days to their home in Columbus, Ohio. We expect them back today with a new sleeping car for the gamblers. I had to give up my berth to one of them and sleep on a pallet made down in the dressing and wash

*room of our coach. I would not sleep three in
a bed in this warm weather, so I took the
pallet on the floor.*

*Mrs. Brown sends her regards to you and
says tell you she feels sorry that painting is
injurious to your health as she wanted to have
you paint that dress front for her ever so
badly. Well dearest, I would like to go horseback riding with you, though I can't help but
be uneasy every time I hear of you riding. For
my sake and all that you hold dear, don't ride
any animal that will get frightened at anything.*

*Yes, I would have liked very much to have
heard that sermon by that Baptist brother you
wrote of.*

*Well, dearest, it is useless for me to try to
make my pen express how glad I am to get
your letter. Oh, . . .*

Jennie feels her mama and papa's eyes on her.   She
knows they are watching from behind the cracked kitchen
door.   "Major had to give his bed to some gamblers," she
says softly and reads further. "He says he's afraid for me to
go horseback riding."

"I wonder what else that letter says," Layton growls. "It
sure is long enough."

"Oh, hush and listen," Julia orders as she places her ear
closer to the cracked door.

Jennie smiles and her heart melts as she continues
reading. "Oh, Mama listen to this!

' *. . . it thrills me with a new life. It inspires
my whole heart and soul with a love that I*

> *had never known before in life and makes me*
> *long to bask myself in the sunshine of your*
> *beautiful smiling face forever. Undoubtedly, I*
> *am the happiest little man on earth, for I have*
> *the whole heart of a pretty little fairy queen all*
> *for my own . . . . '*

Have you ever heard anything more *romantic?*" she sighs.

"Makes me sick," Layton mumbles under his breath. "The man sure has a slick way with words. At least on paper."

"Oh, hush! I think it's sweet. You never wrote anything like that when you were courtin' me," Julia snaps.

"Hey, I brought you some flowers one time. Did you forget that?"

"Heavens, no! Who could forget the look on my mama's face when she found out someone had cut every one of her prize roses off at the base!"

Jennie smiles, never looking up, as she listens to her parents quietly tittering. Jennie continues reading.

> *Well, dearest, according to the program of*
> *the farmers picnic and parade laid down in*
> *your letter, it will be grand indeed. I would*
> *like to have a copy of your speech, if it is not*
> *too much trouble to send me today. I belong to*
> *the agriculture wheel.*
>
> *I will send you some of those paint cakes*
> *the first I see. I would, if it were possible,*
> *accompany you to the ice cream party. I visit*
> *an ice cream parlor every night after the show*
> *sharing warm weather and eating ice cream.*

I am glad you like your white rat and also glad to hear your brother's jackrabbit is getting along all right. We have two of the most cunning little rabbits in the side show you ever saw. One is black with a white nose and the other is yellow with a black nose. They are very tame and playful. One belongs to Mrs. Brown and the other to a little boy performer in the Big Show.

I was glad to hear that you liked your music teacher so well. I am glad to hear you are taking instrumental music lessons. My dearest love, I will not wear any long faces if I can help it but will think of you without ceasing and will be glad in knowing you are enjoying yourself, and are happy. I will think of you on the 31st and 2nd, and trust you may have, as you expect, a grand time.

"She's awful quiet," Layton says. He is unable to see Jennie clearly. "What's she doin' now?"

"She's still reading. What do you think she would be doing?" Julia answers rather sarcastically. "Now, hush and just listen."

"Major asks about Joel's jackrabbit and hopes it is getting along well. He also says he's glad to hear that I'm enjoying my music lessons and all," she says aloud for her parents to hear, and then returns to her reading.

I wish you had the little black pony I saw a little five-year-old boy riding this morning in the procession. It just came to the top of my shoulder and was the most beautiful specimen of miniature horses I ever saw in

> *my life. And I have seen a great many small*
> *horses in my life.*
>
> *So your papa wears long faces sometimes.*
> *Well, the prospect is good as you say for him*
> *to wear a longer face than he has yet, for I*
> *mean to send you the ring as soon as I can get*
> *it made. He would open his eyes sure enough*
> *if he could only read my last letter to you. I bet*
> *he would not say pshaw. I can't help but*
> *think your papa is joking with us both. Of*
> *course it is natural for your parents to want to*
> *keep you as long as they can. Oh, how glad I*
> *am to hear your dear mama stand up for your*
> *rights and as your papa does not interfere*
> *with you and I. So, your mama told you*
> *when I wrote about the engagement ring, she*
> *thought it was going too far did she?*

She smiles as she reads to herself about the engagement
ring he will soon send her and how sorry he is about
Papa's attitude. Then, her face grows solemn as she reads
the words . . .

> *"Well I don't see but one thing that could*
> *hinder us from being happy in married life,*
> *and it is no fault of yours. It is a very delicate*
> *subject, but you should know it before we join*
> *hands in matrimony."*
>
> *I learned Mrs. Brown told your mama all*
> *about it. (The lady that wanted you to paint a*
> *dress front for her.) If she did not tell your*
> *mama, let me know, and I will write to your*
> *papa and tell him and he can tell you of it. If*
> *you wish, I can tell you. . .*

"What is it? He says Mama may know," she mutters to herself.

> . . . *Just as you request I want you to know me. I am good and am of good parents as I have told you before. And, I am a man of honor. I want you to be sure and tell me if Mrs. Brown told your mama or not. If not, you must know it. You may not wish to renew our engagement after you have heard all, and it will be almost heart rending to me should your love cease for me. But my duty is clear to me, and I will know that you know it before we are united. I love you with a pure and holy love, and I don't want to put the least obstacle in your way. In the future, if my love was weak, I would not tell you my secret. I realize that I stand a chance of losing you after you know all of it. It will almost kill me to lose you, but on the other hand, after you know all and love me still, I will feel like I was in paradise. It is right for you to know all before hand.*

"Something's wrong," Julia tells Layton. She sees the expression on Jennie's face grow serious. Jennie no longer smiles. "I wonder what Major *wrote* in that letter."

"I don't know," Layton answers. "But all of it had better be good. If that half-pint charlatan breaks my little girl's heart, I'll break him in two!" Julia and Layton watch Jennie as she reads on.

> *My dear little darling, your being blind in one eye and being a poor man's daughter*

> doesn't decrease my love for you in the least.
> If you were ten times poorer than you are, I
> would still love you with all my heart. I am
> poor myself, but if I win you, after you have
> heard all, I will be rich. Yes, I love you as I
> never loved before. As for you being a Baptist,
> that don't matter. We are all trying for heaven
> sure and are brothers and sisters just the
> same.   There is nothing in the name of a
> church. We are all one in Christ. . . .

"He noticed my blindness," Jennie whispers to herself as Major's letter reveals not only her physical impairments, but her religious belief as well. She is relieved to know that nothing matters but his love for her and her love for him. Anxiously she continues reading.

> I was sorry to hear that you had to con-
> tend with chronic hecklers, too, but glad to
> hear that your mama stands up for your
> rights and says you have the same right to
> love and get married as the largest girl in the
> county. It gives me pleasure to know that you
> will be glad to get the ring. And I shall be
> sure to see and be with you next Christmas if
> you still love me after you have heard my
> secret. Give my love to your parents, brothers,
> and sister and tell them I thank them all for
> their good wishes for my welfare. . . .

"I think maybe you should go in there and see what that letter says!" Layton declares. "She don't look too happy."

"You may be right," Julia agrees. "I'll see what's goin' on." Julia pushes the door open, leaving the kitchen to sit next to her seemingly troubled daughter.

"Is everything all right with Major?" Julia asks, trying not to let her motherly concern be too obvious.

"Yes, ma'am. Everything's fine," she lies. "Major says he'll be here around Christmas, and he's glad to know I'll be happy to get his ring."

"Well, that makes two," Julia states sarcastically. "Jennie, I just don't think a ring is quite appropriate right now."

"Oh, Mama. You worry too much. Besides, I'm gonna wear Major's ring anyway, whether you or Papa approve or not."

"I know you will, but at least you know how we feel about it," Julia says sternly.

"I've only got a page or two left to read," Jennie tells her mother.

"Oh, sure," Julia answers, looking around the room. "Don't let me interrupt. I'll just sit here 'til you're through."

. . . . *Well, dearest, I noticed in yesterdays town Cameron in this state, that the fair community offered a great many presents to any couple who would get married at their fair. Among the list of presents were a parlour set valued at $160.00, a kitchen set $60.00, and a dining room set $55.00. Well, there were several other presents too numerous to mention.*

Well, an idea struck me to go and see him, and I did. I told him of our engagement merely to see how great an inducement the

*community would make us to get married
there. They said they would call a meeting
and see, but before I had told them what we
would take, I told them, if it was all right with
you, we would get married there and remain
there all through the fair as an attraction for
the fair for $500 and all the presents which
would amount to over $1,000; with the
privilege of selling our photos. He seemed to
think it was cheap enough.*

*The fair comes off in October. What do you
think of it dearest? Do you approve of it or
not? Let me know as I promised to let him
know by mail if you agree.*

*I will see or write to your parents for your
hand in marriage providing you will have me
for your little husband after you know my
secret. Write immediately to your truest love
and please answer all those questions with
my whole heart's love to you. I am yours
truly.*

> *Major Willie Ray
> of Sells Brothers Circus
> and Menagerie Inc.*

After reading the letter, she places it in her lap and calls
out to Layton. "Papa, Major says that there's a county
fair in Cameron, Missouri that's offerin' a whole list of
presents to a chosen couple who will get married there at
the fair."

Layton quickly enters the living room and sits in a chair
near Jennie and her mother. "Yeah, what about it?" he
asks coldly.

Jennie carefully studies Layton's facial expressions. She quickly continues, "Major also says that he spoke with the man in charge of the fair and told him we would get married on stage and remain on exhibit at the fair for an extra $500, along with the other items offered. Mama, look! That adds up to over a thousand dollars!" Jennie shows that part of the letter to Julia.

"No!" yells Layton, quickly standing up. His face reddens as the blood rushes to his temples.

"But, Papa, the fair is in October and . . . "

"No! *I said, NO!*" he screams, his fists clenched. "No daughter of mine is gonna be placed on a stage and displayed like a freak for a bunch of people to come in and stare at. No! No! *No!*"

"But, Papa, you don't understand! That's what we'll be doing in the circus. That will be our job. Our occupation. How we'll make our money," Jennie cries, trying to make him understand.

Jennie watches her father's eyes fill with tears as he sees his little girl slipping away from him. Layton Meadows walks out the back door and stands on the rough, wooden porch. Julia follows him. Jennie moves closer to the door, listening to the conversation between her parents.

"Now, Layton," Julia places a loving arm around him. "You have to let her go."

"I know, but Julia, she's so tiny and fragile. I don't want her to be scoffed at and glared at, especially on her wedding day." He casually wipes the tears from his cheeks.

"Explain that to her, Layton. Don't just tell her *no*, without a reason."

THE SUN, NOW FALLING BEHIND THE DRY KANSAS landscape, casts a red hue across the land and sky. Jennie cautiously joins her father.

"Papa?"

"Yes, Jennie," her papa answers softly.

"Major says he will either write to you or come in person and ask for my hand."

"Well, I won't give my consent unless that man comes to me in person." Layton Meadows, strong in his word, is weak when it comes to the wishes of his daughter.

"All right, Papa," she agrees sadly. "I'll make sure Major comes here and I'll also tell him we can't get married in October." Jennie touches her father's hand tenderly, tugs on his shirt, and urges him to kneel beside her.

"Jennie." He lowers himself to her level. "I love you, honey, and I just don't want any harm, physical or otherwise, to come to you."

"I know Papa. I love you too." Jennie leans closer to her father and lightly kisses his cheek. She touches his shoulder tenderly and then joins her mother in the kitchen, but before she enters the house Jennie turns, smiles, and softly says, "Papa, supper's ready."

Chapter Seven

Unanswered Questions

With supper over and the dishes done, Jennie wipes the hardwood kitchen table, a gift to her parents from her grandparents when they married twenty or more years ago. Julia's father chopped the trees down in Illinois, carved each board himself, and placed them together with wooden pegs. He crafted six hand-carved chairs to match.

Jennie runs her hand over the shiny wooden table and thinks about the family who sits around it. Without stooping, she scans the top, searching for crumbs and smudges, then stands on a chair to wipe it clean. After the dishes are put away, Jennie confides in her mother.

"Mama?"

"Yes."

"I need to talk to you about something Major wrote in his letter, but you have to promise you won't mention it to Papa. All right?"

"I'll try."

"No. You have to *promise* you won't mention it to Papa," Jennie pleads.

"All right, I won't mention it to Papa. Now what is it?"

Jennie motions for her mother to follow her out the back door to sit on the porch and talk. Jennie sits in a little wooden rocker her father made for her from cedar. Julia joins her in the larger rocker next to it. For a moment Jennie quietly studies the beautiful August moon that hangs overhead, illuminating the countryside. Breaking the silence, she takes the letter from her skirt pocket and begins questioning her mother.

"Mama, do you know a Mrs. Brown that works with Major in the circus?" Jennie asks curiously. Fumbling with the letter in her lap, and rocking slightly, she swats at a mosquito.

"No. Why do you ask? Jennie, somethin' *is* wrong. I knew earlier when you were readin' that letter. Now, do you want to tell me what it is or am I gonna have to find out for myself?" Julia waits for her daughter to share the letter's disturbing contents.

"I don't doubt Major's love for me," Jennie says. "But there's something about him that he's afraid for me to know—something he believes will change my feelings toward him."

"What do you think it is?"

"I don't know. That's why I'm asking you." Jennie opens the letter and reads, "He writes: 'I learned Mrs. Brown told your mama all about it. If she did not tell your mama, let me know and I will write to your papa and tell him and he can tell you, or if you wish, I can tell you.' "

"I don't know Jennie. I haven't heard from any Mrs. Brown."

"I can't believe anything about him would make any difference to me or change the way I feel about him, Mama."

"Exactly what does he say about this secret?"

"Not much. Just that he'll come and ask for my hand in marriage, providing I still want him after I know about his 'secret'." Jennie stares out across the Kansas farm as though the answer will come through the dried corn patch or the parched wheat fields.

"Mama? Has Papa ever done anything to make you ashamed of him?"

"Heaven sakes, no! What makes you ask that?"

"Well, I don't know. You weren't ashamed of Papa and what he did for a living?"

"Honey, haulin' four-hundred-pound water barrels to people who need it is nothin' to be ashamed of. I know it's nothin' like bein' a big farmer or a banker, but it pays the bills and puts food on this family's table. Your papa is an honest man doin' an honest day's work, and I'm sure Major is the same kind of man."

"Mama? If Papa decided today to pack up and take off across the country to . . . say, California, would you pack up and go with him without saying a word?" Jennie searches for answers through her mother's actions, because she knows her mother loves her father like she loves Major.

"Sure I would. Why?"

"That's all I need to know." Jennie stands on the tiptoe and places a light kiss on her mother's cheek. "Thank you, Mama. I believe I'm ready to go to bed now. Good-night."

"Good-night, baby."

LYING IN BED, JENNIE THINKS ABOUT MAJOR'S strange and troubling letter. She turns to look at the large hope chest she bought to hold her wedding trousseau, positioned at the end of the bed. She has filled it with delicate hand-stitched dresses, along with the beautiful little white hat Major sent her several weeks ago.

The trunk was too costly for her family's meager earnings, but with the money she saved from painting dresses, and a little public speaking, she had more than enough. Beautiful varnished oak slats adorn the outside of the chest. A padded floral cloth lines the interior. The metal latch on the outside shines like solid gold and has a lock and key to protect all her valuable possessions.

Getting out of bed, Jennie takes the key which is hidden inside her Bible between the pages of the "Twenty-third Psalm," and quietly unlocks the trunk. Struggling to lift the oversized lid, she finally opens it, swinging it back to rest against the leather straps that help hold it together.

Carefully she places the letter under the stack of clothing to hide it from anyone who might become curious about its contents. The "secret" will remain a "secret" until Major, himself, reveals it to her in its entirety. She wants no one second-guessing about some secret she doesn't herself even know about yet.

Stretching on tiptoe, Jennie reaches to grasp the edge of the heavy lid and slowly closes it. She turns the cold steel key, locking the letter and its secrets safely away from bigger hands and prying eyes. God would never take away this dream-come-true. Never.

After placing the key back in her Bible, she quietly returns to her bed. Looking out the window into the star-studded sky, she knows God is responsible for her happiness.

Bright beams of light from the full moon filter through the open window and across the bed, casting a spiritual light upon her. Kneeling by her bed, with hands folded, Jennie humbly speaks to God. "Father who art in heaven," she prays. "Please, if it be your will, let me understand

and accept whatever it is that troubles my poor little
Major. I love him so and I thank you for leading me to
him, Lord. . . ."

Chapter Eight

Confessions

The circus has traveled through fourteen states in thirty weeks and railed 12,168 miles during the season before finally coming to an end on November 25, 1890, in Water Valley, Mississippi. Business is good, but the weather turns cold as a north winds blow in suddenly, keeping many people from the eight o'clock show that ends at almost eleven o'clock.

The sideshow and its performers pack their belongings and prepare for the long journey home. Major leans against a large, beat up, old trunk with torn leather straps that for the past several years has followed him like a shadow. Holding an array of letters in his lap, he thinks about Jennie and the life he hopes to share with her.

"Major?" calls a soft, sweet voice from the opposite side of the old trunk.

"Yeah, I'm down here." He knows the person who speaks will follow his voice and find him sitting on the ground.

"What are you doing down there?" Henrietta asks. Her dark green bonnet, tied tightly under her chin, and her matching waist jacket keeps her warm, protecting her from

the winter wind that developed during the night. She
holds a lantern high in her hand to light the dark corner
where Major sits. "Letters from Jennie?"

"Yeah. All here and accounted for." He holds up a large
bundle of letters, tied in a pink ribbon. "All declaring her
love for me as I did in letters to her," he says with a smile.

"Are you going back to Missouri now, or Kansas?"

"I guess I'll catch the first train back to Missouri and
visit my family."

"I know they'll be happy to see you."

"What are you going to do?" asks Major. He stands and
places the bundle of letters into the old trunk.

"I'm going home. I got a letter from my sister, saying my
mother isn't doing well, so I think I need to stay with her
for a while. I'll catch the first train to St. Louis." Henrietta
starts to turn and leave, but before taking a step, she
speaks once more to Major. "Remember, if you love her
and she truly loves you, nothing will destroy that love, because if it does, it was never meant to be."

Major says nothing. He only watches as the light from
the lantern Henrietta holds in her hand disappears
around the corner. He watches several men throw his
trunk into the back of the baggage car, "No wonder it looks
like it does," he mutters to himself. "Lord, I hope I don't
look that bad."

"Don't worry. You don't," laughs Lizzie, after overhearing the conversation between him and Henrietta.
"You ready to get aboard and head for home?"

"Yeah, I'm ready."

THE KANSAS TERRITORY IS FULL OF ROUGH TERRAIN
and cold weather as Major makes his journey from the
Kansas City train station to the small town of Yates

Center. Wrapping his coat tightly around him, Major fights back the cold as the crisp December air flows freely through the rocking stage coach.

His visit in Missouri with family was not long because of his anxious heart and urgent need to be near Jennie. He arrives in Kansas City and takes the first stage destined for Yates Center.

Major sits and remembers the embarrassment he suffered as he boarded the stage. Because of the height of the steps, Major slipped and tumbled to the snow covered ground. With a bit of help from the young man next to him, Major managed to climb into the cold stage.

Cold air whistles through the drafty coach, but Major is so happy he barely notices. Passengers—heading home for Christmas—fill the stage's cramped cabin, while curious eyes watch Major, whose feet dangle uncomfortably, never touching the floor.

"Are you goin' home for Christmas?" Major asks the young man who helped him into the coach. The young man's dark suit and expensive overcoat label him a highly successful and educated man.

"Yes sir," he answers, noticing Major's size and manner of dress. While Major's perfectly fitting blue suit, top hat and cane depict a professional man, his mannerisms and colloquial form of speaking suggest otherwise. "Sir, may I be forward and inquire as to your profession?" the young man asks reluctantly The need to satisfy his curiosity overcomes his socially polite upbringing.

"I work with the circus," Major replies, holding his head high.

"What do you do in the circus?"

"I work with the sideshow."

"That must be fun. When I was a boy my father took me to the circus once, and after that, I always wanted to join.

My father had other plans for me—law school. You travel extensively, don't you?"

"Yeah, we travel constantly. Sometimes it's all right, but there are times when it gets old."

"Where are you going now?"

"I'm going to see my fiancee´ who lives in Yates Center," Major answers proudly.

"Oh, that's nice," the young man nods and smiles, unable to think of anything else to say without sounding awkward and inconsiderate of the little man's feelings. Nothing more is said until they pull into Yates Center. The stage stops in front of the depot which is next door to the Sunflower Hotel, the only hotel in town.

Emerging from the unsteady coach, Major cautiously grasps the sides of the door as the horses' movements continually rock it. He finally stands firmly, feet planted on the hard, cold earth beneath him. He immediately sees Jennie standing on the wooden sidewalk in front of him.

His eyes brighten, his heart jumps, and his stomach gets the normal "Jennie butterflies." She is a vision of pure loveliness. The fur coat she wears enhances her beauty, and he aches to hold her in his arms. Jennie smiles broadly as Major approaches her.

"Jennie," Major speaks tenderly, wanting only to hear the sound of her name roll off his tongue. Taking her hand in his, he tells her, "Six months ago when we first met, I thought you were the most beautiful woman I had ever seen. You *are* indeed the most beautiful woman in the world."

"Major?" Jennie blushes, and pointing to her father says, "I believe you remember my father, Layton Meadows."

"Yes, I do. How are you, Sir?" Major says politely, looking up at the stern face staring down directly into his eyes. "It's good to see you again." Major extends his hand, waiting for Jennie's father to receive it in kindness and respect, which after a few moments' hesitation, he does.

People gawk at the tiny couple standing together on the sidewalk. Some point and snicker, others are just curious.

"We had better get on outta here," Layton Meadows says, picking his daughter up and placing her into the wagon. He turns to lift Major, but is surprised to find him climbing the spoke wheels like a ladder to sit next to Jennie. With Major's trunk in the back of the wagon and the three comfortably seated, they ride to the Meadows' farm.

Jennie's brothers, sister, and mother receive him well, but Layton remains cold and distant, still unable to accept Major as a future son-in-law. While Julia busily prepares the evening meal, Major takes the opportunity to speak with Jennie before talking to her father about their forthcoming marriage.

They sit in the living room of the Meadows home near the large fireplace that provides heat for the small, but tidy dwelling. The constant stares from Jennie's father and brothers, who sit across the room, create an uncomfortable environment for Major. Stretching his neck and changing his position, he imagines a noose growing tighter and tighter around his throat.

"Layton, I need you and the boys to come in the kitchen to help me and Maggie get supper ready," Julia urges the three to leave the young couple alone for a few minutes. The hint is not taken. The three sit steadfast in their chairs.

"Layton, I said I need some help from you and the boys!"

"That's woman's work," Layton snaps.

"Yeah, woman's work," mocks the two young boys sitting next to him.

"I need wood brought in, now! That's man's work!" Julia replies sternly.

Layton knows his wife is making a point. "Come on boys. Let's go see what those women need."

Major welcomes the time alone with Jennie, but at the same time, dreads it. The time has come to tell Jennie his secret. He silently prays it won't change her feelings toward him.

"I saved all of your letters," Jennie says, breaking the silence. "They're locked safely inside my trunk where no one will ever see them. I read them every night."

"I also kept your letters with me. They were my only reason for going on day after day."

The room, filled with a golden glow from the fire that crackles and sparks in front of them, grows darker and smaller to Major as he prepares to unleash his horrible secret. Jennie is everything to him. His heart races as he tries and fails several times to approach the subject.

"What is it dear, sweet Major?" Jennie asks softly, seeing the torment and sadness in his eyes.

"Dear, dear Jennie. I'm afraid to face you with the words I need to speak for fear of losin' you forever. However, as I wrote you, I believe you must know about a deep, dark past that I've tried to forget for many years." He bends his head. Holding Jennie's hand tightly in his, he continues while she sits quietly, embracing every word.

"By your actions, I gather neither your mother, nor you, know anything bad about me."

"No, Major. I asked Mama if she knew a Mrs. Brown in the circus. She assured me she didn't, so I let it go."

With the rest of the family busy in the other room, Major hopes they cannot hear him speaking to Jennie. The room seems uncomfortably warm.

Tugging at his tie, Major swallows hard. "Jennie, as I said before, I am a man of honor and would not hurt you for anything, but the truth still remains that I am a man. I am thirty years old and am not so virtuous, and I have known many women of a not so virtuous backgrounds."

"What are you trying to say to me?" asks Jennie innocently. Her eyes wide and curious, she takes her hand from his and sits straight as if expecting her world to come crashing down.

"What I am trying to say is that I have had relations with other women in the past." Major doesn't know quite what to say but tries to explain his sordid past as best he can.

Jennie remains quiet for a moment. Then with her eyes fixed on his, she speaks confidently, "Is that all? Sir, I am quite aware of the promiscuity of the male species. I may be pure, but that does not make me ignorant to their sinful activities. However, I do not condone such ungodly behavior, and I don't think I want to hear about it, either!"

Her response surprises Major. He sits watching the fire in her eyes as she speaks with strong conviction in reference to not only her own intellect, but her moral values and principles in relation to promiscuity and infidelity as well. He is both intrigued and attracted to Jennie's forthrightness, which at times is a mirrored image of his own strength and confidence.

"That's not all," he says sadly. Pausing a moment, he swallows hard, allowing the huge lump in his throat to pass, then continues, "During my days of promiscuous behavior I discovered I am unable to father children. Any woman I wed will be without a family of her own."

Jennie sits quietly. The sound of the crackling fire becomes deafening in the silence. "Jennie?" Major waits for her to comment on what he has said, but she doesn't immediately respond.

"Did you hear what I said?" he asks. "I cannot give you a family of your own. Can you still love me knowing this?

Jennie looks into his eyes. The tears roll down her cheeks as she gently reaches out and touches the side of his face. "Major, all I need is you."

"But, after what I have told you, the other women and all . . . "

"I don't care. That was before me. What is important is *now. Here. Tonight. In this room.* God has brought you to me, and if it is His will that there be no children for us, then so be it."

With a sigh of relief, Major realizes how true Jennie's love is for him. Even his past mistakes cannot change the way she feels about him. He knows there will be no more secrets between them—only love forevermore.

"Tonight I will ask your father's permission to marry you," Major promises, wrapping his hand tightly around hers.

"Major, don't say anything to Mama or Papa about, well, you know. Do you understand?"

"Yeah, I understand," Major agrees, relieved that he will not have to explain anything more to Jennie's father.

DINNER IS OVER. MAJOR AND LAYTON GO TO THE front porch. Layton scrapes a match down the rough wooden post and lights the pipe he pulled from his pocket. Major watches the large man suck the flame of the match into the tobacco-stuffed object, filling the air with its sweet aroma. Major pulls a wad of chewing tobacco from his pocket and stuffs it into his mouth.

"Jennie know you chew that stuff?" Layton   asks, breaking the silence.

"I don't think so. Why?"

"I wouldn't let her know, then. She hates the stuff."

Major hesitates for a moment allowing the dark, wet tobacco to lie in his mouth, then slowly pressing it into the side of his jaw, he feels the sweet juice soak into his tongue. "Mr. Meadows, I need to speak to you about an important issue that I know you are well aware of." Major spits the dark substance into the yard and continues talking, while Layton sits quietly listening. "Sir, I love your daughter, and I want to marry her."

"You do, huh? Well, just what do you think you can give her?" Layton asks, blowing a large cloud of smoke into the night air. The bright moon reflects off a foggy ring creating a large halo above his head.

"I can give her a good life, Sir."

"How? By dragging her across the country?   Letting people stare at her while she sits miserably on a stage every day?" Layton's voice is calm, but tense.

"Sir, you don't understand. It's not like that at all. I love Jennie and she loves me. I'd never do anything to hurt her."

"Oh, I *do* understand. You want to make a mockery of my daughter! Well, I'll not see her stared at and teased. I will not see her hurt by some circus charlatan who wants to display *my baby* like a two-headed goat!" Layton's voice roars from the Meadows' porch, echoing across the Kansas fields.

"No!" Major shouts back, his high pitched voice straining as he tries to explain his feelings. "It's not like that at all. Don't judge all by a select few!" he cries. Growing frustrated by the inability to convince Jennie's father that the circus is not all bad, Major turns away from him, afraid of saying something he will regret.

Hearing the voices of the two men who are still just shy of a shouting match, Jennie and her mother run out to try to calm them. "Layton Meadows, what in the good Lord's name is going on out here?" Julia shouts, demanding an answer from her irate and overly protective husband.

"This charlatan wants to drag *our Jennie* across the country with him and his bunch of deceiving Gypsies," Layton blurts out, his hands shaking and tears welling in the corners of his eyes.

"But, *Sir*," Major protests. "I love Jennie. I told you, I'd *never* do anything to hurt her. The circus is not what you think. Yes, we do have a few that are, as you say, charlatans, but they are not all charlatans. These people are my family."

"I said, 'No!' And I mean every word of it! I'll not have it!" Layton yells once more and turns his face away.

"But, Papa!" Jennie screams. Her heart sinks as her father continues to forbid the marriage between them. "Papa, I'm nineteen-years-old and I'll marry Major, with or without your blessing!"

Layton Meadows calmly empties his pipe on the rail, softly tapping it against the wooden banister, watching the hot tobacco fall to the ground and scatter with the wind. Quietly, he turns and walks into the house. Julia follows her sullen husband. She closes the door, leaving Major and Jennie alone on the porch.

"Don't worry. He'll be there. You'll see," Major assures Jennie softly. Holding her in his ams, he tries desperately to dry the tears that flow like running water down her cheeks. "I love you, sweet, sweet, Jennie," he whispers, takeing a tiny diamond solitaire from his vest pocket.

Gently, he slips it onto Jennie's finger and kisses her long and passionately.   "When I see you again, it will be our wedding day when you become my wife—Mrs. William Ray."

Jennie smiles, but her heart still aches as Major leaves her standing alone.   *"Papa will be at the wedding, and everything will be wonderful. I know it will,"* she whispers to herself as she watches the evening sun kiss the horizon.

Chapter Nine

For Better or Worse

Major and Jennie prepare for their February wedding. Jennie, Maggie, and Julia finish Jennie's miniature trousseau. Each stitch, sewn with accuracy and care, brings pure happiness to Jennie as she watches her life fall almost perfectly into place. Her only sadness is that her father will not be at the wedding to see her marry the man she loves.

"Mama, do you think Papa will come?" Jennie asks sadly. Her hands carefully fold each piece of clothing. Stretching, she stands on tiptoes and delicately places the clothes, piece by piece, into her trunk.

"I don't know, Jennie. You know how stubborn your papa can be at times. I do know he loves you. You're special to your papa, because you're the eldest and the first to leave the nest. Talk to him, Jennie." Julia knows her husband and knows Jennie is his favorite because she is just like him—determined and stubborn.

"All right, Mama. I'll try again, but I don't think it'll do any good."

Jennie's eyes stray absently to the wedding dress hanging on the miniature dress form standing in the corner of the bedroom. Papa carved the wooden form with his strong, loving hands. Now he speaks to her only when he finds it absolutely necessary.

"I saw your papa go into the barn a few minutes ago," her mother says casually, sewing another stitch in the little dress in her lap. "I think maybe we need some more wood."

Jennie understands what her mother is saying, and quickly wrapping herself warmly in a heavy shawl, she walks hastily to the barn. She can barely reach the latch positioned high above her head, but she sees the stool Papa made from an old log laying close to the door. Dragging it underneath the latch and standing on it, she opens the door with ease. The stench of the animals in the cold, musty barn takes her aback for a moment before she spies her father unloading empty water kegs from the wagon.

"Papa," she calls softly. "Papa," she repeats, approaching the large, intimidating figure standing near the wagon.

Layton carefully sets the large wooden keg he carries in his arms near the edge of the horse stall. "Yes, Jennie," he answers, rather coldly.

"Mama says we need more wood in the house."

"All right, tell your mama I'll bring it in a few minutes."

"I'll tell her." Her head barely reaches the top of the wagon wheel as she stands steadfast. Jennie knows she has to convince her father to attend the wedding and give her away, but sometimes he is so overbearing and demanding that her courage seems to melt at her feet.

"Papa?" Her voice quivers slightly as a small tear rolls down her pink cheek.

"Yes," he answers. "Is there something else I can do for you, Jennie?"

"Papa, I want you to come to the wedding," she blurts the words out quickly.

"Now, Jennie, you know how I feel. You may be almost twenty years old, but I still don't want you marrying some circus freak."

Shocked at his words, Jennie explains, "But, Papa, what am *I?*"

"You're my little girl. Jennie, if I let you do this, you will be miserable for the rest of your life."

"No, Papa. I'll be miserable if I *don't.*"

"I'm sorry, Jennie. Nothing you say will change my mind. I don't want you to marry this man, and I'll not be there to watch any fiasco that's gonna ruin your life."

"Papa, I love Major, and I want you there with me on the happiest day of my life," she sobs. "But, if you are so sure fired set against coming, then so be it," she cries, tugging gently at his shirt.

Layton squats near her and Jennie plants a kiss lightly on his bearded cheek. "I love you anyway, Papa," she says. Jennie leaves her father still kneeling in the hay as she walks out of the barn and closes the door behind her.

A HARD NORTH WIND WHISTLES THROUGH THE cracks around the poorly sealed windows of Jennie's bedroom. The excitement of her wedding day prohibits any possibility of a good night's sleep. Quietly, she slips slowly from her bed, removes the key from her Bible, and opens the trunk. Sliding her hands beneath several layers of clothing, Jennie pulls out the stack of letters she had tucked safely away. Careful not to wake Maggie, Jennie carries the letters to the window, and using the moon as a lantern, begins to read them again.

"Jennie?" Maggie calls, softly. "You're not ailing or anything are you?"

"No, Maggie, go back to sleep," Jennie whispers.

"Well, what are you doing up at this hour?"

"I couldn't sleep, and I thought I'd look at Major's letters again, just for a little while." Jennie stares out the window and catches a glimpse of a star falling from the heavens. She quickly makes a wish before its long, fiery white tail disappears from sight.

The room is quiet except for the occasional sound of a mouse gnawing on the rafters in the attic. Maggie joins her older sister at the window. She blows a light breath of warm air onto the window, fogging it over ever so slightly, and with her right index finger she traces a large heart with, "J.M. loves W.R." in the center. Jennie smiles at her sister's playful gesture.

"Are you excited?" Maggie asks. "That's really a dumb question. Of course, you're excited. But, are you *scared?* You know, about the wedding night and all."

"No, I'm not afraid. I love Major and our wedding night will be the most wonderful night of our lives."

"Is it Papa and the fact that he says he's not coming tomorrow?" she asks. "That's what's bothering you, isn't it?"

"Maggie, do you really think Papa won't come to the wedding?"

"No. I bet he'll be the first one to show up."

"Thanks," Jennie cries, and reaching up, wraps her arms around her younger sister. "I'm going to miss you a lot."

"Yeah, I'm going to miss you, too, but I won't miss finishing all of those jobs you start," Maggie laughs, trying to hide the tears that slide down the sides of her nose.

"Go on back to bed, Maggie. I'll be there in a minute." Jennie gives her a slight nudge. "I just want to read a few more lines from Major's letters, then I'll go to bed."

"Okay, whatever you say." Maggie returns to bed and within minutes is fast asleep.

Jennie reads to herself:

"It inspires my whole heart and soul with a love that I had never known before in life. It makes me long to bask myself in the sunshine of your beautiful smiling face forever. Undoubtedly, I am the happiest little man on earth, for I have the whole heart of a pretty little fairy queen all for my own . . . "

Jennie reads Major's letters earnestly through the night. When morning comes, Maggie finds her sister not in her bed but asleep, propped against the cold window pane. Her fragile body lies limp on the tall stool. Her head rests on her bent arm, and she still clings tightly to Major's letters.

"Jennie," Maggie whispers. "Jennie, it's morning." Maggie gently lifts her older sister from the stool and places her carefully onto the bed.

"I must have fallen asleep," Jennie moans, stretching her sore back. "I've got to get started. There's so much to do before the wedding."

THE SMELL OF THE WEDDING CAKE BAKING IN THE kitchen is wafting throughout the house, awaking the senses with its wonderful aroma. While Jennie's mother busily prepares the wedding feast for the coming evening, Maggie and the boys take the wagon to town and decorate the small Baptist church, preparing for the eight o'clock ceremony. Jennie's siblings set about making decorations.

Joel and his little brother, Harold, gather several small pine limbs and pine cones to weave into wreaths. Maggie arranges holly and beautiful pink and white velvet ribbons for the bridal bouquet.

MAJOR STANDS AT THE WINDOW OF THE MERCANTILE that doubles as the stage depot, impatiently waiting for the noon stage to arrive from Kansas City. The cold, dry Kansas air blows under the large crack in the door, sending a chill through his body.

"How 'bout a cup of coffee?" asks Mr. Jenkins, the proprietor. He stands beside Major, holding a pot of coffee in his old wrinkled hand. Although his hair is gray, it is full and long, matching the beard that covers his withered face. Major guesses his age to be about seventy.

"Yes, thank you," Major answers, caressing the cup with both hands.

"Aren't you and little Miss Jennie gettin' married today?" Mr. Jenkins asks.

"Yes, Sir. I'm waitin' on my mother to ride in on the stage from Missouri."

"Me and the Missus have been married almost fifty-two years now."

The old man's eyes light up when he speaks about his wife and the hard years they endured while raising a family of eight boys and two girls. Major thinks of Jennie, and he can only pray that married life will be as fulfilling for the two of them as it obviously has been for the aging couple he has come to love and admire during his stay.

"I understand her pa don't want her to marry." Mr. Jenkins says, wiping the dirt from the window with a towel. Without waiting for a response he continues, "Well, I wouldn't worry too much. When I married Mrs. Jenkins, her pa was just as dead set again' it as Layton is, but he came around after a while, and I suppose Layton will too."

"Thanks." Major takes another sip of the steaming brew.

"Well, looks like the stage is right on time." Mr. Jenkins glances at the watch hanging from his vest pocket. "I guess I'd better get some more coffee ready for the passengers. They're gonna be mighty cold when they get here."

MAJOR OPENS THE HEAVY DOOR AND STANDS ON THE snow-covered wooden sidewalk to welcome his mother. The frozen ground has eliminated the usual dust that follows the horse-drawn stage as it rolls into town. Major pulls his coat collar closer to his neck, attempting to keep out the cold wind.

"Willie!" his mother cries, stepping from the stage. Her aging body, now bent and fragile, still towers over her young son's. She grasps his round face in her hands and plants a light kiss on his forehead. The woman he remembers as young and beautiful now stands before him looking a hundred years old.

"Ma," he cries, holding her hands gently. "Come in from the cold and get warm before we go to the hotel." Mother and son sit in the store and reminisce about home and family.

JENNIE USES ONE OF THE SMALL CLASSROOMS in the country church to dress for her wedding. Maggie holds a large oblong mirror in front of her, while Jennie looks in awe at her own stunning reflection. Her mother carefully braids several long pieces of white ribbon through her long, dark, silky hair. Twisting it into a delicate loose bun at the back of Jennie's head, she places a small star-shaped comb on the side.　Julia places the veil on Jennie's head. It trails down her back and flows several feet behind her across the floor.

Her dress, white with three-quarter puffed sleeves and delicate lace covering the bodice front, accentuate her wee, but full, figure.　Jennie painted the beautiful pink roses with green leaves that trail down　the front of the dainty, floor-length skirt.

"Jennie, here is something old to wear.　It belonged to my mother, and I wore it when your papa and I married." She carefully pins an old silver brooch to Jennie's high collar.

"Here is something new and blue," says Maggie, carefully laying the mirror aside.　Slowly, she hands a beautiful little blue cotton handkerchief trimmed with white lace to her older sister who stands teary-eyed in front of her.　Tiny embroidered rosebuds accent each corner, and a slight scent of rose water emanates from it.

"It's beautiful, Maggie.　Thank you." Jennie accepts it and　tears well in the corners of her eyes as she reaches up to hug her younger sister.

"Are you ready?" asks her mother, hearing Aunt Tess play several　notes of the "Wedding March" on the piano. "I believe that's your cue."

"I'm ready," Jennie answers.　There is a note of sadness in her voice as she remembers that her father will not be there to give her away.

Maggie stands　in front of Jennie as they prepare to walk down the isle of the Baptist church which is now filled with family and friends standing with anticipation to get a glimpse of the bride.　The door opens.　Major stands at the end of the long isle which leads to where the preacher is standing.　Joel stands next to him.

Illustration 2: Jennie in front of oblong mirror. By the design on the dress in this photograph and description of the wedding dress as described in the February 13, 1891 Yates Center Newspaper, this is a wedding photograph.

Photo courtesy Imogene Young

Major is handsome in his dark blue tailed suit. His image, dwarfed by Joel, looks odd to family and friends but to Jennie, Major is the tallest man on the face of this earth.

"Well, come on, Jennie-girl," blusters a deep, familiar voice. A large hand appears from the side of the doorway, lowering to meet hers. "You haven't changed your mind have you?"

A smile quickly spreads across Jennie's face as she looks up to see her father standing waiting to walk her down the aisle. "Thank you, Papa," she cries. Tears run softly down her cheeks as she takes her papa's rough hand, and they slowly start down the isle. Remembering the wish, she looks up and whispers, "Thank you, God."

"I hope those are tears of joy," Layton says. The top of Jennie's head barely meets his waist, and looking down he is awed by her beauty. He gently places Jennie's little hand into Major's and whispers so everyone can hear, "Take care of her, Major. She's special."

"I will. I promise," Major answers with a loud whisper as Layton turns and joins a smiling Julia.

Looking into Jennie's eyes, Major tenderly squeezes her hand. Tears glisten off her rose petaled cheeks, like tiny diamonds, when she looks into his eyes.

The image of Jennie as she first emerged from the opposite end of the isle repeats itself in Major's mind: Silhouetted in the soft candlelight, an angelic vision in white glides toward him.

"We have come together on this joyous occasion to join together this man and this woman in holy wedlock," says Reverend McDole. His lanky figure seems even thinner in his black suit. The hard lines etched in his face tell a story of pain as well as a life in the ministry. His soft, deep voice reveals a gentle, kind man who enjoys spreading the gospel and caring for the Lord's lost sheep.

"Let us pray: Our Heavenly Father, we ask thy blessings on William Ray and Jennie Meadows. May their life together be forever a shining example to all who know and love them. Amen. Who gives this woman to this man?"

"Her mother and I do," Layton answers as a tear forms in the corner of his eye. He wipes it away casually with back of his hand. The smile on her father's face tells Jennie he no longer denies her marriage but blesses it sincerely.

Reverend McDole motions with his hands for the congregation to be seated, and asks, "If there is anyone here who has just cause that this man and this woman should not be joined in holy wedlock, speak now or forever hold his peace."

The congregation is silent.

Suddenly, the door opens, and a large man enters, shouting, "Stop the ceremony!" He shakes the snow from his shoulders, and in long strides, walks eagerly down the isle. His seven-foot-nine-inch frame captures the attention of the congregation as they watch him approach Major. "You didn't think I'd let you get married without me, did you?"

"Singleton!" Major yells. The two men shake hands like old friends. "How did you find me?"

"Never mind that. We'll have plenty of time to talk later. We don't want to put these poor people off any longer than we have to!" Singleton looks down at Jennie and smiles. To Joel he says, "Excuse me son, do you mind if I stand here next to you?"

"No, Sir," Joel answers politely. "Here, I think you're the one that should be standin' next to Major." Joel moves a few steps to the right, allowing Singleton to act as best man.

Jennie stands with her mouth open, unable to speak. Major gently places his index finger under her chin and closes it. "I'll explain later," he whispers. Aloud he says, "Reverend, you may continue."

"Well, shall we try this again? If there is anyone here who has just cause that this man and this woman should not be joined in Holy wedlock, speak now or forever hold your peace." Reverend McDole holds his breath for a brief moment—no response—he lets out a sigh of relief. "William Ray, do you take this woman to be your lawful wedded wife? To have and to hold from this day forward, for better, for worse, in sickness and in health, forsaking all others until death you do part?"

Major looks lovingly at the angel standing before him. Holding onto every word the minister speaks, he pauses as if to think about his answer. Jennie pokes him teasingly in the ribs to coax a smile as he answers with a sincere and elated, "I do!"

"Jennie Meadows, do you take this man to be your lawful wedded husband. Do you promise to honor and obey, to cherish and keep him, in sickness and in health, forsaking all others until death you do part?"

"I do," she vows, looking romantically into Major's eyes.

"The ring, Major." Reverend McDole holds out his hand.

Joel pats his pockets as he searches for the dainty band of gold. "I know it's here, just give me a minute . . . *please!*"

"Harding Joel, so help me if you've lost that . . . " Jennie whispers, embarrassed at yet another interruption. "Find it!"

"Joel, is this it?" Singleton asks, holding the young man's hand up to reveal a tiny gold band on Joel's little finger.

"Oh, yeah. I forgot. I didn't want to lose it, so I put it on my finger. Sorry." Quickly, he slips the ring from his hand and gives it to Singleton who then, with an open palm, gives it to Major.

"Thank you," Major takes it from Singleton's hand and gives it to Reverend McDole. "Here you go."

"This ring. A gold circle, signifies Major's undying and ongoing love for Jennie." He hands the ring to Major. "Place it on her left hand and repeat after me. With this ring, I thee wed . . . ."

"With this ring, I thee wed. Hereto I plight thee my troth and do endow thee with all my worldly goods," Major repeats and slowly slips the ring onto Jennie's finger.

Joyfully and relieved, Reverend McDole announces, "I now pronounce you man and wife. You may kiss the bride."

Taking her into his arm's, Major gently kisses his bride.

The couple turns to face the guests as Reverend McDole introduces them, "Ladies and Gentlemen, Mr. and Mrs. William Ray."

Aunt Tess finishes playing the wedding march, and the newlywed couple run down the isle toward the church doors. The guests stand as Reverend McDole announces that the wedding reception will be held at the Sunflower Hotel.

THE DINING HALL AT THE SUNFLOWER HOTEL IS beautifully decorated with holly, pine wreaths, and pink and white velvet ribbons. A variety of delicious food is spread across a long table at the end of the room. Major and Jennie stand at the side of the large room welcoming their guests who file through in a line congratulating the happy couple.

"Singleton!" Major yells to his friend standing across the room. He waves and motions for the large man to join them.

"The bride is beautiful," Singleton says, bending slightly to speak to Jennie.

"Jennie, I want you to meet Frank Singleton," Major says, introducing his friend. "Singleton and I worked together for years with the Stowe Circus."

"It's very nice to meet you Mr. Singleton. I've heard many stories about you and Major in regard to the circus. I'm glad you could make it for the wedding," Jennie says, extending her hand.

"Thank you," Singleton answers. "Major, I know you have other guests to greet, and we'll talk again before I leave."

"I want to know what you've been doin' and how in the world you found me way out here in Kansas," Major says.

Suddenly, the door opens and a hearty voice blares throughout the room, "Hey, we missed the weddin', but we're here for the party!"

Before a startled crowd stand several members of the Sells Brothers band, including the clowns William Burke, Spader Johnson, George Kline, and Charles Bliss.

"Well, aren't you gonna invite us in," yells John Stein, the large man whose music always sets the mood for the circus. "Great! You've got a piano. Sorry couldn't bring the calliope. Too big, you know."

"Sorry we're late, Major," hollers William Sanger, clarinet player and leader of the circus orchestra. With his instrument in hand, the thin figure hurries past Major and follows Stein straight to the old upright piano in the corner. "We had a heck of a time gettin' a wagon at this time of night, especially with that snow storm."

"Now what?" Jennie cries loudly. "Major, who *are* these people?"

"They're friends of mine from the circus," he answers proudly. "They must of traveled for days to get here!"

"Great," she shouts and throws up her arms. "My wedding has been interrupted by a bunch of . . . charlatans!"

"No," he responds quickly. "A bunch of clowns and musicians."

"Wonderful!" she sighs sarcastically.

"Jennie," Layton yells, standing near the door. He watches each character, short and tall, thin and fat, loudly ramble past him. "Who are these charlatans?"

"Not charlatans, Papa," she answers, and smiles at Major. "Musicians and clowns."

"Oh," Layton answers, his voice calms as he turns to his wife. "Julia, what are we going to do now?"

"Enjoy the music and cut the cake," she happily replies. "And get used to your new son-in-law."

The music strikes up as the band plays a medley of circus tunes. Guests gather around the happy couple as they stand on a small platform behind the table to cut the cake. Standing next to her older sister, Maggie laughs at Major and Jennie as they carefully feed one another a piece of the sweet substance.

"A toast," Papa says, holding his glass of apple cider high in the air. The music stops for a moment while he speaks. "I know I didn't cotton to this idea . . ."

"Layton," Julia warns under her breath.

"Now, Mama," he says. "Let me finish. . . . in the beginning, but, after seeing how happy my little girl is today, I must admit I was wrong and give my blessing. To my lovely daughter, Jennie, and her new husband, Major, may their lives always be filled with good fortune and happiness."

"Thank you, Papa. I love you."

"I love you too, Jennie-girl," Layton tells her with tears in his eyes. "Be happy for your old Papa."

"I will," she answers with a smile.

Layton hears Maggie giggle while she talks to John Stein and William Burke. "Oh, no you don't," he says and pulls her from the company of the band. "One daughter mixed up with the circus is enough."

Reverend McDole leaves a group of guests and approaches the band. "Can you gentlemen play a waltz tempo in the key of C?" he asks the circus orchestra.

"I think we can handle that, Reverend," Stein answers .

"This is a song I wrote especially for Major and Jennie." The band strikes up a waltz tempo, and the Reverend sings, "Just a moment ago, I placed my wedding ring on your finger . . ."

"Jennie," Layton says. "Would you dance with your Papa. It may be the last one for a long time."

"I'd love to," she replies, holding her arms out. Layton must bend over to hold her tiny hands. Being sure to take small steps, he waltzes across the floor with Jennie. Soon, Major stands beside them and taps Layton on the leg. "Sir, may I cut in."

Layton nods and places Jennie's hand in Major's. Her father steps back.

"I believe he said this is our song," Major whispers. Before Jennie can say anything, he guides her onto the dance floor.

By the end of the evening, Layton joins in with the circus orchestra, playing his country fiddle, while Maggie dances a few waltzes with several clowns.

Nobody seems to notice as the tiny bride and groom slip out the door and up the stairs to their hotel room.

Chapter Ten

The Morning After

The hotel lobby is quiet. Major sits sipping his coffee, reflecting on the previous night and all its enchantment.

"Well, you're out early this morning," Singleton says. He grabs a chair and pulls it up to the table and sits down across from Major. "I figured you wouldn't be up and out 'til at least noon." Singleton pulls his watch from his pocket and checks the time.

"What time is it?" Major asks.

"Shoot far, it's only seven-fifteen."

"I never could sleep late."

"Where's the little bride? Excuse me, where's Jennie."

"That's all right," Major says with a smile. "She's still in bed. I thought she could use the sleep. You know . . ."

Singleton winks and nods. He motions for a waitress to bring him a cup of coffee.

"How in the world did you find out I was here in Yates Center?" Major asks, watching the large man stir a spoonful of sugar into his coffee. "And where have you *been* all these years?"

"I'm still in Kentucky. After I left Sells Brothers that year, I went back home. I married and settled down on a farm just outside Paducah."

"That still don't explain how you ended up here last night."

"I'm getting to that. Several weeks ago, I just happened to be up in Columbia when I ran into some old circus buddies. They told me where you were, so I hot-footed it this direction. I figure better late than never."

"This is great! I just couldn't believe it when you came a bustin' through those church doors. You were a sight for sore eyes."

"You were a pretty good sight yourself."

"Seeing you here like this, drinkin' coffee in the hotel lobby, reminds me of Memphis, when we were with the Stowes. Remember?" Major asks thinking about the good ole days.

"Yeah. I remember that swanky hotel with all the red trimmings. I'll never forget having to take care of Birdie, the Stowes little girl. She sure took a shine to you."

"She was a cute little thing." A note of sadness creeps into Major's voice. "She could sure stir a lot of trouble, that little one."

"Yeah, how about New Orleans and that bunch of people that followed you two through town to the fair grounds."

"Yeah, I had to cover Birdie's eyes as we passed the brothels. She kept wantin' to know why the ladies were hangin' over the banisters in their underwear."

Singleton and Major enjoy the morning reminiscing about circus days together and catching up on the time spent apart.

JENNIE WAKES TO THE SUN SHINING THROUGH THE
lace curtains that cover the window. The room is bright as
she turns over in bed and sees the vacant spot next to her.
She remembers the previous night and smiles.

Looking across the room she spies a note on the
dresser, propped against the mirror. Carefully, Jennie
slides from the bed. The floor is cold, but the fire in the
fireplace warms the room, making it comfortable to walk
around without her robe. Picking up the note, she reads:

> *Dear Sweet Mrs. Ray,*
> *I woke early from a most glorious night*
> *filled with love and tenderness and did not*
> *want to wake the fair princess who slept by*
> *my side. I am in the lobby enjoying a cup of*
> *coffee and many memories of our first night*
> *together. I love you dearly, sweet Jennie.*
> *Your loving husband,*
> *Major*

Jennie holds the letter to her bosom and happily whispers,
"I love you too, Major." She wishes Major would come
back to the room—just for a little while.

Dancing lightly around the room, she is overwhelmed
with excitement as thoughts of married life play in her
mind. Jennie pulls a dress from the trunk her mother and
sister helped pack. Standing in front of the mirror, she
holds the dress up to see how it looks.

Suddenly, she realizes that when she leaves the room,
everyone will know about her night with Major. "Oh, my!"
she gasps. "I can't go down there."

Jennie envisions the stares from people in the lobby as
she descends the long staircase. Her face turns red with

embarrassment. But she can't stay in their hotel room forever.

"I'll act like nothing happened," she says to herself. "Oh, that's ridiculous. Who would believe that? Why should I be embarrassed? We *are* married, after all!"

Jennie continues to talk to herself as she dresses, and after fastening the last button on her shoe, she smooths out her dress with her hands and leaves the room. The hall is empty and her tiny footsteps echo throughout the long walkway. Coming to the top of the staircase, she stops and takes a deep breath.

"Okay," Jennie mutters to herself. "Hold your head high and act the lady." Slowly, she descends the staircase. All eyes are on her.

Major notices the whispers that circulate through the room, and looking toward the stairs, he sees Jennie. "She is even more beautiful this morning," he says to himself as he watches her approach his table.

"Good-morning, gentlemen," Jennie says, standing next to Major and Singleton. "Do you mind if I join you?"

"Good-morning, Mrs. Ray," Singleton greets politely. "I hope you slept well."

Jennie blushes and avoids the man's eyes—and her new husband's as well—and answers, "Yes, I did. And please, call me Jennie. Everyone does."

"Would you like a cup of coffee and perhaps some breakfast this morning?" Singleton asks and waves for the young waitress who is busy doing nothing across the room. "Could we have some more coffee and a menu for the lady, please?"

The waitress immediately brings Jennie a menu and pours more coffee for the two men. Trying not to stare, the young lady takes Jennie's order for ham and eggs.

"Have you two been talking about old times?" Jennie asks.

"Yes, we were. In fact, we were just talking about the first circus we worked with and the tragedy that fell on it," Singleton answers.

"Oh, really. What happened?" she asks curiously.

"Major knows more about that than I do. In fact, that's where he acquired the title, Major. The owner, William Stowe, gave him that name the night he joined the troupe."

"You never told me that, Major. I'd love to hear more about your adventures with the circus."

"I'll tell you about it someday, but it's a sad tale and now's not the time," Major tells his wife as he takes her hand in his and gently squeezes it.

Noticing the strain in Major's voice, Jennie quickly changes the subject. "Singleton, when must you return home?"

"I need to be going right now," Singleton answers, looking at his watch. "Because the stage leaves for Paducah in about an hour, and I must be on it."

"We'll be living in Missouri," Major says to Singleton as the large man stands. "I'm at the same place. If you're ever out that way, you and your wife must stop and see us."

"We will," Singleton answers and shakes Major's hand. "And it was nice meeting you, Jennie. I wish all the happiness in the world for you and Major."

"Thank you, sir," she replies. "And have a safe trip home."

"Singleton, I want you to know how much I appreciate you traveling all that distance to be at my wedding," Major says, as tears well in the corners of his eyes and a large lump forms in his throat. "I've missed you terribly all these years. Keep in touch."

"I will," Singleton answers, placing a large hand gently on Major's shoulder. "I promise."

Standing next to each other, Major and Jennie watch Singleton leave the lobby. "I don't believe I'm hungry right now," Jennie tells Major. "But, I do believe a short walk in the cool, brisk morning air would do me a lot of good. How about you?"

Understanding Jennie's timid smile, Major, pleasantly surprised at what he is hearing, quickly answers, "I believe you're right. A walk would do us both good."

"I'm going upstairs to get my coat and hat," she says, and teasingly walks up the stairs with Major following close behind.

Chapter Eleven

A New Adventure

Major and Jennie return with Mrs. Ray to Cotton Plant where they remain until a letter arrives from Sells Brothers announcing the need for Major to rejoin the circus. Within a few weeks, the young couple pack their bags and board a train bound for Cincinnati, Ohio.

It is a long journey for Jennie, and Major constantly worries about his fragile bride. With each day and each mile they grow closer, one living for the other—inseparable.

As the train nears its destination, Major grows excited. He speaks often about the circus, and for the past few days it is the only subject to pass his lips, except for a thousand I love you's to his new wife.

Major continually watches Jennie as she sleeps, reads her Bible, even while she sits cross-stitching. He marvels at her spiritual strength and wishes he had such faith in God.

"What are you looking at?" Jennie asks, smiling.

"A miracle. A miracle."

"Oh, you are so silly." Jennie giggles.

Illustration 3:

On the front porch of his mother's home, Major poses with his mother and his wife Jennie.

Photo courtesy Johnny and Lavada Jones

"I love you, Jennie Ray." The softness in his voice and the tender squeeze he gives her hand shows his love for her.

"And, I love you," she whispers softly, placing a gentle kiss on his warm cheek.

AFTER MANY LONG HOURS, THE TRAIN PULLS INTO Cincinnati. A circus wagon waits nearby to escort the couple to the winter headquarters where Major will introduce Jennie to a new way of life.

The wagon passes under the great Sells Brothers Circus banner that stretches above the entrance to the circus headquarters. Major watches as performers and animal keepers busy themselves preparing for the coming season.

"Major?" Ephraim Sells yells from across the lot. "I'm glad you made it safely." He walks swiftly toward the wagon, dodging acrobats and clowns who jump, somersault, and flip their way around the grounds.

"Hello, Mr. Sells." Major says, jumping from the wagon and landing solidly on his feet. "Come here. I want you to meet my lovely wife."

"Hey, you're getting pretty good at the jumping stuff. We may have to hire you as an acrobat instead of a Midget," Ephraim laughs, approaching the wagon. "You must be Jennie. Major's told us all so much about you, but you're even more beautiful than he described," Ephraim says, taking Jennie's hand and lightly kissing her wrist.

"Thank you." Jennie can feel her cheeks grow hot with embarrassment.

"Mr. Ephraim Sells, this is my wife, Jennie," Major announces, formally introducing the two. "Jennie, this is Mr. Ephraim Sells."

"How do you do," Jennie says politely. "I'm very pleased to meet one of Major's employers and friends."

"Thank you, Ma'am. Let me help you down." Carefully he lifts her from the wagon and sets her on the ground. Her head barely reaches his waist when she stands beside him.

"Where do you want us to stay?" Major asks, reaching out and gently taking Jennie's hand.

"I thought you and Mrs. Ray might want to stay in one of the houses reserved for families. You know where they're located, Major. It'll be house number fifteen. I'll have your things delivered if you want to wander a bit."

"Thanks. I think I'll give Jennie a tour of the place. I'll come by and speak with you later about business."

"I'll be in my office when you're ready," Ephraim assures Major before getting into the wagon and giving the driver instructions. "There's no hurry. We'll be here for a few more days."

Gray clouds overhead indicate that the April showers of yesterday and today will probably continue. Making sure Jennie's delicate black leather laced shoes remain dry and untouched by muddy water standing stagnant along the way, Major guides her safely through the paths that separate train cars and circus tents.

"Get outta here!" A tall, thin man scrambles out the large cookhouse door, stumbling down the stairs to the ground. A short, slightly bald man stands behind him, waving an iron skillet in the air and yelling, "Don't you be givin' me orders 'round my own kitchen!"

"Uh-oh, stand back," Major says, placing his arm in front of Jennie to keep her from getting any closer to the cookhouse. "They're at it again."

"Who?" she asks.

"Don't cause me any trouble, Sam Goodwin!" shouts the tall, thin man at the end of the steps who is standing ankle deep in mud and water. Shaking his fist high in the air, he continues his insults to the fat little man. "That may be your kitchen, but it's *my* cookhouse, and don't you forget it!"

"Don't you shake your fist at me, Will Swiggers!"

"I'll do anything I darn well take a notion to," Swiggers replies, shaking his large fists even harder.

"That's who," Major answers, pointing to the two feuding men. "They go at it several times a year."

"One of these days I'm gonna let you have it," Goodwin yells to Swiggers.

"Oh, yeah. With what? That skillet you're always wavin' in the air?"

"You're runnin' from it, ain't ya?" Goodwin laughs sarcastically and disappears through the cookhouse door.

"You old pig!" Swiggers angrily stomps off, leaving a trail of mud behind him.

"But that's what's nice about this place," Major says smiling. "It never really changes."

"Who and what was *that* all about?"Jennie asks, curiously watching the furious Mr. Swiggers stomping madly down the path toward the front gate.

"That, my dear, was William Swiggers, the cookhouse man, and Sam Goodwin, the cook. There's been an on-going feud between those two for years. One minute they're fightin' like two old sore tailed tomcats, and next thing you know they're buyin' each other beers."

"Why are they always fighting?"

"Well, Swiggers likes to think that because he runs the cookhouse, he also runs the cook. Sam don't see it that way."

Major and Jennie continue their conversation as they walk past several animal houses. The smell of animals, manure, and straw remind Jennie of the farm she grew up on.

She sighs. "That smell takes me back home to when Papa was tending the horses in the barn."

"It only reminds me of an old smelly barn." Major teases.

"Oh, you! You know what I mean!"

"Come on. I know someone who's anxious to see you again." Major smiles broadly, tugging at her slightly. The two run like children down the fairway.

The rain begins to pour like water from a pump as they enter the large open-ended building. Raindrops play a crude melody as they hit the tin roof overhead. The roof leaks in several places, but straw which has been scattered across the dirt floor soaks up the water which is now seeping into the dark and aging barn.

Jennie's hair falls loosely around her shoulders as her comb falls to the ground. Major picks up the pearl covered object, and touching the rain-soaked strands that hang carelessly in her face, he takes her gently in his arms and kisses her long and passionately, his heart beating furiously as it always does when he holds her close. Their souls themselves seem to join.

They stand almost motionless, like statues carefully sculpted by an Italian artist in a timeless state—a world composed only of them. Suddenly, the high pitched cry of an animal startles them back to reality.

"Where exactly are we?" Jennie asks, noticing the strong smell of animals and the strange size of the stalls around them.

"You'll see," Major answers mysteriously, leading her deeper into the old barn. They stop and stand in front of a large stall filled with a vast amount of hay.

"Where *are* we?" Jennie stands near the entrance of the huge stall, her back to a gate. The cool, damp air chills her, but not nearly as much as Major's silence as he stands motionless in front of her.

Soon the sound of straw stirring behind her becomes evident. Heavy footsteps follow. Turning, she screams and jumps behind Major, crying out, "My, Lord, what is *that?*"

"Hello, old friend." Major strokes the huge rough, gray trunk which is already reaching out to search the little man's pockets for peanuts. "Yeah, I've got a couple for you, right here." Removing several of the elephant's favorite morsels from his pockets, Major carefully feeds them to Dick, the circus' favorite pachyderm.

"Oh, you scared me!" Jennie sighs, clutching her chest. Reaching out, she gently runs her hand along the rough trunk that yearns for attention. "I remember you," she whispers.

"I sure have missed you, boy!" Major exclaims, rubbing the elephant's long trunk. "Dick here is my best friend. We have a special bond, don't we boy?"

Dick raises his head, and with his trunk high in the air, roars loudly as if to agree with Major. The elephant again rubs against Major, searching for more peanuts.

"See," Major says to Jennie. "I told you we have a special bond."

"Yeah," she answers, laughing. "And I think it's in your pocket."

"Watch this," Major says as he picks up a stick from on the ground. Gently tapping Dick on the back of his right front leg, Major orders, "Up! Dick, up!"

Dick obediently sits up with his front legs high in the air as if reaching for the rafters overhead.

"That's great," Jennie says, clapping her hands together. "Bravo!"

"Down, Dick! Down!" Major orders. The elephant quickly stands on all four feet. "Good boy!" Major praises the animal and slips him another peanut.

"Okay, big boy, it's time for your bath," orders a young boy who rounds the corner of Dick's stall. With a large brush in one hand and a bucket in the other, he addresses Dick with much love, "Sorry folks, but it's time for this bull's bath."

"That's all right. We have to go anyway." Major motions for Jennie to move close to his side by reaching out for her hand. "Who are you?"

"I'm Ben. I give the elephants their baths and make sure they're cared for properly." His voice cracks when he speaks as mother nature plays her games with the adolescent who is going through the natural stage from boyhood to manhood. "Who are you?" he asks, curiously staring at the miniature couple in front of him.

"I'm Major Ray, and this is my wife, Jennie. We just got here. I've been with Sells for years, but this is my wife's first year."

"Hello, it's nice to meet you." Jennie reaches out to greet Ben. He quickly wipes the dirt on his trousers before graciously accepting her hand.

"I guess I'll be seeing you around quite a bit, Ma'am."

"Ben, you seem awfully young to be here alone. Where are your parents?" Jennie wonders if his family works for the circus or if he is, indeed, alone.

"Ma died several years ago. Pa just packed up and rode off one day about a year ago. I guess the pressure and loneliness was a bit much for him, so he left me and my little sister alone."

"Where's your sister?" Jennie asks, saddened by the abandonment the boy must feel.

"She's with Mrs. Franklin here in town. I stay here on the lot so's that Mattie, that's my little sister, can go to school and get the proper raisin' for a girl." Ben kicks the hay around his feet as he continues his story. "I work for the circus takin' care of the animals, and I send what little money I get to Mrs. Franklin."

"Ben, I want you to know that anytime you need someone, you know, a mother figure or anything like that, you can come to me." Jennie reaches up, and taking the young man's rough, calloused hand, gently squeezes it.

"Thanks. I appreciate that, Ma'am." He picks up the tin bucket at his feet and signals the elephant with a flip of his hand, "Well, gotta go. Come on, Dick. Here's your pail. Let's go."

Dick lifts the pail with his trunk as Ben taps him on the back of the legs with a thin switch. "Come on, Dick. Let's go." Before leaving the barn, Ben shouts once more to Jennie, "Thanks again, Mrs. Ray."

Jennie watches as the boy, dwarfed by the elephant next to him, walks through the large double doors. Silhouetted by the afternoon sun breaking through the clouds, his image is that of a man—not a boy.

"I sometimes forget in my own selfishness how lucky I really am," Major says sadly, watching the orphaned boy disappear from view. "I am truly blessed because, no matter what happens, good or bad, I can endure what life hands me as long as I have you by my side, Jennie," he whispers, unaware of the trials and tribulations that lie ahead of them.

Chapter Twelve

First Experiences

Dawn finds circus performers, kinkers, and roustabouts busily loading the Sells Brothers train, preparing to leave the winter headquarters for Tiffin, Ohio, the first stop of many this year. The April rain continues through the last day of the month, but the show must go on.

Jennie watches the beautiful trunk she treasures being hastily thrown onto the train. She knows that with time and the accumulation of miles, its loveliness will soon fade.

The steam billowing out beneath the great steel wheels of the engine reminds Jennie of the giant fire-breathing dragons in tales her father told her as a child. She misses her family, and she is unsure of the life that is ahead of her—only a step away.

"Are you all right?" Major touches her shoulder softly and sees the sadness in her eyes as she watches the strangers loading their luggage.

"Yeah, I'm fine." Jennie loves Major with all her heart and soul, but she has mixed feelings about the decision she made, and can only hold onto the Bible she keeps with her for comfort and assurance.

"Hey, Squirt," a familiar, but dreaded voice booms from behind. "Move outta the way before I step on you." Robinson's large frame overshadows the young couple like a dark cloud. The Giant shoves Major to one side with his heavy hand.

"Stop it!" Major cries out, falling helplessly to the wet ground.

"Major!" Jennie screams, quickly stooping next to him. Holding tightly to his arm she helps him to his feet. "You brute!" Her shrill voice carries through the air and circus performers gather in haste to assist.

"What's going on here?" asks Alonzo, the Strong Man. His dark complexion and muscled body are no match for the aggravating Giant who constantly bullies everyone but Alonzo and the Sells brothers.

"Nothing," Major answers, as he tries to wipe the mud from his suit. "I just fell—that's all."

"No, you didn't!" Jennie shouts. "He intentionally knocked you down!"

"Is that right, Robinson?" Alonzo asks.

"Maybe." Robinson turns to board the train. Stepping around Major and Jennie, he whispers under his breath, "You just wait, Little Man."

"The next time I catch you roughing up anyone smaller than you, Robinson, I'll take you apart myself," Alonzo warns, swinging the Giant around by the shoulder.

Robinson jerks from Alonzo's grip and boards the train.

"Are you two hurt?" Alonzo asks.

"No, we're fine. Thank you." Jennie appreciates the kindness her new friend in the circus offers and is thankful for support in regard to their cruel co-worker.

"Jennie, why did you do that?" Major's voice is angry and aggravated, not by just the interference of others but the embarrassment as well. "I could have handled the situation just fine."

"No you couldn't. I know how hard you want to keep your independence," Jennie speaks sincerely. "But, you sometimes have to swallow your pride and accept help from others."

"That's all right, Major," Alonzo says, hearing the conversation between Jennie and Major. "You have to remember, Major, we're a family, and as a family, we have to look out for each other. One day, I may need your help, and I'm sure you'll be there for me."

"Alonzo, you're a large and strong man. I'm extremely small. What can I do for you that you can't do for yourself?" Major never felt more inadequate than at this moment—not because he's unable to defend himself, but because he can't protect Jennie from the threats of the likes of Robinson.

"I don't know, but I bet there are many things you can do that I can't," Alonzo says, trying to ease his friend's mind. "Come on. Get settled on the train. We have a long day ahead of us."

The sun's rays peer over the horizon, scattering a red hue across a partly cloudy sky. "Look Major, isn't it beautiful?" Jennie points to the streaks of heavenly rays that dart from the ground, stretching upward, disappearing from view.

"Red sky at mornin', sailor take warnin'," Major dismisses the thought from his head, agrees with Jennie, and carefully helps her onto the train.

Although the trip only takes a few hours, it seems longer. The train rocks back and forth roughly while speeding down the hard, cold, steel rails. When the locomotive arrives in Tiffin, Ohio, people gather around to watch the train unload.

"Look, Mama!" a little boy yells, pointing to Major and Jennie as they step from the train.

Major worries that the stares from the boy and his mother will trouble Jennie, but he is pleasantly surprised when she steps from the train and approaches the curious duo. "Hello. I'm Jennie Ray and this is my husband, Major. What's your name?" She looks at the child standing next to his mother, holding tightly to her hand, and cautiously hiding behind her for protection. Jennie repeats her question, "Come on, honey, I won't hurt you. Won't you tell me your name?"

Slowly, the little boy peers from behind his mother. "I'm four." he says, holding up three fingers. He is as tall as the two adults in front of him.

"Do you mean you are four years old." She carefully takes his fingers and forms the number four. "My, but you're a big boy!"

"Come on, Johnny, we need to let the nice people get ready for their performance." The young woman takes her son's hand and apologizes for the inconvenience he may have caused them. "I am sorry about his questions and pointing, but he is young, and I'm afraid good manners is one thing I'm having a hard time teaching him."

"Nonsense, Major and I adore children. I hope you're taking him to see all the circus sights."

"Oh, we will. It was very nice to meet you, Major and Mrs. Ray." The young woman, tall and slender, wears a moderately plain dress. It is obvious she does not come from a wealthy family. More than likely, she is a farmer's wife. Major and Jennie watch her take the child's hand and guide him in the opposite direction.

"Well, I see you handled that very well," Major says surprised.

"Did you have any doubts about my ability to cope with this lifestyle of yours?" she asks.

"No, because you never cease to amaze me." Grinning, Major plants a kiss on her cheek, and the two venture toward the sideshow tent.

Within a few hours the circus tents are assembled and in place. By noon, the fairway already stirs with excitement. Children and adults who revert back to the reckless days of their youth, run chaotically through the muddy lot, each one trying to catch a glimpse of everything the circus offers in entertainment. Soon the day will be gone, and along with it, the giant tent town, leaving behind only memories of clowns, cotton candy, and exotic animals of every kind.

Accustomed to the stares of townspeople, Jennie is not prepared for the looks from people who file through the sideshow tent and stare at her as if she were an animal in a cage. The knot in her stomach grows, and the stench of people crowded into a small area permeates the air. Taking a rose scented lace handkerchief from her pocket, she gently holds it beneath her nose and takes a deep breath.

"It's bad, isn't it?" Major says, wrinkling his nose.

"Is it always this way? The smell, I mean?"

"Yeah, but you'll get used to it. Give it another couple weeks and you won't even notice."

"Hello, again, Major and Mrs. Ray." Jennie hears a familiar female voice and looks down from the platform to see Johnny and his mother standing on the opposite side of the rope.

"Hello! Johnny, are you having a good time here at the circus?" Jennie asks.

He nods shyly. The candied apple Johnny holds in his hand and the pink remains of cotton candy covering his face show he is having a wonderful time.

"Oh, he has seen every animal here. And, of course, he always wants to take them home with him," his mother laughs.

Major feels a breeze blow through the warm shelter, then a strong gust of wind shakes its canvas walls. Although it is three in the afternoon, the inside of the sideshow tent becomes dark.

"The wind is gettin' up. Must be a storm a comin'," Major says, stepping down from the stage to peer out the opening at the back of the tent.

"I know. It was beginning to darken a few minutes ago," the young woman says. "But, I didn't think it would blow in this fast. Come on, honey, we had better go. Major and Mrs. Ray, you two be careful." She takes Johnny's hand and quickly exits the tent.

Major stands at the back opening, watching Johnny and his mother bolt from the tent. The little boy's short legs and light weight make it almost impossible for him to keep up. As the storm grows stronger and the wind swifter, his mother sweeps him up into her arms and runs for a better shelter.

"Jennie, I think you had better come over here! Quick!" Major stares into the stormy skies, never taking his eyes away, even as he speaks. "Jennie! Get over here, now!"

"What is wrong with you?" Picking her Bible up from the floor at her feet, Jennie quickly joins Major at the tent exit.

"Look!"

Peering out the flapping canvas door, Jennie sees circus equipment blowing across the midway. People are screaming as huge tent poles break like toothpicks and are hurled across the lot by the ravaging winds.

"Major, what is happening?" From living in Kansas, Jennie is accustomed to stormy weather, but she has never seen a storm of this velocity.

"Jennie, watch it!" Major screams as he grabs her arm and pulls her away from the tent opening as it, too, collapses. Darkness surrounds them. Still holding onto Jennie's hand he can hear her breathing. "Jennie, are you hurt?"

"I'm fine, but what happened?"

"Evidently that last gust of wind shredded the tent."

Major clings to his wife and tries bravely to find a way out of their potential canvas grave. "The poles fell so as to make a kinda lean-to. Come on. Let's find our way outta this."

Major knows they were near the opening of the tent when it collapsed. They will have to make sure they crawl out toward the opening; otherwise, they will never find their way out. Carefully, Major guides Jennie through the dark, feeling his way, searching for the slightest ray of light. He hears Jennie quietly praying. "The Lord is my shepherd, I shall not want. He maketh me to lie down in green pastures, he leadeth me by the still waters . . . " Major is unable to see her, but he knows she still holds her Bible in her free hand.

Climbing over broken tent poles and boards from the stage, Major finally locates the opening. The weight of the heavy canvas is almost unbearable as he guides Jennie along the muddy ground. He must get his wife out of the frightening hole that swallows them.

"Major, do you think we will ever be free of this darkness? Will we ever see light again?" She continues to pray.

The tent moves and Major hears the sound of people running and shouting. "Anybody in there?" calls an urgent voice from the outside of the pile of heavy canvas.

"Yeah! Under here!" Major begins to beat the cloth roof that crushes them. The air is thin, and it is difficult to breathe. He tries desperately to keep his senses about him, but the sense of another time in his life overcomes him, and he can almost feel the cold, dark, Mississippi River that once tried to possess him. Like the light and warmth that drew him out of the darkness then, it is here for him again. The tent is peeled back, exposing the two little people to the elements as strong arms lift them and carry them to safety.

Rain and wind pound the backs of the men who are working to save all they can. Animals run free. Trainers try desperately to secure them safely in train cars. Winds whip the canvas dwellings like laundry on a clothesline in March. The skies remain dark. The storm continues to ramble through the tent city. A heavy rain falls with such force that it stings Jennie's delicate skin with each drop.

Looking around, Major notices the devastation of the once beautiful tent city that brought life and merriment to the people in the quiet little town of Tippin. Running for the train, Jennie steps over several toys lying in her path. She thinks about Johnny and his mother and hopes they reached safety before the storm hit with full force.

Major sees the Big Top shredded like pieces of rotten cloth wrapped around a stick. The wind pushes and pulls at the two little people who run to the train for shelter.

"Major!" Swiggers yells as he runs across the lot. "Major! We need your help!" The strain in his voice tells Major something is seriously wrong.

"What is it?"

"Alonzo's trapped in an abandoned well, and we can't get to him!"

"Jennie, you go on to the train, and I'll join you as soon as I can." He tells her as he turns to follow Swiggers.

"I will not!" she screams back. "I'm coming with you!"

"No! Go to the train and wait for me!" Major orders. "It's too dangerous out here!"

Jennie says nothing as she watches Major follow Swiggers across the lot. "I waited too long to find you William Ray and hell nor high water is going to keep me from your side!" she yells out and follows the two men.

Trying to keep up with Swiggers, Major doubles his pace but still cannot keep up with the long-legged man. "What happened?" he shouts.

Swiggers, who keeps running and looking back, briefly answers, "He was running to help some people over by the Big Top. He didn't see the abandoned well in the field. The old boards couldn't hold his weight, and he fell through."

"Didn't someone throw a rope to him."

"He's wedged in with his arms down. He can't move."

The rain continues to pour down, and Major knows it won't be long before the water will be rising in the old well where Alonzo is imprisoned. Looking back across the lot toward the train, Major sees Jennie following close behind him.

"Jennie!" he screams. "I told you to wait for me at the train! It's too dangerous out here!"

"I won't leave you out here!" she screams back. She pushes her wet hair from her face and she stands firmly in front of her husband. "And you can't make me leave! Not unless you come with me!"

Knowing her strong will, Major takes his stubborn wife by the hand and leads her to where a crowd gathers around a spot in the middle of the field. The cook tent is gone and the only thing remaining is the heavy cook stove.

Ephraim stands near the hole and shouts, "Alonzo? Are you all right?"

"Yeah, but you've gotta get me outta here. It's gettin' hard to breathe." His voice breaks—silence.

"Major, I don't know how much longer he can stay down there," Ephraim says.

"Have you sent someone down there to try to get him?" Major asks.

"Yes, we tried sending Swiggers down, but he's too wide and can't move his hands when he gets down there."

"You're the only one small enough to do it." Lewis steps from the crowd. He has several ropes in his hands. "We're going to tie a rope to your feet and lower you in head first. Then, you take the other rope and hook it around his waist."

"Do you think you can do that?" Ephraim asks.

"I'll try," Major answers and yells down the well. "Alonzo, I'll have you outta there before you know it!"

"You can't do that!" Jennie yells at Major. "It's too dangerous!"

"Jennie, I have to. Alonzo's life depends on it. Now if you can't stand there and wait quietly," he orders, "then go back to the train like I told you to, and wait for me there."

Frightened but steadfast, Jennie shakes her head and stands back. She holds tightly to the Bible in her hands and closing her eyes, she says a silent prayer.

Major lies on the ground. Lewis ties one rope around Major's feet and then hands him the second. "You ready?" Lewis asks.

"Yeah, I'm ready."

Lewis lifts Major and carefully lowers him into the dark hole. The moist walls brush against him and dirt begins to fall. It smells stale. The air is thin. Major fights back the urge to scream as he is lowered farther down. Water continually trickles down the sides of the well as the rain pours.

"How you doin' down there, Major?" Ephraim yells, overshadowing the opening of the deep hole.

"I'm all right! Stand back! I can't see!" The blood rushes to Major's head, and he can feel it pounding against his temples. He sees Alonzo wedged tightly between rocks jutting from the sides of the dirt well. Small rocks fall. He hears nothing—then they hit water. "How you doin', ole friend?"

"See, I told you I'd need you one day," Alonzo says, looking up at Major. His face is dirty and blood trickles from a cut on the right side of his forehead.

"Can you move at all?"

Alonzo tries to move his arms. He slips farther down. "No. I can't without fallin' more."

"All right. I'm gonna try and slip this around you." Major threads the rope with his small hand up under Alonzo's arm. He cannott reach the other side to grab the rope. "Move me a little more to the left!" he shouts to the men above. Lewis moves him to the left.

Major's head pounds harder, and he realizes he cannot remain any longer. "Alonzo, I'm gonna hook this around your arm right now, but I'll be back. Lewis, get me outta here, quick!"

Lewis pulls Major up and out of the hole. His face is blood red and the veins in his forehead show through the skin.

"What happened?" asks Ephraim.

"You try standing on your head for a long length of time and see what happens." Major sits at the edge of the well for a brief moment to rest. His head still pounding, he orders Lewis, "Lower me back down."

Again, the cold, damp air of the deep well surrounds Major. He can hear Alonzo's heavy breathing. Major's lungs fight to fill with clean air. His head still pounds at the temples, but the need to set his friend free is greater.

"Alonzo, are you still all right?"

"Yeah." Alonzo's voice is weak, but his will is strong. "I'm just hangin' around," he laughs a little, trying to break the tension and keep up a good front. He coughs. He slips a little more. Dirt falls. Splash.

"I know you're having a great time down here, but I think you need to save the jokes for later."

"I think you're right."

Major moves to the left and carefully shoves his hand under the great man's arm, threading the rope like thread through the eye of a needle. Quickly he pulls the hook through and tries to hook it to the other end of the rope. It's too short.

"Hey! Give me a little more rope! I need more rope!"

"He needs more rope!" echoes Ephraim from the opening of the hole.

Major can't see anyone, but he can hear the buzz of conversation on the surface. He again pulls more rope through. It slides roughly under Alonzo's arm pits. Alonzo flinches with pain as it burns his skin. The dirt loosens. The rocks that Alonzo is wedged between slip from the walls around him. He slides down the damp walls that hold him. He falls farther.

Major's heart jumps. His hands are quick. The hook is in place. "Got it!" he yells. "Pull!"

"Pull!" shouts Ephraim. "Pull!"

The line of men standing on the surface pull the rope with all their collective might. Suddenly, it tightens and jerks. Alonzo stops falling.

Major breathes a little easier. "I've got him! Now, get us outta here!"

Slowly, Lewis pulls Major to the surface and places him easily on the ground. Major's head spins; he sways. Then he sits and waits for the world to stop spinning.

"Are you okay, Major?" Ephraim asks standing over him while Lewis removes the ropes from Major's feet. "You did good, Little Man! You did good!"

"Major!" Jennie cries, and relieved that he is safely out of the well, kneels to wrap her arms around him. "I'm so proud of you."

Major says nothing. He watches the line of men who look like they're one side of a game of tug-o-war stand strong, pulling Alonzo to the surface. Carefully, after he is free, they place him next to Major.

"Hey, I owe you my life," Alonzo tells him.

"No, we're family. Remember?" Major answers.

Alonzo smiles and nods. Several men quickly load him onto a stretcher and carry him to the train.

"Major, can you walk?" Lewis asks, helping him to his feet.

"Yeah, I was just a little dizzy at first, but I'm fine now."

Thunder roars throughout the heavens as bolts of lightening streak across the sky, reminding those standing nearby of the dangerous storm that surrounds them. Quickly, Major grasps Jennie's hand and runs to the train for shelter.

Breathless, tired, and wet, Major and Jennie finally board the locomotive. The rain still beats heavily on the metal roof overhead as deafening claps of thunder boom outside.

After changing clothes, Major and Jennie lie in their sleeping quarters, listening to the storm that still rages outside. They are relieved to be safely inside, but dark visions of a devastated circus still weigh heavily on their minds.

"Major, how do you do it?" Jennie asks, her voice trembling even as she lies in the safety of her husband's arms.

"Do what?"

"Live with this every day?" she cries silently. A tear falls from her cheek and lands on Major's chest. "First, it's the attitude of those rude people you have to work with. Then, there's the people who come to gawk at you. Actually, most of those are nicer than the ones you work with. Then, you have the weather. It either blows you away, or drowns you, or both!"

"You take your licks and go on," he answers. "You become stronger with each tragedy, with each death, with each rude comment. You just take it as it comes to you."

Jennie snuggles closer to Major and whispers, "I love you."

"I love you, too," he answers and squeezes her gently. "Try to get some sleep, and don't worry. You're safe now."

Chapter Thirteen

A Letter Home

Gradually, Jennie grows accustomed to the fast pace of the circus as it travels through town after town, state after state. Days turn into weeks and weeks into months as the steel rails guide the great iron locomotive farther west toward California.

It is July 18. The hot summer sun is still behind the western horizon when the train arrives in Ogden, Utah. The workers unload animals, performers, and tents to make ready for another day. Jennie sits near the corral full of horses watching the sun rise, dreading the heat that will soon make the sideshow tent almost unbearable.

"Jennie?" Major approaches his wife. She sits, almost motionless, watching the beautiful show horses run circles in the tiny space allowed them.

"I'm here," she answers sadly. "I was just sitting thinking of home and how nice it will be to see Mama and Papa. Oh, Major as soon as the tour is over can we go to Kansas and see them? Please."

"Jennie, I've been talking to Ephraim, and we aren't going straight home when the season's over."

"What do you mean. We're not going home?'" The tension in her voice is mixed with anger and disappointment. She moves to stand near the ropes of the make-shift corral. She may be small, but the temper she holds inside is larger than any giant on the lot. Turning to look into her husband's eyes she demands, "Answer me, William Ray! What do you mean we're not going home?"

"Jennie, calm down, and I'll tell you why." He puts his arm around her waist. "Jennie, have you ever wondered what it would be like to go to faraway places?"

She looks at her husband. Her eyes widen and her right brow rises like it often does when she knows Major is up to something. "Like, *how far* away?"

"Well, is Australia far enough?" He lets the words roll off his tongue quickly. He closes his eyes and waits for the wave of wrath he knows is coming.

"*Australia?*" Jennie yells. "California is far enough, but Australia! Are you *crazy?*" Desperately, she tries to calm herself and overcome the urge to shake some sense into the boy-like man standing next to her. "God, give me strength," she whispers under her breath.

"Come on, Jennie. Admit it. It'll be great. Traveling across the ocean to Hawaii, Samoa, Australia. It's the chance of a lifetime."

"No. Major, I have endured heat, tornados, embarrassment and sometimes loneliness. I've seen people bitten, beaten, and trampled the past several months. And now, you tell me that you're going to drag me half-way around the world on a boat to . . . Lord knows where . . . " she stops in mid sentence and thinks for a moment. "How long? How long are we gonna be on this, so called boat, traveling through all of these wonderful places?" she finishes sarcastically.

Major looks around and sees a crowd beginning to gather. Jennie is outspoken, but she usually overlooks Major's antics and his uncanny ability to get into trouble.

"Now, Jennie. Calm down." Considering the crowd, he takes her by the elbow and leads her behind the Big Top.

Jennie wiggles free from his grip and stands impatiently with tears in her eyes. "*How long,* Major? How long will we be gone?" she cries, aggravated because he has not mentioned it to her before now.

"We're scheduled to leave in October, and we should return around June, next year."

Jennie says nothing. She turns away from Major and looks across the back lot. The silence between them is deafening. A barrier has formed to separate them for the first time.

"Jennie." Major speaks her name softly, trying to ease the tension and break the silence.

"I need to be alone right now." She walks away slowly, leaving Major helplessly alone. "I must think about this."

BACK AT THE TRAIN, JENNIE FINDS HER LUGGAGE IN the baggage car. With great effort she carefully opens the trunk that holds her most prized possessions. Its once beautiful oak slats are growing dull from traveling and harsh handling. Tears leave trails along her cheeks as she stands on the tips of her toes and bends over the edge of the trunk. Reaching beneath several layers of clothing, she removes a small, square box.

Holding the box to her chest, she cautiously slides down along the trunk and sits on the hard ground. Gingerly she removes the slightly worn lid and pulls a small tin photograph from the box. Running her fingers over the delicate frame, she whispers, "Dear Mama and Papa, how I miss you. Will I ever see you again?"

"Jennie, are you all right?" asks Lizzie, appearing from around the corner of the boxcar. She is concerned and tries to ease Jennie's pain of longing for her family.

"Oh, yes. I'm fine." She quickly wipes the tears that glisten on her cheeks. "I just needed some time alone. That's all."

"Major's worried about you."

"I know."

"Is that a picture of your family?" Lizzie sits next to Jennie and reaches for the photograph. "May I?"

"Yes, it's my mama and papa."

"Oh, what a handsome couple." Lizzie admires the photograph, hands it back to Jennie, and tries to comfort her a little. "Jennie, what's wrong?" Lizzie can see the tiny tears flowing uncontrollably.

"I miss my family, and now Major tells me I won't see them for another year. "

"You'll get used to it. I promise." Lizzie sympathetically wraps an arm around the child-like figure next to her. "I tell you what. I'll stall Major while you sit here and think."

Jennie nods in agreement. She watches the tall, white-haired woman with the strange pink eyes, rise and leave. Once again Jennie reaches into the box that sits next to her. She removes several sheets of paper, a quill pen, and a bottle of ink. Setting the ink bottle beside her and placing the box in her lap for a table, she begins to write:

Ogden, Utah

July, 17 1891

My Dearest Mama and Papa,

> *I seat myself to write this much needed letter to let you know all is well with Major and myself.   I hope this letter finds you the same.*
>
> *There are some good times, but I find it hard sometimes, because I miss you very much. I was hoping to see you as soon as the tour was over, but the Lord has other plans for Major and me.*
>
> *Mama, Major is becoming a better Christian. He joins us for church on Sunday when the lot of us come together for worship. Mr. Sells never works on Sundays. He says that is the Lord's day and no money will be made for ourselves on that day.*

Jennie realizes that the circus life is not what she envisioned it would be. She remembers sitting on the bleachers, watching her first circus, and thinking how exhilarating it was to see the beautiful equestrians and trapeze artists perform. She thought it would be a wonderful life, full of fun and excitement. She was wrong. The circus to a spectator is full of life and merriment, but to the performer, it is a hard life full of disasters and sometimes, death. She continues writing to her family.

> *. . . In June, while we were in Nebraska, a parade horse attached to a cart jumped from a bluff down onto a crowded street. Mama, it was terrible. Several ladies and children were killed.   It seems like there is always some type of tragedy that besets us; however, I pray every day that the good Lord will look upon us and bless Major and me.*

And He has blessed us by keeping us safe, but as I wrote earlier in this letter, The Lord has other plans for us and I can only accept what He hands us without question. As part of this new plan we will be setting sail for Australia in October and will not return until June the following year. Major says we will be sailing to Australia, Samoa, and Hawaii. I must say I am afraid to travel that far and across water, but I must put my faith in God always because he has a set plan for everything.

Tell dear sweet Maggie hello for me and tell Harold Dewitt to behave himself and not to pester poor Harding Joel too much.

If it be the Lord's will, I will see you upon our return in June. I have enclosed the route for the remainder of our tour in the country. I wait earnestly for your letters to reach my loving hands. God bless you all. Your most loving daughter,
Jennie

"Jennie," Major calls. "It's time for the show to begin. Are you ready?"

Hearing her husband's voice, Jennie holds the box to her chest. Then she quickly places it into the trunk. Stretching to reach the lid, she lowers it, securing her most precious recollections from the past and says, softly, "I'm ready."

"Jennie, I'm sorry I didn't tell you earlier about the overseas tour." Major sees the sadness in her eyes and the dampness on her delicate cheeks from tears that, only moments ago, fell like rain.

"I'm sure it will be exciting," she wraps her arms around Major's neck, forgiving him. She plants a tender kiss upon his lips. "Major, as long as I'm with you, I will be happy. I don't care where we go as long as we're together."

Chapter Fourteen

Letters From Home

Jennie stares off into the distance at the September sun as it sets along the horizon. She leans against the small makeshift corral for the circus horses, while her thoughts wander to home and family as the time to set sail grows nearer. Jennie has not heard from her family in over a month, but she knows the mail has to catch up with the traveling troupe, and by the time she receives a letter, it's old news.

"Jennie!" Major shouts across the circus lot. "Jennie! A letter from your folks!"

Jennie's eyes brighten and a smile replaces the sad frown she wore only moments ago. "A letter from Mama and Papa?" Jennie yells back to her husband as he runs toward her. "Hurry!"

Major quickly hands Jennie the letter she so anxiously awaits. Sitting on the ground, she hurriedly opens the en-

velope postmarked several times from each post office it
was delivered to.

August 15, 1891

Dearest Jennie and Major,
   *We quickly answer your letter that came to
us this day, and we sincerely hope all is well.
We worry about you continually, but know as
long as you are faithful to the Lord, He will
keep you safe.*
   *It is good to hear from you and to know that
you are having a good time traveling with the
circus. But of course you realize that all good
times are impossible without some bad, and
Maggie was especially sorry to hear the sad
news about the wagon and horses going over
the cliff.*
   *We, too, were hoping to see you and Major
as soon as the season is closed. But my darling Jennie, we talked about this before you
married, and you knew what to expect when
you married a man who was with the circus.*

   Jennie stops reading long enough to remember the
conversation she and her mother had that afternoon in
the kitchen then again that night after supper.   It was
then that Jennie realized how much she loved Major, and
it didn't matter where they traveled, as long as they were
together. But Mama was right about one thing, it is hard
to continue each day as hundreds of people file through to
stare and gawk.

"Jennie, is it bad news?" Major asks when she stops reading. "Somethin' hasn't happened to your Mama or Papa has there?"

"No," she answers, smiling. "Everything is fine. I just stopped to think about something Mama said. That's all."

> . . . *Maggie has been seeing Jedidiah Smith's boy, Samuel. He's a nice boy, but I don't think we need to look for any preacher yet. Your papa isn't all that excited about the courting Samuel's been trying to do. Your papa hasn't quite gotten over your marriage yet.*
>
> *Everyone at church misses your preaching once a month, and the kids miss having you teach Sunday school. Perhaps you'll be home soon and you can do it again. . . .*

Jennie stops smiling as she reads the last few lines of the letter, and a tear slips from the corner of her eye. She wipes it from her cheek before Major sees it.

> . . . *Jennie the place just isn't the same without you. We all miss you terribly, especially Papa. He misses coming in and picking you up in the air, listening to you bicker about how old you are, but soon you will be home.*
>
> *Maggie and the boys are pea green because you are sailing across the ocean to faraway places while they sit on a dirt farm in Kansas. Enjoy it Jennie, while you can. Be happy with Major and always remember that home is where he is.*

We all love and miss you. Be safe and if
you keep the Lord in your heart, you will re-
turn to us soon. Tell Major we love him too.
Your loving Mama, Papa, and Maggie.

Jennie holds the letter close to her heart as she thinks about the words on the pages. Major sits patiently waiting to hear the news from home.

"Well, what did they say?" he asks curiously. "I gather all is well?"

"All is well," Jennie answers, handing him the letter. "And, Mama's right. As long as I'm with you, I am home."

Chapter Fifteen

The Monowai

The October sun has not yet risen. Major wakes to the smell of the salt air of San Francisco Harbor. Even with the window closed, the Harbor Hotel room still reeks of salt and fish. Quietly, he slips his arm from Jennie's resting shoulders and watches her sleep. Without waking her, he eases his legs carefully over the side of the bed and jumps to the cool, hardwood floor with a slight thud.

Staring out the window at the sleepy harbor streets below, Major realizes that months have passed so quickly he cannot remember when summer ended and fall began. The 1891 season is over, at least here in the United States, but the memories remain—memories of joy and grief among the company of circus people who travel daily trying to support their families.

The sound of water lapping in the harbor brings back a terrifying memory from another time when Major traveled by water with another circus: the cries from the people, helpless on a showboat floating like a lit torch down a cold, dark river. This horrifying image of the past fades as he realizes the fire he sees is only a lantern held high in a fisherman's hand as he gathers nets in the pre-dawn hours.

Major looks again at Jennie, still sleeping like a little angel. Her long dark hair lies loose on the pillow. Gently, taking a few strands into his hand, he lets the silken threads slip through his fingers. Careful not to wake her, he pulls the satin spread over her to keep her warm. The October mornings are cool, especially by the sea.

"Morning, my love," Jennie whispers as she stretches her arms over her head. "Have you been standing there long?"

"No, only a few minutes."

"Did you sleep well?"

"No, but I didn't disturb you, did I?" He wants her to believe the excitement of the trip is what interrupts his nights, and not the horrifying memories of a burning ship that grips his soul.

"No, I always enjoy sleeping in your arms," she smiles, extending a loving hand. "What's wrong? You're not having second thoughts about us, are you?" Her smile fades as she sees the serious expression on Major's face.

"No. It's not that," he reassures her. "Do you remember when you asked me about the Stowe Circus and I told you I would tell you about it some other time? "

"Yes," she answers curiously. "Why?"

"I believe it's time for you to know." He climbs back into their bed and takes Jennie into his arms as he tells her the tragic story.

"I was twenty-one when my father died, and to support my family, I was compelled to join the Will Stowe Showboat circus. We traveled along the rivers on several different charted steamers, but the last and most beautiful of them all was the *Golden City*.

"Frank Singleton and I were with Will and Lizzie Stowe for only about four or five months, but we came to love them all like our own families, especially their children, four-year-old Birdie and her older brother, Willie. I took a real likin' to their little girl because she reminded me of my nephew, Thomas. She was about his age, too."

"You keep referring to them in the past," Jennie interrupts. "Why?"

"I'm gettin' to that," he says, and continues with his story. "It was in March, and the showboat was steamin' down the Mississippi River on the way to meet up with Dan Rice, the Stowe's partner, at Cairo, Illinois. I remember lookin' at the stars that night and thinkin' how beautiful they lay against the black sky. Reminded me of diamonds on black velvet, and the moon was so big and round that it looked like a huge circus balloon suspended in mid-air. Before Singleton and I went to bed that night, we waved to the night watchman who held his lantern high in the air so we could see our way to the second deck safely.

"I still hadn't quite gotten used to the rockin' of the ship and Singleton's earth shatterin' snorin', so I didn't sleep well. It was March 30, 1882. A quiet mornin' just before dawn at about 4:40 a.m. We were on the outskirts of Memphis. I was lyin' in bed listenin' to the water slap the sides of the ship and dozin' when, suddenly, I heard the captain yell, 'Fire! Fire on the main deck!'

"I'll never forget being trapped on that ship as it burned. Singleton saved my life that mornin' when he carried me out of our cabin and then jumped from the burnin' upper deck. The whole ship was engulfed in flames. People were jumpin' into the icy cold river to escape the fire. Most died that mornin'. Very few of us survived."

Jennie holds Major's hand tenderly and continues to listen as he unleashes his tragic memories. "If you were so close to Memphis, couldn't anyone help?" she asks sympathetically.

"Oh, there were a lot of people who tried. In fact, we floated right past the Southern Transportation Company dock there in the Memphis port, but each time the men threw ropes and tried to dock her, the fire burned clean through 'em and the ship just kept goin'. It was no use; nothin' could be done.

"I can still hear the screams of people and animals, and I can still smell the burnin' flesh. It was horrible, like a nightmare you can't wake from."

"How did you escape?" Jennie asks, stunned by what Major is describing to her. "And what happened to the Stowes?"

"The boat sunk outside President's Island, and I had no idea where Singleton was because we got separated during all the commotion. I didn't find out until later that he even survived. Me, Frank Stowe, and several others where rescued by several men in a small dinghy. The Stowes weren't that lucky. Everything and almost everyone was gone," he finishes his story sadly. "So you see, my reason to worry has nothin' to do with you."

"I'm sorry for the painful memories, but I'm glad I have you," Jennie tells Major, sitting up and looking into his tear filled eyes. "I love you, and while we're on that ship I want you to know you are not alone because I am with you, and God is with us both."

THE LIVESTOCK, HOUSED IN CENTRAL PARK SINCE THE arrival of Sells Brothers, is moved to a beautiful steamship, the *Monowai*. She is unlike any vessel Major has ever seen.

Her huge hull rises above the murky waters of San Francisco Bay while she sits majestically like a queen on her throne. The towering black stacks, wearing crowns of gold to accentuate her royal image, grow from her deck. Her crew, the royal court dressed in white, are busy making preparations for her guests who wait anxiously to meet her.

"Look at the people," Major says. He scours the area as a crowd of several thousand gather to bid farewell to the popular Sells Brothers Circus. "I've never seen this many people in one place before. At least not just for us."

"This is unbelievable." Jennie says uncomfortably. The carriage stops unsteadily in front of the huge ship, allowing the miniature couple to exit safely and board the great vessel untouched by the pressing crowd who want a closer look.

The long plank leading to the ship's deck is steep. Major and Jennie have difficulty crossing it.

Standing on the huge deck of the vessel, Major places a protective arm around Jennie. They watch the harbor full of people, consisting of friends and spectators, shouting "bon voyage" and "farewell" to those already aboard.

Bands play. Big banners of red, white, and blue wave high in the air. Voices break out in a chorus of "Olde Lang Syne".

Ephraim, his dark hair slightly graying with age, stands at the top of the long plank addressing the enormous crowd gathered below him. Raising his arms high in the air, he quiets those anxiously congregating on the cramped harbor dock.

"Friends," he shouts enthusiastically. "We have over 7,000 miles of hard sailing ahead of us, but your presence here today will truly make our journey easier." Shouts and cheers of the crowd partially drown out his words. He can barely be heard, but he continues, "Our travels will take us to Hawaii and then on to Samoa. From there, we will sail to Sydney, Australia, where we will perform for those 'down under'. But, we set sail with the thought of you in our hearts this day."

The whistle blows and steamy white clouds of smoke rise from the black stacks on deck. The ropes holding the ship in place at the dock are loosened, the anchor hoisted, and the ship slowly leaves the harbor.

Major and Jennie wave to the crowd below. A tear falls from the corner of Jennie's eye as the land she loves disappears from sight.

"Are you all right?" Major asks, gently wiping Jennie's tears with his handkerchief.

"Yes, I'm fine. It's just I've never been this far away from home before." She continues sadly, "Especially on a boat bound for a foreign land. I'm just a little uneasy."

"We're together and that's what's important." Major doesn't want her to worry about setting sail on a ship with no land in sight. Holding her head between his hands and looking into her eyes, he tells her, "As long as I am alive, I will always protect you. You are my queen, and I will always be your most humble servant."

"Oh, Major. I love you and you are not my most humble servant. You're my knight in shining armor." Jennie closes her eyes and silently says a prayer for their safe journey and return home.

THE CONTINUOUS UP AND DOWN MOVEMENT OF THE ship on choppy waters is difficult for many and causes a great deal of sickness the first few days. Once they acquire

their sea legs and become accustomed to the continued
movement, the circus people stroll on deck to enjoy the
view or play a few games. During the day, the ship's crew
is entertained by acrobats and jugglers practicing their acts
on deck. At night they dance, both crew and guests, while
Professor Merrick's band plays beautiful melodies that float
across the waters.

IT IS THE MORNING OF THE SEVENTH DAY, OCTOBER
24. The air grows warmer as the ship moves farther into
the South Pacific.

Major wakes and decides to walk the deck while Jennie
sleeps. The ocean breeze blowing across the port side is
refreshing. Standing near the rail, he sees several young
dolphins jumping through the water, silhouetted by the
sunrise.

"It looks like they're following us, doesn't it, Lad."
Captain Charles Carey says, as he stands behind Major.
The beautiful, sleek, gray dolphins swim alongside the
ship, never falling back.

Captain Carey is a tall Irishman in his late fifties. His
hair is white as snow; his eyes as blue as the ocean he
sails. He stands straight and tall, never letting his shoulders fall for even a moment, always prideful in his ship and
crew. He holds an ivory carved pipe between his fingers
while he talks. Every now and then he puts it in his
mouth and inhales the rich foreign tobacco.

"What are they doing?" Major asks, curious to the ways
of the sea.

"Some say the dolphins have actually saved the lives of
shipwrecked sailors by guiding them to land. And some
ships lost at sea have been led to safety and set on course
by them."

His Irish brogue reminds Major of Nathan O'Donald, who lived near his family at Cotton Plant. He remembers the day he borrowed the wagon from Nathan to join the Will Stowe Circus as it came through Caruthersville. It seems a lifetime ago, but then again, he remembers it as if it were yesterday.

"How long will they follow the ship?" Major asks. He has been watching the dolphins for several hours and they never slip back, but remain close, parallel to the ship.

"Oh, they may stay with us for days, at least till we spot some land. Then, they'll leave and go somewhere else."

The dolphins continue jumping and follow single-file one behind the other. With such grace and beauty, they can almost hypnotize anyone watching.

"The sea is beautiful, isn't she?" Again, the captain speaks. His voice is deep, but his feelings for the sea run deeper.

"Are you married, Captain?" Major asks.

"I'm married to the sea, little man, and I'm a dedicated husband. One day I will die in her arms—the only woman who can keep me. The sea can call any sailor to his death with her song of love."

"Captain!" shouts a crewman from the upper level of the ship. "The Island of Molokai is in sight." The captain signals in response to the information and turns to leave.

"Captain, is Molokai the island where we'll be stopping?"

"Oh, no. That's where the leper colony is located. We'll land on Oahu, about thirty miles from here," he responds quickly and leaves to join his crew.

Major continues to stare at the tranquil island as the ship passes. He sees pure white sand along the beaches, high mountain ridges covered with green ivy, wooded valleys and streams that encircle the island paradise. Molokai is beautiful, but it is also a prison, shut in on one side by the sea and on the other by a fifteen-hundred-foot wall also covered with beautiful green vegetation. To keep the island secluded and free from curiosity seekers, there is no wharf to dock a boat.

"Major, I've been looking for you." Jennie joins her husband and together they watch the island disappear. "I was worried when I woke up and you weren't there."

"It's beautiful isn't it?" He says, looking out across the ocean as the sun rises higher, and light dances off the rippling water around them.

"Yes, it is," she replies. "I don't think I have ever seen anything more lovely. Major, I'm glad we made the trip."

Soon they see the volcanic points of Mokapuu and KoKo Head, and at 8:30 a.m., Diamond Head comes into view. At 9:10, a pilot boards the *Monowai* to take her safely through the coral reef of Oahu's harbor.

All the guests and crew are on deck of the huge ship when Captain Carey makes his announcement. "Listen up," he instructs. His voice is deep and authoritative. "We will be here for twelve hours. During that time you may enjoy the fine company and sights of the island. Stretch and regain your land legs, but remember be back by ten o'clock because we will hoist the anchor and set sail for Samoa with or without you."

The ship's deck is crowded, and Major senses Jennie is uncomfortable with the crowd of anxious passengers eager for a look at the island paradise. Carefully, he guides her to the edge and waits for the boat to clear.

Major notices the ship-filled harbor contains the *U.S.S. Pensacola,* an American war ship. While in San Francisco, Major read about the unrest of the Hawaiian government and how the United States was slowly trying to take over the Hawaiian islands.

After catching Major's attention, Ephraim tells the young couple about the queen's request to see them. Overjoyed by the news, Jennie and Major return to their cabin and quickly dress for the occasion.

Jennie nervously pulls several dresses from the closet, and holding them up to her asks Major, "Which one?"

"What?" he asks while slipping on a black coat and top hat.

"Major!" she cries, trying to get his attention. "Look at these dresses and tell me which one I should wear!"

"Oh, I don't know. That one," he says, pointing to a dark blue cotton dress with a white blouse and short waist jacket. "I always like you in that one."

"I'm so excited!" Jennie declares, as she pulls the dress over her head. "Just think, the queen wants to see us!"

"I've never met a queen before," Major mutters. "What will I say?"

"I don't know," she answers, smoothing out her dark hair and tucking in several loose locks that fall from their pins. "But I do know if we don't hurry, we won't see her at all. How do I look?"

"Beautiful," he states proudly. "I just hope you don't outshine the queen."

"Oh, you!" she exclaims, planting a light kiss on his cheek as she walks past him on her way to the door. "Let's go before Ephraim and Fanny leave without us!"

After meeting Ephraim and Fanny on deck, the four leave the ship. At the foot of the plank they are greeted by several beautiful natives with leis draped over their arms.

"Aloha!" greets a young woman, smiling and placing a lei around Major's neck. The scent of orange ilima, the feathery red ohia, and the fragrant maile leaves envelop him.

"Thank you." He accepts the necklace graciously, but is bewildered by the customs of the Island natives. "What did she say?"

"'Aloha' is Hawaiian for 'hello.'" Ephraim tells Major. "The lei is a symbol of love and friendship."

"Oh, 'aloha' to you too," Major says, bowing low, and tipping his top hat.

The young barefoot girl giggles at the funny little man. She backs away and places another lei on a sailor who comes ashore to drink in the pleasantries of the island. People divide into groups, excitedly scattering in different directions.

A carriage waits for Ephraim and Fanny, Jennie and Major to take them to the palace.

SEEING THE ISLAND, OAHU, FOR THE FIRST TIME FROM the comfort of the carriage, Major and Jennie are amazed by the beautiful sites the island has to offer. It is like driving through a gigantic hothouse in a botanical garden with trees and beautiful flowers on either side. The carriage takes them to the Iolani Palace (the royal palace), surrounded by a large garden of tropical trees and flowers. A royal escort meets them at the palace gate and guides them to the front entrance.

"Is this the queen's house?" Major asks. Jennie sits beside him excited at the prospect of meeting the famously daring Hawaiian queen.

"It is the palace of Queen Liliuokalani," Ephraim explains. "According to the newspapers in the United States, the queen was placed on the throne earlier in the year after her brother King Kalakaua died in San Francisco while staying at the Palace Hotel."

"I know you said she requested to see us," Jennie's voice cracks. "But, why?"

"Yeah, we're just a couple of midgets from the farm," Major replies, still shocked by the queen's request.

"Hey, speak for yourself!" Jennie snaps, shoving an elbow into her husband's mid section. "Do I look all right?" She immediately begins primping, straightening her dress, and adjusting her hair.

"You look beautiful, Jennie," Fanny replies reassuringly.

The carriage stops in front of the palace at the foot of a long line of steps that lead to a large set of double doors. A young native, uncomfortably dressed in a suit and tie, escorts them to the Royal Throne Room. "Mo'i wahine Liliuokalani will see you soon," he says and slowly backs through the large double doors behind him.

"What did he say?" Major asks. The native language is unfamiliar to him.

"He said Queen Liliuokalani will be here in a minute," Ephraim replies.

The four stand in the center of the great room gazing up at the high, hand-carved ceilings from which four exquisite chandeliers hang. An enormous rug, woven in brilliant colors, covers the beautiful hardwood floor. On each side of the room are four massive double glass doors leading to the outside veranda which surrounds the palace. Each door is elegantly decorated with royal blue velvet curtains. The majestically decorated interior captivates the Rays and the Sells.

The royal thrones, one for the king and one for the queen, sit at the end of the room on a carpeted platform. In the center of the room is a large, circular sofa, much like the one Major remembers from the Memphis hotel.

"Aloha, and welcome to my Islands," announces a large woman with a dark complexion. She enters the room

Illustration 4: Hawaiian Queen Liliuokalani, 1891.
                 Jonesboro Sun; Sunday, January 10, 1993

gracefully and introduces herself, "I am Queen Liliuokalani, and I am so happy to meet you."

The queen is a plump, but handsome woman in her mid-fifties. Her dark hair, with streaks of gray, is neatly pinned up with flowers and pearls. She moves gracefully across the room and sits on her throne. She shifts her extraordinary feathered black silk dress out of her way.

Major and Ephraim bow deeply, while Jennie and Fanny curtsey. Jennie's knees shake as she rises politely and smiles at the queen who is now seated in front of her.

Breaking the silence, Major speaks, "I am Major William Ray and this is my wife, Jennie."

"I am pleased to meet you," Queen Liliuokalani answers.

"Queen," Major says, looking up. "We know nothing about royal etiquette, but we will greet you in our own American way." He holds his hand out, and she accepts it. "Have you been to the United States?"

"Oh yes, I have visited your country many times and am most taken with San Francisco. However, I do not know what a country of that size with so many modern conveniences would want with my tiny Islands," she says sadly, referring to the foreign political influence surrounding her, threatening her throne.

"I have never seen anything more beautiful than these islands," Jennie compliments shyly.

The queen is fascinated by the miniature couple and spends most of the afternoon talking with them and showing the couples around her Islands. The open gold trimmed, royal carriage, driven by a native servant, takes the adventurers through colorful gardens and quaint villages.

Jennie is embarrassed by the scant clothing worn by island natives, and often diverts her eyes from their dark, barely clad bodies. Major laughs at the redness in her cheeks when she sees a bare body, but he also sees the excitement in her eyes when she spies a large colorful bird sitting on a tropical tree limb.

"I have planned an evening of festivities for you and your company," Queen Liliuokalani informs her guests as the carriage returns to the palace. "We are having a luau in your honor."

After stopping in front of the palace, the passengers are helped from the carriage and led to the royal garden where a long buffet of food is spread. Jennie's eyes widen as she sees the area which is arrayed with flowers and palms.

"My word!" Jennie mutters. "Major, have you ever seen anything like it?"

"Just look at all that food," Major declares as he eyes the feast set before them.

"What is *that?*" Jennie asks, pointing to a large pig with an apple in its mouth, lying in on the ground in front of them. "I do believe it's staring at me."

"That's part of the feast," Queen Liliuokalani explains. "It is cooked in the ground for several days before serving."

"Is that raw fish?" Major asks, seeing a large wooden bowl full of white uncooked meat. "Down home the only fish we eat are pan fried."

"Yes," the queen answers. "Try it. It is very good."

"This is something I have heard a lot about," Ephraim says, pointing to a bowl of a pasty light pink substance. "This is supposed to be one of the native favorites."

"Yes, Mr. Sells. Poi is part of our native cuisine," Queen Liliuokalani replies. "Here, taste it." Carefully, she also passes a dish of poi to Jennie. "Eat like this, with your fingers," the queen tells her, as she scoops up the Hawaiian treat with her fingers.

"Emmm, delicious," Jennie lies, choking down the pasty substance. "Here, Major. I believe you will love this."

"I don't think I want any," he answers, trying to refuse his wife's offer. "You can have it."

"Oh, no. It's yours," Jennie says sweetly, sliding the bowl toward him. "Eat! Go on! Enjoy!"

Major lifts the sticky fermented mixture to his lips and puts it in his mouth, swallowing quickly so as to taste as little of it as possible. "Ummm!" he shivers and wrinkles his nose. "Raw fish and poi. What a treat!"

The queen smiles with pleasure, thinking Major and Jennie are enjoying every bite of their Hawaiian buffet. After the food is served, several young native girls clad in long grass skirts entertain their American guests with dancing.

"What are they doing?" Jennie asks, watching them dance, sing, and move their hands to music. "They are so graceful."

"They are telling the story about the island's history and how our people came here," Queen Liliuokalani explains, translating the story to her guests as the natives dance.

Soon, several acrobats join the festivities by performing for the queen. Hours pass like minutes, and much too quickly it is time for the American troupe to leave the island and return to the ship.

"We hate to leave," Major tells the queen. "We are delighted with our visit with you today. Thank you for your kindness."

"Thank you, sir," she replies. "And if you come back this way, please stop again for a longer visit."

"Good-bye," Jennie says to Queen Liliuokalani as she steps into the carriage. "I have never met anyone as nice and gentle as you and your people."

"Travel safely, my friends," Queen Liliuokalani says as she waves to Ephraim, Fanny, Major, and Jennie. "May the gods watch over you."

"Aloha!" Their new native friends yell as they leave.

"I thought you said, 'Aloha' means, 'hello'." Major says, perplexed.

"It also means, 'good-bye'," Ephraim says with a chuckle.

"Ain't that rather confusin'? I'd think a person wouldn't know whether he was a comin' or a goin' if he had only one word to say it with."

"Forget it, Major," Jennie laughs and places her arm around his. "Let's just enjoy the ride back to the ship."

All the passengers are aboard the *Monowai*. At ten o'clock the anchor is hoisted and the ship sails down the harbor which is marked with electric lights. Standing on deck, Major and Jennie watch the island fade into the distance.

"Isn't it lovely, Major," Jennie says, staring at the bright lights that reflect off the harbor waters. "The lights look almost like the stars overhead."

"Yes," he answers. "And once the man-made stars are gone from view, the stars in the heavens will provide us with the only light we need to guide us through the night."

Jennie places her head on Major's shoulder as they stand arm-in-arm gazing out across the ocean.

Chapter Sixteen

Samoa

The *Monowai* plows through the South Pacific, bound for Tutuila, the chief island of American Samoa. Good weather stays with them.

They leave Oahu and steam for over a week. The tension between those aboard increases with each passing day. Even the animals are restless in the confines of such a small area.

Finally, they are only a day from Tutuila. They will remain there overnight while the captain prepares for new provisions.

Each night there is entertainment for the guests aboard the ship. On Saturday night, the ship holds a dance in the music hall, and most of the passengers waltz through the night.

Major and Jennie enjoy each other's company and quietly stroll along the deck. The stars shine brightly like tiny diamonds on dark velvet. The moon is full and bright, casting romantic shadows across the hardwood deck. Music fills the air.

Major takes Jennie in his arms. They waltz. The deck is their dance floor, the stars their orchestra. Gracefully, he leads her in circles. To him, her feet seem to never touch the deck as she glides like an angel. His heart races as he holds her close and gazes into her huge, dark brown eyes.

Neither notice the audience that has slowly gathered around them. The music stops and Major gently kisses his wife. Suddenly, the sound of applause brings the couple out of the world they created for themselves. Embarrassed, Jennie covers her eyes with her hand. Her cheeks redden, but Major simply turns to the crowd and bows.

IT IS EARLY SUNDAY MORNING WHEN THE CREW sights Tutuila at the edge of Samoa. Within the hour, everyone is on deck as the ship steams through the channel. A whale boat moves close to the port side and prepares to guide the steamer through the dangerous reef to the Samoan harbor.

"Grab that line!" an officer orders. Several crewman secure the whaler to the side of the ship. A rope ladder is lowered to the pilot who comes aboard to take the helm and navigate the *Monowai* safely through the harbor.

On the upper deck, Major observes the crewmen busily working to secure the lines of the visiting vessel. "Come here, Jennie, look at this." Major motions for her to join him.

"What?"

"Look, have you ever seen anything like this before?" Major points to four half-naked natives boarding the ship with the navigator. Their hair is light brown, almost red as it lies against copper skin. An embarrassingly small swatch of calico material, about a yard long, wraps around their finely developed bodies to cover their loins. It is the only clothing they wear. "Oh, my word!" is all Jennie can say, observing the scantily clad natives standing on the main deck.

The lines are loosened and the whaler moves ahead. The pilot takes the helm of the *Monowai*, safely maneuvering the steamship through the dangerous coral reefs.

Major and Jennie join other passengers on the main deck as the ship slowly steams toward the harbor. Looking through the rails, the first thing they see are the remains of U.S. warships scattered across the bay.

"What happened to them?" Major asks Captain Carey who stands nearby.

"They were damaged by a hurricane that hit the island about six months ago."

"I don't understand why the United States has ships here anyway." Jennie is curious. "Remember several ships on the island of Oahu? The Queen didn't seem too happy with their presence, either."

"It's political and you wouldn't understand," the captain answers sharply. "There's been a lot of unrest among the natives."

"So, the U.S. and German forces are here to make sure there's no fighting," Jennie says as she tries to understand the situation fully. She is politically active in her hometown of Yates Center, something that most men cannot accept from a woman.

"Yeah, something like that," he answers, his Irish brogue more apparent when he is aggravated. "Nothing for you to worry your pretty little head over, Lass. Tie her down!" Captain Carey yells as the ship pulls into the dock.

Suddenly, hoards of half-naked natives selling trinkets and shells board the ship. Sailors looking for mail, swim to the large vessel and crawl aboard from all sides.

Frightened, Jennie steps back. A large native shoves a shell necklace at her. He speaks in a language she cannot understand.

"Get back!" Major yells, shoving him back with one arm, while trying to protect his beloved Jennie with the other. "Leave her alone!"

"Major!" she cries. The crowd of natives and sailors surround her. A copper body presses against her, pushing and pulling her away from the arms of her husband.

"Jennie!" Major calls, panic stricken.

Shadows of people close in. Desperately, Major grabs for Jennie's hand. It slips from his grip. Anger replaces panic. Suddenly, he attacks the barrage of people surrounding him. His hand lands on bare skin as he kicks and claws his way through while he tries to locate Jennie. She screams, terrified of the strangers who press against her.

"Hang on Little Buddy!" Major hears a voice from behind. He is hoisted above the crowd. "We'll get you outta here in a jiffy."

"No!" Major protests. "Jennie's in there!"

"Don't worry," the man says, trying to keep a safe grip on Major. "We've got her."

"Major!" Jennie screams.

Major can see his wife above the crowd, as a pair of strong arms hold her safely, high in the air. She clings tightly to the hands that wrap around her waist.

"Don't worry Ma'am," a young voice tells her. "I'll have you outta here in a minute. Just hang on."

It seems an eternity before their feet are planted on the second deck of the ship, and they face their rescuers. Behind Major stands a young man in his twenties. He has the face of a boy. His blond hair is ruffled, and his white shirt hangs slightly out of his trousers. "You two had better stay up here until that crowd clears," he tells them, stepping back to give Major some room.

"Jennie!" Major grabs his wife and holds her tightly in his arms. "I was afraid you would be trampled. I'm so sorry. I shouldn't have taken us there."

"That's all right. I'm fine now," she reassures him and turns to her rescuer. "Thank you."

The young man at her side stoops to speak to her, "You're very welcome." His voice is soft. Jennie detects a slight Southern accent. "I've always wanted to rescue a fair maiden in distress. I'm just glad we heard your screams and you weren't hurt."

She introduces herself to the young man, "I'm Jennie Ray, and this is my husband, Major."

"I'm Joe," he says, offering his name in return. "And this is my shipmate, Al."

Jennie is taken with Joe. He stoops politely next to her. His dark hair curls uncontrollably and hangs several inches down his neck, unlike his friend Al's hair which is short and neatly groomed.

Joe's shirt sleeves, rolled high, reveal a large tattoo on his right arm between his shoulder and elbow, of a Polynesian woman wearing a grass skirt "Do you like it?" he asks Jennie, and pulls his sleeve up a little more to expose the image. "Watch." Slowly he flexes his muscle making the island girl's grass skirt move as if she is doing the hula.

Jennie giggles, "Look, Major."

"We need to get back to our cabin," Major almost snaps. Jennie thinks she detects a note of jealousy in his voice.

Turning to the young man, Major says, "I want to thank you again for your help. Come on, Jennie. We need to go."

"Yes," she agrees, but not before she extends her hand of thanks to her hero. "Thank you again for your help."

Joe carefully holds her tiny hand against the tips of his large fingers, "It was my pleasure to help a fair damsel in distress." He places a light kiss on her wrist before releasing her hand and saying good-bye.

"You were rude," Jennie scolds after Joe and Al disappear around the corner.

"I was not," Major's voice squeaks in aggravation. "I thanked them. Besides, they had work to do, and I don't think the captain would appreciate us takin' up his crew's time."

"You're jealous, William Ray!" she laughs.

"I am not!" he protests.

"You are too!"

"Am not!" He paces back and forth across the ship's upper deck.

"Are too," she teases. "If you're not jealous, why are you pacin' back and forth like a lovesick puppy?"

"Well," he answers, his voice low. "You didn't have to giggle like a love struck school girl."

"I did not!"

"You did too!"

"Did not!"

"Then what would you call gigglin' when that young man showed you that ridiculous tattoo?"

"I thought it was cute," she smiles shyly. "Besides, you know there's no man but you for me." Jennie wraps her arms around his neck, places a kiss on his lips and whispers in his ear, "You're my only hero."

MAJOR DECIDES THE OVER ZEALOUS NATIVES ARE too threatening for two people of such small proportion, so he and Jennie wait for the others to return from their tour of the small island. The couple stands on the second deck watching the trainers bring several animals onto the main deck for fresh air. Jennie loves the horses and misses riding them like she used to do on her family's farm. She yearns to ride the beautiful show horses on the deck below, but Major is afraid for her to ride and forbids her to even go near them.

The *Monowai* remains berthed overnight. The increased political tension on the island worries Captain Carey who orders the crew to load provisions throughout the night.

Major lies in the dark and listens to the footsteps outside his cabin become louder, pass his window, and fade away into the night. The noises do not bother Jennie. She sleeps peacefully and never flinches at the sound of a falling crate or a yelling seaman. She knows she is safe in her husband's arms.

THE MORNING SUN SLOWLY RISES ABOVE THE WET horizon, casting a yellow glow throughout the cramped cabin. With it comes cries of rebellion. Native followers of Chief Mata'afa, recently exiled, are trying to overthrow the governing King Malietoa. Major can smell the smoke as it drifts through the air and rises high above the burning village. Soldiers are firing guns in an attempt to push the invaders back.

"What is that?" Jennie cries, springing upright in bed.

"Evidently there's a civil war taking place in the village." Trying to reassure her of their safety, he adds, "Don't worry. It won't affect us."

"Get that anchor hoisted," Captain Carey orders. "Let's get outta here. Now!"

"Aye! Aye!" his crew replies almost in unison. The engines roar, and the ship slowly pulls out of the bay and away from the dangerous fighting on shore.

"Hey, watch it! They're comin' over the sides!" yells a seaman.

"What's going on, Major?" Jennie asks. Frightened half to death, she nervously pulls the blanket close to her chest. She reaches for the Bible that lays on the nearby table.

Major spies a number of natives trying to board the ship, but they are intercepted by crewmen who shove them back into the rough, white capped ocean.

"Don't worry, Jennie," he reassures her. "We're headed out to sea now. We're safe."

Major turns to Jennie. Her Bible is open to the Twenty-third Psalm. She prays faithfully for their safety and salvation. How Major wishes he had faith that strong, but it has been a long time since he talked to God. He is uncertain whether or not God will hear his prayers, the prayers of a sinner. Quietly he moves to the bed and holds her in his arms while she continues to pray.

The sound of gunfire and the screams of rebellion soon fade. So does the primitive island. Several hours tick by, and now the only sound is the rythmic chug-chug of the ship's engines.

Finally, passengers venture onto the main deck for fresh air and the chug-chug of the engines is joined by the buzz of conversation. Major and Jennie stroll out among the other passengers who are enjoying the sun and watching jugglers and acrobats practice their routines. All is well again.

ALMOST TWO WEEKS HAVE PASSED AND THE *Monowai*
steams toward Sydney, Australia.   Major, while walking
along the upper deck, notices Captain Carey staring across
the ocean.   He holds his pipe between his lips with his
hand and rests his elbow on the railing in front of him.   He
never notices Major standing near him.

"Captain?" Major calls softly to get his attention, but
does not want to disturb his train of thought.   "Is something wrong?"

"Oh," he answers, startled.   "Hello, Major.   And what
can I do for you?"

 "Is something wrong?"

"Can't you feel it?"

"Feel what?"

"The air.   There's a certain restlessness in the air."

Major stops and listens to the ocean.   He tries to sense
the restlessness the captain speaks of, but he can't.   "No.
What are you talkin' about?"

"The air is so still.   There's not even a light   breeze.   And
have you noticed there aren't any birds flying about the
ship."   Suddenly, the clouds   swirl relentlessly above the
steel vessel, and in the distance they see a storm rolling
toward them, like a wall of water.   "Quick! There she is,"
yells Captain Carey.   "Get back to your cabin and stay
there."

The storm hits with surprising force.   The passengers
have little time to prepare, and run chaotically for safety
when they feel the hard-hitting wind and hear the captain
yell.

Major, unable to keep his balance as the ship heads
into the storm, bounces from the rail to the steel hull in
an effort to reach his cabin door.   Waves crash against the
sides, sending water rushing over the main deck.   A loud

bell rings out as a signal to crew and passengers that rough weather and an angry sea loom ominously ahead.

The high wind blows Major around like a feather in a whirlwind. Desperately clinging to the railing, he pulls himself closer and closer to the cabin door. Crawling on his hands and knees with the rain beating against his face, Major feels his way to the door. He grabs the knob above him and pulls with all his might.

"Major!" Jennie screams as he falls through the open door.

"Quick!" he orders. "Help me close this door before we're swept out and drowned!" Working together, they finally push the door shut and latch it securely. Leaning against it, they slide slowly to the floor and cling to one another for dear life.

"If we ever get home," Jennie cries. "I will never board another ship as long as I live!" Her wet hair falls from the combs that usually hold it in a small bun on top of her head, and clings to her face. She feels the weight of her rain soaked dress. The storm beats against the huge door they lean against as it threatens to enter and drag them into the sea.

Monstrous waves threaten the passenger carrying steamer, as chairs overturn and personal items fall from table tops. Lamps sway. The ship lurches. Grabbing a blanket and pillows from the bed, Major makes as comfortable a place as possible while they sit and endeavor to ride out the dangerous storm.

"I promise," Major whispers, holding Jennie tightly in his arms. "We will never do this again."

That night Major and God develop a new relationship. He finds himself praying harder than he has ever prayed in his life for the morning to find them safe.

RAYS OF SUNLIGHT FILTERING THROUGH THE WINDOW
overhead awake Major from a troubled sleep. His back is
stiff from sitting on the floor, and his right arm is numb
from holding Jennie so tightly throughout the night.
Softly, he whispers into her ear, "Jennie."

Her eyes open slowly, and realizing where she is, Jennie
moans sleepily, "Is it over?"

"Yeah, " he answers. "It's over. Come on, let's get up
and see what the storm left." Carefully he helps Jennie to
her feet and tries to smooth out her wrinkled dress with
the palm of his hand.

Slowly, Major opens the door. Sunlight fills the dark-
ened cabin.

"Leave it open," Jennie begs when Major starts to close
it. Her eyes say what her lips do not. She needs freedom
after being trapped in the steel cage overnight.

Major, Jennie, and the others survey the damage on
deck. Furniture is scattered about, some missing, some
floating out to sea, some broken and lying in a crumpled
heap behind a piece of heavy equipment that saved it from
being swept away.

"Are you two all right?" asks Allen Sells, his brown hair
hanging several inches beneath his worn brown hat.

"Yeah, were fine," Major replies.

Concerned for the animals below deck, Jennie asks,
"Have you checked on the animals?"

"They're a little shaken, but I believe they'll be all right."

Major detects worry in Allen's voice. "What's wrong?
You act like something's botherin' you."

"Well, I don't know if it's the weather last night or something else." He pauses a moment to think, then continues,
"but the horses seem awful restless for some reason."

"Maybe they'll be as glad as we will to get their hooves on solid ground again," says a voice from around the corner. Alonzo, the Strong Man, appears with a broken deck chair in his hand. "Well, I guess we don't need this for anything but a good fire."

"I have to check on a few other things before we get to Australia," Allen says when he spots Ephraim on the port side talking with Captain Carey. "I'll see you later." With a raised upturned hand, Allen hails his brother.

"Attention!" shouts Ephraim to the passengers roaming the decks. "Could I have your attention, please." They gather around and listen to Ephraim, who is standing on several crates like a vote-gathering politician.

"Captain Carey has informed me that because of last night's storm our arrival in Australia will be delayed one day." The disappointed crowd moans. "Now, I know you were hoping to reach Australia today." The circus leader's words carry loudly through the salty sea air, "But we had to turn around in the middle of the night to avoid getting hit full force by the storm. Therefore, we've been delayed." The moans turn into belligerent epithets.

"Come on everyone," Major yells as he runs quickly to the stacked crates, climbs them, and stands beside Ephraim. "We've been ridin' this floatin' tub of steel for a solid month now. What's one more day?" Major spots Jennie shaking her head at his boldness and lack of sense by jumping in front of the fretting crowd.

"Major's right," interrupts Jennie. Walking slowly toward the front of the crowd. She holds her Bible high in her right hand and speaks, "What good does it do to get angry about it? You forget that it was by, and only by, the grace of God that we got through this terrible storm in the first place. You should be happy He gave the good captain here the sense to turn around and take you away from the worst of the storm." The angry crowd quiets.

"We should all be down on our knees thanking the Almighty for His gracious power and kindness that saved us, thereby giving us a second chance at life. Would you rather be lying in the deep, dark depths of the cold ocean floor or be alive now and able to complain at a day's delay?"

Major is surprised to see his wife join him in his attempt to calm the disgruntled group. He knows she is a very impressive and persuasive speaker, but the only time he has ever heard her get wound up is when she is persuading him in private. Major is aware of the aggressive speeches she gave at benefits and social functions before they were married, but this is his first opportunity to see her in action before a crowd. Major, proud as a peacock, watches Jennie almost hypnotically turn the riot rooting crowd into a group of productive and energetic citizens.

"Why don't you use this time the good Lord gave you ladies and take advantage of it along with the facilities? You won't have them later. And don't you men have animals to prepare for docking, equipment that needs gathering, and plans that need to be made? I believe instead of standing around complaining, we should all be praying and singing praises to God for our salvation from the hands of the devil who tried to send us to our death. Let us pray."

Silence covers the deck as each head bows to pray.

Silhouetted by the rising sun behind her, the miniature Joan of Ark prays, "Our most gracious and kind Heavenly Father, we come to You humble and thankful for Your loving heart. We thank You for delivering us from harm's way, blessing us with Your almighty presence, and protecting us through the night. Help us to accept those things we don't understand with clear heads and kind hearts. Take us through the rest of our journey safely and deliver us into the bosoms of our families back home, but most of all, forgive us of our evil ways that sometimes overtake us. Bless us, oh Lord, throughout our journey, not only here but through life on this earth as well. This we ask you in Your Son's most Holy name. Amen."

Suddenly, a woman begins to sing in a beautiful soprano, "*Amazing grace, how sweet the sound . . .* " Then others join, " *. . . that saved a wretch like me . . .* " until a chorus of thankful voices ring out the hymn across the ocean waters.

"How does she do that?" The surprise in Captain Carey's voice tells Major he is very impressed with the tiny woman standing on the stacks of crates in front of him.

"I don't know," Major answers proudly. "But put her on a soap box, and you've got a keg of dynamite."

"I've never seen anyone change the attitude of a crowd like that."

"Yeah, she could talk the devil into repentin'," Major laughs.

"Well, I'll tell you now," Carey's Irish brogue stronger as the crowd continues to sing. "I don't welcome too many women speaking out the way she did, but I've never seen one control a crowd that way, either. She was born to stand on a pedestal."

"I know," Major agrees proudly as the crowd begins to leave, still singing. "I know."

Jennie joins her husband and the captain. Major says, "And that's where she'll always be as far as I'm concerned––on a pedestal. Good-day, Captain." Major escorts Jennie away from the startled crew and leaves Captain Carey standing wide-eyed.

Chapter Seventeen

A Land Down Under

The ship arrives at the Union Steamship Dock in Sydney, Australia, the following morning. The mid-November air is warm.

Major remembers the cold, winter air that chilled his bones and froze his breath on the family farm in Missouri. There the family will soon gather around warm, cozy fires to celebrate Thanksgiving and a white Christmas, but in Australia it is early summer.

Stepping off the dock onto solid ground, Major and Jennie are excited to be away from the rocking steamship and wait with the others to gather their luggage. Ephraim is busy making preparations with an Australian guide, while his brother Allen unloads the livestock and arranges to stable the horses until the show is ready to travel north on the railroad from Sydney to Bundaberg.

"Good Day, mate," welcomes a young Australian. He has an unmistakable outback accent. "Can I help you with your stock?" he offers.

"That's kind of you, young man," Allen says. His long, lanky body is not characteristic of his brothers, but the same handlebar mustache he sports reveals a strong family resemblance. "Can you tell me where I can find the port authorities to inspect the livestock?"

"Sure, I can," he answers. "I'll be right back."

Quickly he moves down the wharf. A few minutes later he returns with an older man who is dressed casually in loose fitting pants and a white shirt, sleeves pushed above his elbows. He pulls a handkerchief from his pocket and lifting his suede hat, carefully wipes the fine drops of sweat that bead on his forehead from the hot mid-morning sun. He is overweight and Major figures he enjoys a visit to the local pub more than once a day.

The man introduces himself to Allen as William Kelly. The local people call him "Walley." Hired by the port authorities, Walley inspects all livestock coming into the country, making sure they are free of diseases.

Major sees the sparkle in Jennie's eyes as the horses trot by her. "I miss riding," she sighs. Several large, white Arabians are led from the ship to a small corral where livestock are inspected. "Aren't they beautiful?"

"One day you'll have a whole corral of horses for your own," Major promises.

"Do you think we'll ever own any like those, Major? "

Jennie's love for horses runs deep, and watching them circle the rough wood corral promts memories of riding on the Kansas prairie. The animals move gracefully. Their full manes, always groomed magnificently, float freely in the wind. Their beauty and grace would cause envy among the most powerful kings.

"What do you mean they all have to be shot?" Allen raves. His face is red from both anger and despair. "These animals are the finest show horses in the world, and you're telling me they have to be *shot*?"

"Yes, sir," Walley answers regretfully. "There's nothin' I can do. Your fine horses are diseased, and we cannot allow them to remain in the country. Look at this horse, " he explains. "Don't you see the blood here in the eyes and in the nose of this horse? This horse has cattle fever."

"But that doesn't mean the whole lot is diseased."

"Mr. Sells, cattle fever is a highly contagious disease, and if one of these animals has it, the whole lot has it. Just be glad they were housed in a area separate from the rest of your exotic group, or we would have to destroy the whole bunch."

Allen can't believe his eyes and ears. He watches as each horse is harnessed and led to another area several hundred feet away from the corral. "Wait a minute," he pleads. "These horses are more than just animals; they're part of a family. Are you sure they can't be saved?"

"Yes, Sir. These animals must be completely destroyed," Walley commands.

Major and Jennie see the desperate look on Allen's thin face as several men carrying guns slowly take each horse away. Suddenly, shots ring out and echo through the air as each magnificent horse is shot and killed instantly.

"No!" Jennie screams. Her voice pierces the air. She runs toward the three men. "What are you doing? You can't do that to these beautiful animals. Mr. Sells, make them stop!" Tears flow down her cheeks as she continues to scream. She pulls at a young man who takes careful aim with his pistol.

"Someone come get this sheila off me!" the young man orders. "I can't aim. I'm afraid I'll only wound the animal."

"Jennie, this is better for them," Major assures her. He desperately tries to calm her. "They are diseased."

Jennie collapses in a small heap at Major's feet, tearing her dress in the desperate attempt to save the majestic beasts. Her face, streaked with muddy tears, looks plead-

ingly at Major. She again begs and pulls at his legs,
"Please, make them stop!" Her voice trails to sobs.

Guns continue to ring out, and the smell of burning
horse flesh fills the air. Black smoke billows, like the
stacks on the huge steamship, almost blocking the sun,
and turning the pale blue sky into a dingy gray.

Major scoops Jennie up in his arms and carries her
away from the sad and gruesome scene.

"Jennie," he whispers softly. Her sobs block the sound
of his voice, and she hears nothing but guns as they are
fired at dozens of hysterical horses.

"Major," she insists between sobs. "I want to go home."

MAJOR AND JENNIE'S LIVES DO NOT ALWAYS CENTER
around the circus. They also enjoy the theater and attend
the wonderful comedies whenever possible. Jennie,
however, prefers the tragedies.

It is November 10. Major and Jennie walk near the
corner of Pitt and Park Street where the Criterion Theater
stands.

"Look at this," Major points to the sign on the double
doors, *Adelaide Photo Company.* "There is a photographer
in the theater. Why don't we go in and get our picture
taken?"

"You really want to?" Jennie giggles.

"Yeah, let's do it." Major reaches up and with a great
deal of strength, opens the heavy door. Bowing low, he
motions for Jennie to enter the great building. The inside
of the magnificent hall is dark, and it only takes a
moment for the little couple's eyes to adjust to the dim
lighting.

"Hello," Major calls softly as if he were entering a mausoleum instead of a theater. "Hello," he repeats a little louder.

"I wonder if anyone is here," Jennie whispers. Her voice echoes through the dark, mysterious auditorium. Beautiful maroon velvet curtains gracefully drape each side of the stage. Large sculpted pillars enhance the background.

"May I help you with something?" The voice comes from behind the dark curtains. Slowly a shadowy figure emerges from the dimly lit corners of the stage. An elderly man—dressed conservatively in dark pants, white shirt, and black vest—steps into the light. "Well, who might you two little people be?"

"Hello, Mr. . . ." Major pauses, waiting for the gentleman to finish the sentence for him.

"Hansen, George Hansen," he answers. "I'm the caretaker of this magnificent hall of fine actors." The old gray-haired man gazes curiously at the extremely well dressed little man in front of him.

Major's light blue suit, complete with long tails and vest, is complemented by a black top hat and gold tipped cane. Jennie, looking like a porcelain doll, wears a beautiful royal blue and white-striped silk skirt with a bustle and a long train. The edge is trimmed with ball fringe hanging along the hem.

"Mr. Hansen, I am Major William Ray, and this is my wife, Jennie. We are with the American circus, Sells Brothers. We saw the sign on the door indicatin' a photography studio, and well—we'd like to have our picture taken."

"Sure, let me get Mr. Appleby. He's the photographer. I'll be right with you."

Illustration 5: Major Ray and wife, Jennie at Adelaide Photo Company in Sydney, Austrailia.

Photgraph courtesy Mr. and Mrs. Charles Miller

Hansen returns with a much younger man whose hair is slicked down with grease and parted on the left side. His huge, black handlebar mustache twists to a point on each side of his upper lip.

"Major and Mrs. Ray, this is Jonathan Appleby. He's the theater photographer," Hansen says.

"It's a pleasure," Appleby replies, offering his hand. He has never photographed anyone like these two. Quickly, he positions them on stage next to a tan wicker chair.

"Now, don't move," he orders and stands under the black hood behind the large wooden box camera. Making sure the photograph will be flawless, he looks through the lens, removes the cap, and says, "Perfect."

AMAZINGLY, WITHIN TWO WEEKS, ALLEN, WHO IS AN excellent animal trainer, has the group of new horses trained and ready to finish the tour. Each horse is in perfect step as if it has performed all its life, and the performance at Sydney is successful.

The *Bulletin,* Sydney's first newspaper, established in 1880, writes about the high wire acts, the acrobats, the animals. The intelligent little couple in the side show, however, receives the best reviews.

After the last performance the train is loaded, and the four-hundred mile trip to Melbourne begins. Major and Jennie are mesmerized by the scenery. Great herds of antelope and water buffalo run across open fields. Dingos feast on strange prey. Beautiful birds, unlike any they have ever seen, soar across the heavens. Neither Jennie nor Major will ever forget the exquisite sunsets along the vast foreign horizon.

JANUARY 6, MELBOURNE, AGAIN TRAGEDY FALLS upon the great Sells Brothers company. William Head, one of the property men decorating the Big Top, loses his footing and falls forty-five feet to an instant death.

It is a solemn occasion as circus friends and family bury William in the Melbourne General Cemetery. Professor Merrick's Band leads the long procession of roustabouts and kinkers who walk two-by-two behind the hearse carrying William's body to its final resting place. Fine circus horses adorned traditionally with black and white plumes pull the hearse while the band plays a sad funeral march.

It is an unhappy time for the family of circus performers and workers, but the show must go on. The show opens. The show closes. The circus packs. They travel almost a thousand miles to Brisbane, and then go on to Bundaberg.

Major, not only a circus performer but a farmer as well, cannot ignore the beautifully prosperous land surrounding Bundaberg. He counts forty plantations in the small community. Most grow sugar because it is the only crop that interests the countrymen.

The group travels five months throughout Australia, performing for the most sophisticated audiences and the simplest aborigines. It is exciting but physically draining for Jennie. One May morning on the way back to Sydney, Jennie, unable to stand up to the constant hard traveling, falls ill.

"Jennie," Major urges, trying to wake her from the nightmare she is having. "Jennie, wake up."

Touching her, he notices the heat emanating from her body. Beads of sweat appear on her forehead. Jennie never moves but only continues her babbling. Jumping out of bed, Major quickly dresses and runs to get help.

Running desperately through each car and battling the constant rocking of the train, Major manages to find Ephraim in the dining car eating breakfast. "Mr. Sells!" he blurts out with and exhausted gasp. "Jennie's real sick! You gotta help me!"

"Now, calm down, Major," he replies. "Catch your breath. Now, what about Jennie?"

"I don't know. She's burnin' up with a fever or somethin'."

"You go back to the car and sit with her. I'll get the doctor."

"Hurry! I don't know how bad it is!"

"You just go on back, I'll be there in a minute." Ephraim scurries to the next car to find Dr. Compton, the circus physician. They are by Jennie's side in a matter of minutes.

"What is it doctor?" Major asks, watching the elderly man carefully check her pulse. He takes her temperature. He listens to her heart. "What is it? Is she going to get well? She's not going to *die* is she?" Major rambles frantically, fearing the worst for the woman he loves.

"Ephraim!" the doctor orders. "Get me some cold towels. Now! We have to get this fever down—and fast!"

"Right," Ephraim agrees and rushes out of the sleeping car.

"Doctor," Major begs. "Is she going to be well again?"

"I don't know."

Hours pass as Doctor Compton works diligently, trying to lower the high fever that came on so suddenly. Major paces and waits for good news, but none in forthcoming. Several women wander in and out trying to help the doctor, replacing warm towels with cold ones.

"Major," Jennie calls out weakly. "Where are you?"

"I'm here, Jennie!" he cries. Rushing to her side, he leans over the bed. "I'm here. I never left." He is torn by her pale, white face and dark circles around her eyes, but to him, she is still as beautiful as the angels in heaven. Tears of joy flow down his cheeks, and he softly caresses her hand. "I love you," he vows.

"What happened,?" she asks feebly. "All I remember is feeling ill last night."

"Jennie," the doctor interrupts. "You've had a very high fever. We'll be in Sydney tomorrow. I believe you'll feel much better by the time we arrive. Major, I need to talk with you a moment."

"I'll be right there," Major answers and turns his attention to Jennie. "I won't be long. Is there anything I can get you?"

"No," she replies. She smiles and closes her eyes. "I think I'll just sleep a little longer."

"You do that."

Major leaves Fanny to care for Jennie and joins the doctor in the narrow walkway.

"I don't know why Jennie developed the fever," Doctor Compton admits. "But it could be something she contacted on the tour. Keep a close eye on her, and when we get back to the states, I'd suggest a full physical, especially if the fever comes back."

"All right, you can bet your last penny I'll do that." Major quickly returns to Jennie and stays at her side until the train reaches Sydney the following day.

Chapter Eighteen

Home Sweet Home

The group spends several days in Sydney while the boat is loaded, and they prepare to depart for the States.

It is May 16, and the *Monowai* leaves Darling Harbor at four o'clock in the afternoon. A full band plays. U.S. flags wave high in the air. People standing on the dock and on the ship sing the "Star Spangled Banner."

"Isn't it wonderful," Jennie says, watching the celebration while the steamer slowly slips from the dock. She is still weak from her illness.

"Yes, it is," Major replies as he places his arm around her shoulder. "But what will be even better is seeing San Francisco."

During the first few days at sea, passengers endure both sickness and bad weather. But the idea of going home is the light that keeps them full of hope and happiness throughout their sometimes perilous journey. The ship again travels across the great ocean, offering nothing to do but look across the blue and endless water. Everyone is tired. Even the animals have endured more than enough of the slow, continual, up and down movement of the vessel. A chimpanzee jumps overboard one morning after giving the Animal Man the slip. Most believed the chimp's full intention was suicide.

Jennie's health improves. Coughing still wracks her body at times, but Major believes with all his heart that as soon as they return home to Cotton Plant everything will be fine.

The steamship pulls into San Francisco Bay June 9, at 3:30 in the afternoon. The wharf is full of people to welcome them home. A large brass band plays, "Home Sweet Home."

"And home it is," sighs Major, holding Jennie tightly, as tears roll down his cheeks. His heart is filled with joy when he steps onto American soil. "I'll never leave it again."

"Nor will I, Major," she cries, happily. "We're home to stay!"

Chapter Nineteen

A Home For Jennie

June, 1892. The circus season is over. Major and Jennie say good-bye to friends and board the train for home. The trip is long and hard with many stops in between, but within several days they are nearing the train station in Walnut Ridge, Arkansas. Almost home, Major is deeply concerned about the dry cough that Jennie developed after her mysterious fever in Australia

"How are you feeling?" Major asks. Jennie coughs into her white laced handkerchief.

"I'm fine, Major," she coughs again. "Really, I believe it must be the dust."

"I don't know. I think maybe you should see the doctor when we get home."

"No. I'll be fine once we're settled in at Mother Ray's. I just need some rest."

"Here, lay your head in my lap and rest awhile."

"I think I will. Thank you." Jennie carefully removes the feathered hat from her head. The seats are large compared to Jennie and Major's size, so Jennie rests comfortably, using Major's lap as a pillow.

Major strokes her forehead softly and moves several stray strands of hair from her face. Breathing deeply, he can smell rose water. Her skin, soft to his touch, reminds him of cotton before it is spun. Jennie is his life, and without her, he could not exist.

"The angels blessed me with one of their own, and I'll never let any harm come to you," he whispers.

Major looks out the window and sees familiar territory. The rocking train slows as it nears the station. The hissing sound of the brakes releasing pressure is almost deafening. Steam blows out from underneath the iron horse. Clouds of white smoke blow across those standing on the wood-planked deck outside the station.

"Jennie," Major gently shakes her shoulders. "Jennie, honey, we're here."

"Walnut Ridge!" The conductor yells as he strolls down the isle. "All out for Walnut Ridge, Arkansas!"

Sitting upright, Jennie is dazed for a moment, but she quickly realizes where she is. Looking out the window she asks, "Do you see Mother Ray?"

"Yeah, she and John are standing next to the station door."

Major watches Jennie tuck each hair back into place and smooth the wrinkles in her dress as she prepares to get off the train. She is always neat and proper no matter where she goes.

"Willie!" cries Major's mother when she sees him step from the train. Holding out her arms, she rushes to gather the man who only comes to her waistline, "We've all missed you. And how is our dear, sweet Jennie?"

"I'm fine, Mother Ray," Jennie answers, clearing her throat. "How are you and the rest of the family doing?"

"We're all just fine," she says, but notices that Jennie has a terrible cold. "We have so many things to talk about. John, get their bags and load them onto the buckboard, and we'll get started toward the house."

Stepping off the platform, Major looks around. Busy people fill the streets of the little town.

John drives the buckboard over the hard, dirt road. The ride home is rough, and the June weather is stifling. The humidity is still high, even though it is late in the day, but the temperature is dropping, making the ride somewhat less miserable.

As they near the old cemetery where Major's father is buried, memories of that day many years ago fill Major's mind and lie heavy on his heart.

A hush falls as they pass the cemetery. Nothing more is said until they pull onto the Ray farm.

The evening is exciting. The family wants to know all about Major's and Jennie's trip to Australia. Naturally, being the great story teller he is, Major tells all and more—his descriptions and gestures embellishing the adventure.

John, his wife, Mary, and their boys bid farewell. Mother Ray retires, and Major and Jennie slip out to sit on the back porch.

"What are you thinking about?" Jennie asks. She detects a slight sadness in Major's eyes as he gazes across the farm. The moon is full, giving a special golden brilliance to the wheat standing in the field, high and ripe for cutting.

"Jennie, we've spent the past two years saving our money for a home of our own, yet I didn't realize how really important that is until now."

"What's important to me, Major, is for us to be happy. I told you before that I don't care where you go as long as I am with you. Nothing else matters."

"I know you said that, but watching John and Mary with their kids made me remember we'll never have a real family of our own. At least we can have a home filled with nieces and nephews."

"Major, we have a wonderful life. We have been places that most people only dream about. When we're ready, we'll settle down and enjoy the years we have left together."

"But wouldn't you like a home now?" he asks. "A place where we can come home to each year? A place that is truly ours?"

"I'd love it, but I want you to know that owning a house is not the most important thing in our lives—*we are*."

"Tomorrow, we're going to take the buggy out and look for us some land of our own," he declares. Pulling her close, he whispers softly, "We're gonna belong somewhere. Somewhere permanent, not just to a traveling sideshow. I promise."

MAJOR WAKES TO THE SOUND OF A ROOSTER crowing, and the smell of breakfast cooking. A slight breeze blows through the window of his old bedroom.

He remembers an excited young boy, many years ago, staring out at a circus as it traveled toward Hornersville. His life changed that day with the Fat Lady's words. While he stood quietly crying over harsh words that were spoken to her, she told him to dry his tears because, she said, "You are special, not different."

The memory fades, and Major slowly slips out of bed. Trying not to wake Jennie, he quietly dresses and leaves the room. Outside he walks around the house. Major surveys the land, breathes in the smells of the farm, and listens to the sounds. Although life on the road with the circus is exciting, Major misses the solitude that comes from living on a farm.

"Hey, Willie!" yells John. He cannot get used to calling him Major. "I see you're up early this mornin'." John is harnessing the mules and hitching them to the iron thrasher used for cutting wheat.

"Yeah," Major answers, "I wanted to get out early to think."

"Think about what?"

"Well, Jennie and I have been savin' our money to buy a farm."

"That's great news. Hey! Earl Johnson over at Cardwell is trying to sell his land. I believe he and his wife are goin' up north to live with their son."

"How much land is there?"

"Oh, I believe it's about two-hundred acres, and its already got a house on it."

"Do you know how much he wants for it?"

"I think he wants eight dollars an acre, but now a great deal of that land ain't farmed. It's pure swamp."

"I'll look at it and then we'll decide whether we want it or not." Major thinks a moment and asks, "John, would you mind hitchin' the buggy for me before you go out to the field?"

"No, I don't mind at all," he replies. "I need to get started, but I'll hitch the buggy before I leave." John starts for the barn, but pauses a moment and says, "Willie, it's good to have you home."

"Thanks, John," he replies. "For everything."

After breakfast, Jennie grabs her bonnet and parasol. Major gets the horse and buggy. Mother Ray has already packed them a lunch.

Soon the two are on their way to Cardwell to look at the land, but Major notices a bit of sadness in Jennie's voice when she speaks. He believes a ride in the country will cheer her and perhaps improve her health. Because the farm is located twelve miles west of Hornersville, the trip takes a little over an hour at a slow trot.

Only about one hundred acres is farmland. The other hundred is uncleared swamp and forest land. It is located at the edge of the Saint Francis river, making it ideal for turkey hunting. The house is a small bungalow, not fancy, but far from being a shack. It is perfect for the young couple who have very little time during the year, but who enjoy their winters hunting and fishing. Major arranges to purchase the land and the house from Mr. Johnson for sixteen-hundred dollars.

By the time they finish their business it is almost noon, and Major's growling stomach reminds him of the lunch basket in back of the buggy. "How about a picnic by the river?" he asks, swatting at a fly that insists on aggravating him. "There will be a breeze that will not only cool us but it'll also keep the flies away from our food."

"I'd love to," Jennie answers. She closes her parasol and climbs into the covered buggy.

They survey the land once more as they drive toward the St. Francis river bank. The wooden, steel-rimmed wheels easily follow the small trail. The trees along both sides of the trail create a giant archway of shade. The sweet aroma of honeysuckle permeates the air.

Major helps Jennie from the buggy. They spread a small blanket to sit and eat on. She positions herself next to Major, who leans casually against a large oak tree.

"Jennie, what's wrong?"

"Nothing," she answers, handing him a piece of fried chicken. "Why?"

"There's somethin' wrong, and I want you to tell me what it is."

"I told you, I'm happy," she answers. A small tear slips from the corner of her eye.

"And *I* told *you* somethin's wrong." He wipes the tear from her cheek. "You know you can tell me."

"You said when we returned from Australia, I could go home," she cries. "I miss Mama and Papa. I want to visit them."

"I'm sorry," he apologizes. "I didn't realize it meant so much to you. I just wanted to get settled in a place of our own. I wasn't thinking."

"I want to go home!" she demands. "I just want to visit my family. That's all."

"And you shall," he promises. "I'll make the train arrangements for you."

"But what about the house?"

"Forget about the house. I'll tend to that. You need to write your folks a letter or send a telegram so they'll know when to expect you."

"Thank you!" she shouts excitedly and throws her arms around him. "I love you."

The coughing starts again, wracking her body with uncontrollable spasms. Her face flushes, and sweat beads on her forehead. Major runs to the river bank. After dipping a cloth napkin into the cool water, he places it at the back of her neck.

Alarmed by the attack, Major pleads, "Jennie, please see a doctor."

"No," she coughs and tries to clear her throat. "I know it's just the dust and the heat. I've always been susceptible to colds, and that's all it is."

"I just don't want anything to happen to you."

"When I get back home, I know I'll be fine," Jennie reassures Major. They gather what is left of the meal and prepare to leave the beautiful wooded area.

"Here let me do that," Major orders. Taking the oversized basket from her hand, he struggles to place it in the carriage. He helps Jennie onto the seat, climbs up, and sits beside her. He turns the horse around and drives toward home.

JULY IS ALMOST GONE WHEN MAJOR DRIVES JENNIE to catch the train bound for Kansas. While she spends time with her parents, he prepares to farm the land and move into their new home. Major wants everything to be perfect for Jennie when she returns.   Walter Perry, a cabinetmaker in Hornersville, makes a miniature bed, a wash stand for the bedroom, and several other pieces of furniture sized just for Major and Jennie.

Finally, the day comes for Jennie's return, and Major happily prepares to meet the train. The mornings are cool, and the days are shorter as the summer comes to a close.

Too excited to eat, Major gulps down a cup of coffee and goes quickly to the barn. During the past several weeks, he has not only decorated the house, but made the barn and corral more accessible for the two of them by lowering the latch.

He speaks to the horse he purchased weeks ago, as he harnesses him to the buggy. "Colonel, ole boy, today's the day Jennie comes home, and she is gonna love you!" He pats the old bay on the nose and carefully places the bit between Colonel's large teeth.

Colonel, too old to plow but too young to pasture, is perfect for Jennie to ride. He is a gentle old horse, and cannot go faster than a slow trot.

Standing on a small box Major built himself, he struggles to finish hooking the horse to the buggy. After he's finished, he pulls another box, with a long, thin, lightweight rope attached, from the buggy floor and places it on the ground. After using it to step into the buggy, he pulls the rope and returns the box to its rightful place on the floor.

The dew lies heavy on the grass, and the air is wet. Major leaves the farm and heads for the train station. Driving down the rough dirt road, he sees the sun reflecting from drops of dew sparkling on the leaves of the high cotton in the fields. Major, feeling exhilaration, lets out a loud, high-pitched, "Yahoo!" that echoes across the lonely fields, scaring a bevy of quail from the fence row next to him. "Come on Colonel, Jennie's comin' home, and we've gotta be there to greet her!" he yells, snapping the reins, and urging the old horse to a trot.

Arriving early, Major paces back and forth at the station. He pulls a plug of tobacco from his pocket and nervously pops it into his mouth.

A few minutes later, Major hears the train whistle. Quickly, he spits out the plug of tobacco, but in his haste to get rid of the nasty substance Jennie hates, he fails to notice a small portion drip onto his white shirt, leaving a dark brown stain.

The train screeches to a halt. Steel wheels lock and skid along iron rails. Smoke and steam billow from the engine's huge stack and brakes, engulfing the platform in a white cloud.

An angel from heaven, silhouetted by the sun, emerges from the billowy haze. The angel is Jennie.

"Major!" she cries running to meet him. "How I've missed you!" She wears a pretty emerald green dress, styled to enhance her delicate frame.

"I've missed you more than I thought I could ever miss anyone." Major holds her close and gives her a long, tender kiss.

"What's this?" Jennie says when he releases her. She points to the brown stain on his white shirt. "Major

William Ray, is that a tobacco stain on your clean white shirt?"

"Now, Jennie. I only had a little chaw."

"You know how I feel about that nasty stuff. Besides, I can't keep your shirts clean if you keep soiling them. It won't come out no matter how long I leave it in the sun."

"I promise I'll give it up." Pulling the remaining tobacco from his pocket, he throws it off the platform without hesitation. He knows he has more hidden in the barn. "Now, no more tobacco. I've something more important to show you."

"What?"

"I'm not telling you. You'll see," he says slyly, escorting her to their buggy. Colonel is busy feeding on some weeds growing around the hitching post.

"Who's horse is that?" she asks. "Where's your mother's buggy?"

"That's part of the surprise," he tells her, watching the expression on her face. "Colonel, this is your new mistress, Jennie. Jennie this is Colonel, your old, but new bay."

"He's beautiful!" She says softly, rubbing his nose. Colonel nudges her affectionately. "I love him. Thank you."

"Madam, your buggy awaits," Major says, doffing his hat.

The ride home is exciting for the young couple, even though they are bouncing over rough, rutty roads and talking continuously about family and friends. Major stops the buggy in front of the house and quickly drops the crate on the ground. He jumps down to help Jennie.

"Close your eyes," he orders sweetly. "I have another surprise for you."

"What is it?"

Illustration 6: Jennie Ray sits on a jenny.
The Daily Dunklin Democrat; Monday, June 15, 1959.

"Just close your eyes." Gently he guides her by the hand up the porch steps, through the house, stopping at the bedroom door. "Now, you can open them."

Jennie opens her eyes and beholds a room exquisitely filled with special furniture. The bed, made to their size, is covered with an elegant lace spread, tatted by Major's mother. Next to the bed sits a miniature stand for a wash basin. A small pitcher and bowl, specially made for Jennie by a shopkeeper in Australia, sits on top of it. The rugs on the floor are those they purchased while on tour. All the souvenirs they collected are unpacked and carefully distributed about the room.

"Major," she says surprised. Jennie sits comfortably on the edge of the bed. Her feet actually touch the floor. "How in the world did you do it? It's *beautiful.*"

"I did it for you because nothing is too good for my angel. You deserve the best."

"You, Sir, are the best." Jennie circles her arms around Major's neck and kisses him passionately. The two lie across the bed—a perfect fit.

WINTER COMES AND GOES ALMOST UNNOTICED. Spring arrives early, and Jennie is busy in the back yard washing clothes, her arms elbow-deep in soap suds and underwear, when Major appears with a letter in his hand.

"Jennie!" he yells, slamming the back screen door as he emerges from the house. "We got a letter from Sells Brothers."

"What's it say?" she asks, wiping her hands on her pastel apron, sewn from a flour sack.

Quickly, he opens it and reads aloud:

March 10, 1893

Dear Major and Mrs. Ray,

We all hope you are well and in good health. If you intend to join us for another season, please respond as soon as possible. Several sideshow performers have decided not to join us this year; therefore, we have re-cruited a great number of new members.

The 1893 season begins in late April; how-ever, we need you to join us the first of the month to prepare for traveling. We would also like to acquaint you with the new additions to the Sells Brothers family.

For easy access and convenience, we have moved our winter headquarters to Fourth and Russell Streets, Columbus, Ohio.

We look forward to seeing you soon.

Yours Truly,
Ephraim Sells
Sells Brothers Circus Inc.

Finishing the letter, Major stands quietly. Jennie says nothing. She looks sadly at the home she loves and the husband whom she knows she must follow.

"Well?" Major waits for an answer.

Paraphrasing the Bible, Jennie answers, "Whether thou goest, I will go. Where thou lodgest I will lodge, and thy people shall be my people—even if those people are a bunch of circus charlatans."

Chapter Twenty

New Friends

The tiny couple stroll along the narrow streets that weave throughout Sells Brothers' new winter headquarters. Major holds Jennie's hand as they walk and talk during the early morning hours. April brings a sense of beauty to the world as the warm spring season awakens mother nature from her long winter nap.

"Do you think Colonel will be all right without me?" Jennie asks, concerned for the old bay she left behind on the farm. "I hope Thomas remembers to brush him every day."

"I'm sure he will," Major laughs. "You left him a list of instructions on carin' for that old horse that'll take him a week to read."

"Don't say that about Colonel," she pouts. "He's a beautiful horse. I just want to make sure Thomas cares for him properly, so he won't miss me."

"Thomas is fourteen years old and very responsible," Major tells her. His young nephew is extremely helpful around the farm, and Major is confident Thomas can do the work while the two of them are traveling with the circus.

"Excuse me." A high-pitched voice cries from a tent nearby. "Can you help me, please?"

Unable to see anyone, Major and Jennie carefully approach the tent. They peer through the open flap. Sitting inside on a heavily constructed bed is an extremely large woman, trying desperately to reach a cup which is lying on the floor. A smorgasbord of food sits on a table in front of her.

"Thank you. I was afraid no one would hear me." Rather amused and surprised by their size, the enormous woman chuckles, "Aren't you a wee pair!"

"We were walking by and heard you calling for help," Jennie tells the woman. Pulling Major with her, she moves closer. Noticing the cup on the floor, Jennie picks it up and sets it on the table. "Is this what you were reaching for?"

"Yes, thank you. And would you mind pouring me another cup of that wonderful coffee there?" she politely requests. She introduces herself as Alice Thompson, one of several new additions to the sideshow. Although Alice weighs eight-hundred pounds, she has a beautiful face, a wonderful sense of humor, and a pleasant personality.

"I'm Major William Ray, and this is my wife, Jennie."

"It's nice to meet you," she replies, holding out a chubby hand. "I don't get much company, and, as you can see, I don't get around much, either."

"Maybe you should," Jennie suggests. She thinks the movement would do Alice good. "We would love for you to join us on our morning walks."

"That's kind of you, but I tire easily, and I try to stay close to my tent."

"We understand, but if you change your mind, you're welcome to join us." Major feels sorry for Alice sitting alone with no one to keep her company. Seeing her brings back memories of a woman, much like her, who helped him understand a world that was all too cruel for an unusually small boy. "We'll come back and sit with you later, if you don't mind, and if you want to talk."

"I'd like that."

"I see you have some visitors, Alice," a man says as he enters the tent. Recognizing Major and Jennie, he introduces himself as John Hamilton, the new sideshow manager. His pants are neatly pressed, and the bow tie he wears at the neck of his starched white shirt, along with a dark blue silk vest, suggest a very ambitious young man. He also seems to be happy in his line of work.

"We were just leaving, Mr. Hamilton," Major tells him. Placing an arm around Jennie's waist, he gently pushes her toward the tent opening. "We'll talk with you later, Alice."

"Good-bye!" Jennie yells over her shoulder. "I'll be back and we'll talk."

"Wait a minute, Major," Hamilton insists, following them. "I was looking for you."

"Well, you found us," Major quips.

"I want to introduce you to Captain and Mrs. Shields, if you've got a minute."

Major and Jennie follow Hamilton past the cook's tent where the aroma of baking bread catches Major's attention. Suddenly, several children with familiar faces surround him. They are anxious for a gum drop or a piece of peppermint they know he always carries in his pockets.

"All right," he orders. "Line up one at a time." Each child holds out a hand, and Major places a peppermint in it. "Now, go on and play," he spouts. "I have important business to take care of."

"I see you're popular with the kids," Hamilton remarks as he watches the children thank the little man before they run off to play. "I think you'll enjoy the Shields. You seem to have quite a bit in common."

"Oh, really," Jennie says. "Are they little people too?"

"Not quite," Hamilton answers with a smile. "You'll see."

Major hears children laughing behind one of the buildings. Turning the corner, he sees a large man bouncing a blond, curly-haired three-year-old on his knee. Several other children are tugging at his shirt and running circles around him.

"Captain!" Hamilton yells over the screaming children. "Captain, I have a couple of people I want you and Annie to meet."

"Annie?" the man shouts. "Come here. Hamilton's out here."

An extremely tall woman, standing approximately seven-feet-nine-inches, appears from the building. Her long blond hair is braided and drapes around her head like a crown. She wipes her hands on the flour-dusted apron she wears to protect her dark skirt.

"Now, who do we have here?" she asks. Her accent tells them she is from Ireland. "I'm Annie O'Brian Shields, and the man playing horsey like a child himself is me husband, Captain Shadrack Shields."

Annie playfully shoos the children away and takes the three-year-old into her arms. "And this is Shade Junior. We call him Shade after his father's nickname," she states proudly. The child squirms in his mother's strong arms. Annie is close to Jennie's age and has a special quality about her that attracts people, even though her height is somewhat intimidating.

Captain Shields is seven-feet-seven-inches tall. The large black-rimmed hat he wears could cover Major's head and face, and Major could fit into one leg of the big man's trousers. Although Captain speaks in a loud bass voice that would scare most people, he is as gentle as a kitten and everyone knows it.

"I guess I don't need to introduce you," Hamilton says, annoyed at how the two men seem to ignore him by leaving him out of the conversation. "I would like to talk to the four of you about how you will be displayed. When we hit the road, you will appear side by side and be billed as 'The Two Extremes of the Human Family: The Largest Couple in the World and The Smallest Couple in the World."

"Whatever you say, Mr. Hamilton," Captain agrees, trying to satisfy the young man who gets on his nerves. "Bossy little coot," he mumbles to Major and jokingly nudges the little man's shoulder with his hand.

"The most ambitious ones usually are," Major mutters.

Hamilton leaves the four of them alone. Jennie enjoys helping Annie with the baking while Major and Captain exchange exaggerated hunting stories.

SEPTEMBER 28, TRENTON MISSOURI. THE RAYS AND the Shields' have spent the last several months together, on and and off stage. A strong bond of friendship has formed, and they are almost inseparable. When the last performance is over, the tents and equipment are loaded onto the train and the circus heads for its next scheduled stop.

Major sits next to Jennie in the passenger car. Captain and Annie sit with them. Jennie is pale and suffers with a bad headache. The train's rocking motion as it travels through the night only aggravates her condition, and she lies across Major's lap while he rubs her temples.

Illustration 7: Annie Shields, Major, Jennie, and Captain Shields.

Photograph courtesy Mrs. Edna Allen

"Jennie, are you sure you don't won't to go to the sleeping car and lie down?" Annie asks from the seat facing them. "I'll go with you."

"That sounds like a very good idea to me," Captain agrees. "I bet Annie can find some medicine that might help that headache."

"I think all she needs is rest," Annie says, holding young Shade in her lap. His eyelids open and close as he fights the urge to sleep. "I think someone else needs to go to bed, too."

"Maybe you're right," Jennie agrees, sitting upright. "I am very tired. It seems like I just don't have any energy these days."

"Let's go, I'm rather tired myself." Annie rises to her feet, and bends over to avoid bumping her head. She steps back, allowing Jennie to enter the isle. "Careful," Annie warns as they walk toward the sleeping car. Before leaving, she looks at Major and promises, "I'll watch her."

"Thank you, Annie." He is grateful for the woman who is a friend to Jennie and helps her overcome the loneliness she often feels without her family.

Staring out the window, Major sees a clear, star-filled sky. The moon shines like a great lantern, illuminating the landscape. His mind wanders back to the past, a time when he looked out a window similar to this one, praying for a miracle. His prayer was answered when he met Jennie, but sometimes he wonders if it is not all a dream and when he wakes, like a dream, she will fade away, leaving burning images in his mind where she once stood.

"Hey, don't look so serious," Captain says, nudging Major's shoulder. "What are you thinking so deep about?"

"I was just thinkin' about Jennie," he sighs. "You know, when we first met, I could have sworn she was an angel. She was so beautiful sitting there on that bench in

front of the Big Top with her Bible in her hands. I looked
for her wings then, and sometimes I catch myself still
looking for them."

Major reveals his innermost emotions to the sensitive
man sitting in front of him. The two men exchange stories
of trials and tribulations. They may be different in size,
but they are similar in spirit—and their experiences of
being gawked at throughout their entire adult lives.

Suddenly, the train lunges forward, jerks and skids to a
stop. Forgetting about the low ceiling, Captain hits his
head when he jumps to his feet. Major darts in front of
him. They both run for the door.

"What's goin' on out here?" Captain shouts, his deep
bass voice echoing through the night. He tries to get the
attention of several brakemen who are already off the train
and running toward the last car.

"Seems we've lost three cages," the engineer explains,
running alongside the train toward the caboose. "We're
gonna have to go back." He never looks back, but continues past Major and Captain, leaving them standing in the
dark.

"Come on, Major," Captain orders, quickly following the
engineer. "Let's find out what's goin' on around here."

Running as fast as possible to keep up with Captain's
long strides, Major follows, jumping and dodging weeds
and rocks. The September night air is cool and damp,
creating a foggy mist that rises mysteriously from the
ground. It is hard for Major to see.

"Back it up! We've lost two black tigers, a pearl antelope, and a horned horse," Major hears Peter Sells yell
through the strange haze that hangs in the air.

"Ephraim!" Captain shouts. He sees the older Sells
standing near the empty car that carried the missing cages.
"What happened?"

"The train was traveling too fast," he answers, "and evidently the jarring movement jolted the cages from their chocks."

"Load em' up!" the engineer shouts. "We'll back it up! You boys stand on the flat beds and keep an eye out for those cages!"

Captain places Major on the flatbed car next to them and joins him as the train moves in reverse through the night. Major and several others search the area for the missing animals and their cages. Major spots what looks like a few scattered bars beside the tracks and sees a piece of wood here and there.

"Captain," Major points to a splintered pile of wood and steel several yards from the track. "Look! There's one!"

"Whoa!" yells Captain. "We got one here!"

The message echoes to the engineer through several men along the train's length. It stops, and the big man carefully lifts Major from the car. The two walk slowly to the rubble and survey the area, hoping to find the missing animals.

"Here's another one," Major hears Peter call out in the distance.

"Major! Look, there!" Captain points to the center of the cage. Walking near the smashed cage they can see the once beautiful antelope lying underneath the wreckage. Major struggles to remove the debris which is laying across the lifeless animal.

"We've found the antelope cage!" Major shouts to the men who search the area. "The antelope didn't make it!"

"There's nothing left of the cage or the horse!" yells Peter Sells from farther down the tracks. "Come on. Let's locate those cats."

"We've found the third cage!" shouts a man in the distance. "There's nothin' in it. Evidently the cats aren't hurt, but there's gonna be some people hurt if we don't find 'em."

"Everyone gather around," Ephraim orders, controlling the group of men around him, as usual. "We're gonna have to go back to Trenton because we can't locate these animals alone. We're not familiar with the territory, and this place is nothing but one big swamp."

"I can help," Major volunteers. "Remember—I live in an area like this, and I've hunted in swamps all my life."

"Are you sure you can do that?" Ephraim asks, thinking about the size of his over zealous volunteer.

"Don't let my size fool you," Major says confidently. "You oughta know that by now."

Ephraim nods and orders the men back onto the train. Within an hour the large locomotive arrives in Trenton, and a party is organized to search for the pair of black tigers. Sport, a large rottweiler, is used as bait to lure the pair to the new cage which has been prepared for them. When Major boards the sleeping car to retrieve his rifle, Jennie is sitting on the edge of the bottom berth waiting for him.

"Where are you going?" she asks, watching him open the long suitcase he always carries with him on his journeys. "Major, answer me. Why have we gone back to Trenton?"

"Nothin' for you to worry about," Major says as he removes a small hunting rifle from the suitcase. "We're just goin' huntin'."

"No! You're not going anywhere until you tell me what you're going to do with that," she says, pointing to the rifle in his hand. "You don't just stop a train in the middle of nowhere to go hunting. Are you going to tell me, or am I going to have to find someone who will?"

"All right," he mutters. "Several cages fell from the train. One of them had a pair of black tigers in it. The cages were found, but the tigers weren't, so we gathered a party together to go lookin' for 'em." He knows his explanation will only complicate matters, but he also knows that Jennie's persistence is limitless. She will not stop until she knows the truth.

Major places several rounds of shells in his pocket. He moves closer to Jennie and plants a light kiss on her cheek.

Her eyes fill with fear as she screams, "No! I won't let you do it! William Ray, I have always encouraged and stood behind you, but I will not allow you to go out there and get yourself killed hunting a pair of cats who could eat you for an appetizer!"

"Jennie." He places a tender hand on her shoulder. "You know I'm more careful than that. I've hunted all my life. I know what I'm doin'."

"No you don't!" she shouts, pushing his hand from her shoulder. "You are only three-feet-tall. You are not a grown man, William Ray. When are you going to know when to stop . . . " Gasping, her eyes widen as she realizes what she said in a moment of anger. Major silently stares into her dark eyes, both hurt and angered by her thoughtless words.

He says nothing, but turns, leaves the car, and joins the hunting party near the caboose.

"Major!" Jennie cries apologetically. "I'm sorry. I didn't mean it like that." Her words fall on deaf ears.

"What was that all about?" Captain asks as Major joins him.

"Nothin'. You know women," he replies callously. "Let's catch us some cats."

Illustration 8: Major Ray poses with his custom-made rifle
while Tige sits at his side.

Daily Dunklin Democrat
Monday, June, 15, 1959

The party quickly disperses to the swampy area surrounding Trenton. Sport is placed near the cage in hopes that the tigers will see him and return where the Animal Handler, John Gibson, a tall nice looking man with a powerful physique, can force them into the cage. The soft, boggy ground often mires under their feet. The glow of lanterns fill the woods like giant fireflies.

Major and Captain hunt side by side. Captain always feels responsible for the little man who is now a dear friend and colleague.

"Major?"

"Yeah."

"Have you ever hunted anything like this before?"

"Ah, sure I have," he lies. "I've hunted plenty bobcats and black bears back home. How 'bout you?"

"Ah, yeah, sure. Me too."

Although the moon hangs high in the sky, shadows from the leaves on the trees create an almost impossible darkness. Shuffling through broken limbs and dead leaves, Major suddenly stops dead in his tracks.

"What is it?" Captain asks the wide-eyed little man next to him.

"You hear that?"

"Hear what?"

"Listen!"

The two men stand still. They listen closely to the noises around them. Major whispers, "Don't move! Look!" A pair of bright yellow eyes glow in the dark.

"What do we do? Shoot it?" Captain asks.

"Lord, no! Ephraim will kill us," Major replies.

"Well, maybe we should back up slowly and head for the trap."

"Yeah, that's a good idea," Major agrees, and slowly, the stumbling duo begins to back away, all the while watching the pair of eyes. The size of the yellow eyes never change. As long as they do not, the men are sure the cat is following at a safe distance.

"I told you we should have brought a lantern," Captain whispers. "But no. Some little smart guy said we won't need a lantern. The moon is all the light we need."

"Hey, you're bigger than me," Major snaps, then quickly lowers his voice. "It's your fault if you listen to what I say."

Major and Captain hear voices as they near the trap that has been set for the tigers. The eyes that follow grow larger.

"I think that thing's gaining on us," Captain informs his partner who is already quickening his steps. "What should we do?"

"*RUN!*" Major screams, and with all their energy, they run for the train.

"Come on!" Captain shouts.

Major's legs may be short, but they are fast. He stays several steps ahead of Captain.

Afraid for his friend's life, Captain scoops Major up under his arm as he lengthens his stride. "Let me give you a lift."

"Hey! We got'em." Major, riding in the crook of the giant's arm, shouts to Gibson who is waiting near the cage. "Get ready. One of 'ems right behind us."

Nearly out of breath, Captain runs past the huge cage. Several men laugh at the sight of the giant running in with the screaming midget under his arm.

Sport immediately takes over. The large rottweiler matches wits with the tiger, carefully dodging the cat's huge claws and sharp teeth. Quickly, Gibson appears with a strong whip to encourage the beast into the cage.

"Thatta boy, Sport," Gibson praises the obedient canine. "Get that other cat in there." Soon, both cats are caged, and the cages are ready to set back on the flatbed car.

Walking toward the front, Major sees Jennie standing next to the train. Still hurt by her sharp and brutal words, Major approaches his teary-eyed wife and embraces her tightly.

"Major!" she cries. "I'm sorry! I didn't mean it! I just didn't want you to get hurt!"

"I know," he whispers tenderly in her ear. "I know."

"No!" she sobs. "You don't understand. I don't know what I would do without you. You are my life. Without you, I have nothing."

"Yes," he tries to soothe her. "I know. I understand because that is exactly how I feel about you."

"Just promise me you will never do anything this dangerous again," Jennie cries, gently shaking his shoulders and embracing him again.

"I promise. No more tiger hunts. Besides, I don't think Captain can keep up the pace."

Chapter Twenty-One

Practical Jokes

The tiger hunt is over. So are the days of chance taken by Major and Captain as Jennie and Annie strive to keep the duo under control and out of trouble. Major enjoys playing practical jokes on many of the performers throughout the company and Captain, now Major's best friend and protector, is always there trying to keep his little friend out of harm's way.

It is 1894, the beginning of yet another season, and "The Largest Couple in the World" is again sharing the stage with "The Smallest Couple in the World." The four grow closer. Many circus workers and performers think it amusing as they watch the two couples become almost inseparable.

Friday's performance in Joplin, Missouri—filled with its usual curiosity seekers—is profitable and very busy. The warm, sunny days of May raise the temperature inside the sideshow tent. After the last group of spectators file through the stuffy old tent, Major suggests to Captain that they take a stroll down Main Street to unwind.

"I bet this place has a great ice cream parlor." Major looks up, stretching his neck to see the expression on Captain's face. "I sure could use a nice cold drink, too."

Knowing the mischievous personality of his little friend and the public reaction the couples always experience, Captain thinks a minute before acknowledging Major's next comment, "I bet this town is just bustlin' with activity."

"Yeah, so . . . ?"

"So, I think a nice, cold ice cream soda would surely hit the spot about now."

"Let's get the girls," Captain says as a sly smile appears across Major's innocent looking face.

Quickly, the two men run to their tents to get their wives. "Jennie," Major yells as he enters their tent. "How about an ice cream soda?"

Jennie is wearing only a small chemise, corset, and pantaloons. Seeing her tiny but perfect and voluptuous figure always causes Major's heart to skip a few beats.

"Major?" she interrupts his daydream.

"I'm so lucky to have you," he tells her, hugging her tenderly.

"Hey, Major!" Captain's bass voice comes from the opposite side of the tent. "You two ready?"

"Great timin'," Major whispers in Jennie's ear. He yells back to the waiting couple outside, "We'll be right with you!" He smiles, drops his arms, and speaks sweetly to the woman in front of him, "We're going into town for ice cream. You want to come?"

"We'll wait out here for you," Captain yells. "That way we can all walk together."

Within a matter of minutes, Major and Jennie appear at the tent entrance, ready to enjoy their walk with friends to the ice cream parlor. The four are a handsome and curious lot, meandering through the busy streets of Joplin. Major's top hat and cane are a reflection of his personality and desire for aristocracy, while Jennie's light summer cotton dress and matching parasol help complete the air of refinement.

The Shields, overpowering the Rays in size, also enjoy dressing up for an occasion. Captain always dresses in a black uniform. Thin, gold military rope decorates the lapel of his coat, and gold stripes adorn the edge of his sleeves. Shiny gold buttons accentuate his black vest. His wide-brimmed black hat, tilted slightly to the side, creates an illusion of prestige. Annie loves delicate floral print patterns and lace for her wardrobe. Her bonnet always matches her dress.

Casually they walk along the sidewalk of the busy town. Major and Captain know what will happen when the public spots the four and enjoy watching the chaos that ensues. Jennie and Annie—innocent of the plan created by their mates—enjoy the late afternoon stroll.

Meeting the unusual individuals walking through town, men tip their hats to the ladies, and women nod and smile. Traffic stops as people back their carriages and wagons trying to get a better look at something they have never seen before and will more than likely never see again.

"Told you this trip to the ice cream parlor would be interesting," Major tells Captain as two wagons coming from opposite directions collide in the street, causing a fight between the drivers.

"Yeah, this is a lot better than sitting around the lot watching a bunch of acrobats jumping about," Captain replies. A crowd gathers behind them, whispering and pointing at the capsulized circus strolling down the sidewalk.

"Here we are," Major points to the ice cream parlor, which is empty upon their arrival. They sit down and wait for the soda jerk to take their orders.

"Hello, and what can I get for you today?" a young man about seventeen asks. His apron, covered in ice cream stains, hangs loosely around his neck. The small white cap he wears tilts to one side. "I don't think I have ever seen you folks around here. In fact, I know I ain't never seen you before."

"Yeah, you're right. We're not from around here." Captain teases the young man. "We work with the circus that's performing here."

"Looks like you may get quite a bit of business today," Major says, pointing to the crowd peering through the shop window.

Several children press their noses to the window, creating small oily circles on the glass. Adults tug at each other, trying to get a better look at the strange people sitting at the table inside the shop.

"I think my wife and I will have one ice cream soda, with two straws, please," Major orders.

"My wife and I will have two ice cream sodas. One apiece with one straw in each, please," Captain orders. Loudly, he says, "Why don't you people come on in. Have a soda and a good look instead of staying outside starin' in."

"Shade Shields, you behave yourself!" Annie demands, pinching her husband on the arm. "Let those people alone."

"Ouch!" Captain squawks, rubbing his arm.

Suddenly, the ice cream parlor is filled with people, eating, talking, and gawking.

Captain and Major motion for the soda jerk. "We have to be gettin' back to the lot. So, how much do we owe you for the sodas?" Major asks, pulling several coins from his pocket.

"You don't owe a thing," the young man answers. "It's on the house. We've never had this much business at one time before."

"Well, thank you." Captain responds, graciously accepting the soda jerk's offer. "Do you have a girlfriend, son?"

"Yes, Sir. I sure do."

"Well, here are a couple of tickets. One good turn deserves another," Captain declares. "Take her to the circus."

"Thank you." The young man looks at the tickets and smiles graciously.

"Are you girls ready to head back?" Captain asks, standing to go.

"We're ready," Annie answers.

Captain and Major doff their hats and bow slightly. Jennie curtsies, as does Annie. The objects of attention march regally out of the parlor.

They return to the lot. While Jennie and Annie prepare for bed, Major and Captain talk, sitting outside the tent on a couple of crates. Captain lights his pipe. Major takes a chew of tobacco from his pocket, and after looking around to make sure Jennie is nowhere near, stuffs the sticky substance into his mouth.

"She's not around," Captain laughs when he notices Major's nervousness. "But I can't believe you're still chewing that nasty mess."

"It's no worse than that stinkin' pipe you keep in your mouth."

"My pipe may smell bad, but at least I don't drool and dribble all over my shirt."

"I like it, but don't tell Jennie. She'll skin me alive if she finds out I'm still chewin'."

"I won't say anything, but she'll find out sooner or later. You watch. Women know everything. You can't keep anything from 'em. They got eyes in the back of their heads," Captain laughs and changes the subject. "I'd say we stirred up a few bees this afternoon."

"Yeah, I knew we would," Major answers, pleased with himself. "What are we gonna do tomorrow?"

"What do you mean, what are we gonna do tomorrow?"

"We gotta do somethin' to stir up some excitement around here." Major sits next to Captain with the same mischievous look in his eyes that always gets them into trouble.

"I don't know," Captain taps his pipe on the edge of the crate, emptying the unused tobacco before retiring for the evening. "But I'm sure you'll think of somethin' before mornin'."

"Where you goin'?" Major asks, spitting tobacco juice several feet to the side.

"I'm goin' to bed. I'll see you in the mornin'." When Captain leaves, Major sits alone, staring out into the dark night. The few lanterns hanging outside the tents dimly light the area around him.

"Major," Jennie calls. "Are you coming to bed?"

"I'll be right there," he answers, quickly spitting the wad of tobacco into a patch of grass.

The night air is warm. Major and Jennie settle for the evening in their tent. The thick pallet they lie on absorbs the coolness of the damp ground.

"Sweet dreams, Angel." Major leans over and places a light kiss on Jennie's forehead before turning over and going to sleep.

MORNING COMES QUICKLY. MAJOR RISES TO THE busy clamoring of circus performers and caretakers. After waking Jennie, he dresses quickly and strolls out to meet the morning. Captain and Annie occupy the tent on the left. Weslie and Lulu Sinclair, the Tattooed Couple, are on the right .

While standing outside, Major catches a glimpse of Weslie standing near his tent, holding a pitcher of warm water in his hand. Major watches the Tattoo Man walk inside and fill a basin full of warm water. Preparing to shave, he turns to hang a mirror on the center tent pole.

Quickly, Major draws a pitcher of cold water from a nearby well and slips unseen into the man's tent. After emptying the basin, he replaces the warm water with cold, and undetected, slips out again. He can barely see Wesley returning for the basin.

"Major!" Jennie yells from their tent. "What are you doing over there?"

Major doesn't answer, but motions with a hard wave of his hand for her to remain silent. He never takes his eyes from the Tattoo Man. Without thinking, Wesley quickly dips his hands into the basin and rinses his face.

"Good God!" he yells, struggling to find a dry towel. "That water's freezing cold!"

Seeing the stunned look on the man's face, Major falls to the ground laughing. "If you could have seen the look on your face," he cries, still laughing.

"You little son-of-a . . . " Wesley is interrupted by his wife's voice.

"Wesley!" she scolds. "Don't you dare say that word in this house!"

"Oh, you little . . . " Too angry even to speak, Wesley cannot find the right words to describe the laughing little imp who is standing at his door.

"What's the matter?" Major yells. "Oh, come on. It was just a joke."

Wesley isn't laughing. "I'll tell you one thing you . . . ," he curses. "If you were a man of normal size, I'd box your ears."

"Oh, really?" Major squawks. Entering the tent, he pulls up a stool. "Here. Now, I'm the size of a normal man. Go ahead. Hit me!" he dares, standing at even height with the aggravated man.

"Don't tempt me, midget!"

"No. Go ahead. I don't think you'll do it."

"No. I'm not going to hit someone smaller than me," he says and turns away. Major continues to annoy him. "But if you insist . . . "

Suddenly, Major feels a sharp blow to the side of his face. Knocked from the stool, he rolls like a ball through the tent door and out into the yard, stopping, stunned at Jennie's feet.

"Major!" she cries. "Are you all right?"

"Yeah," he stammers. "He did it. He really hit me!"

"Well, it serves you right," she replies, after determining he is not seriously hurt. "Now, maybe you'll stop this foolishness and act like a man instead of a silly school boy." She looks at Wesley and angrily shakes her head before stomping back to her tent.

"What happened?" Captain asks Jennie when they meet. "Is Major all right?"

"Oh, he's still alive, if that's what you mean!" she yells back. "You talk to him. I'm tired of trying to talk some sense into him. It's your turn."

Captain bends over to check on Major who is still lying on his back. "Hey, you still alive?" Captain teases. "Did Jennie do this, or were you hit by lightening?"

"Funny!" he growls, waiting for the world to stop spinning. "Help me up."

"He asked for it," Wesley yells as he walks back into his own tent.

"Did he do this?" Captain asks. "Why, I'll . . . "

"Never mind." Major shakes his head and very slowly walks away. "Believe me, I asked for it."

Chapter Twenty-Two

Circus Wars

Allen Sells dies suddenly, soon after the company returns from Australia. Ringling Brothers, a new and rapidly growing circus, is taking over the corn and wheat belt, an area that for years was considered Sells territory.

Needing to speak with Ephraim, Major starts up the steps of the office. He hears loud voices coming from the small trailer, and stops before entering. Major does not want to eavesdrop, but he cannot help overhearing the argument taking place between the three Sells brothers in the office trailer.

"I told you we should have stayed in the states!" Lewis yells at Ephraim. "All that tour got us was a lot of people killed, including Allen!"

"Oh, come on, Lewis," Ephraim shouts back. "That trip had nothing to do with Allen's death."

"No? When he watched those horses shot in Australia, he died then." Lewis paces. "And now the whole show is dying."

"Peter was supposed to make sure something like this wouldn't happen." Ephraim blames his youngest brother for the financial calamity currently affecting the corporation.

"Hey, don't blame me," Peter says defensively. He stands near the closed door. "It's not my fault some other young, ambitious brothers like us started their own circus."

Peter is young and not as business minded as his older brothers. When the new circus gained business in Sells territory, he did not realize it was going to affect them so severely. He hangs his head apologetically. "I'm sorry. I just didn't realize."

"What are we going to do?" asks Lewis. "Every time we make our contacts, Ringling is already booked or has already been through."

"The only thing left to do—declare war!" Ephraim pounds his fist on the desk in front of him. It is piled high with Ringling Brothers' fliers. "Declare war! We will hit every city they roll into, and we'll hit at the exact same time they do."

Major realizes this is not the time to speak to the brothers, and slowly backs down the stairs. He never mentions the incident to anyone because he fears it will cause trouble for the traveling group.

FOR THREE YEARS THE WAR RAGES BETWEEN Ringling Brothers and Sells. The circus plays each town with enthusiasm, but the financial strain becomes almost unbearable. The Sells Circus is losing too much money and cannot support itself.

The brothers call the performers and workers together to discuss the only possible solution. They meet in the large cookhouse. Ephraim is frazzled from worry, and his health is failing. He stands uneasy in front of the crowded room. The talking stops as he gets their attention.

"For the past three years," he begins. "The war has raged between Ringling Brothers and us."

"Yeah," yells a kinker in the back. "What's goin' on, anyway?"

"We're slowly running low on funds," Ephraim explains. "In order to continue, my brothers and I have taken drastic measures."

"What kind of measures?" another worker hollers. "We're not closing the show are we?"

"No, I've talked with Mr. James Bailey of Barnum and Bailey, and we have decided to consolidate the shows."

"Did he say, 'Bailey'?" Major asks Captain. The two stand close to the back of the room. "I thought those two were arch enemies."

"Yeah, he said Bailey." Major cannot see what is going on, but Captain describes the scene as he has a clear view. "He looks nervous. His color's not too good either."

"I know Barnum and I had our differences," Ephraim continues. "But since his death, James Bailey has taken over management, and after speaking with him, we plan on producing the biggest and best show ever seen on earth."

"What's the catch?" Captain asks Ephraim. "A big show like that. There has to be a catch."

"We run the Adam Forepaugh title in return for a third interest in not only Bailey's show, but Buffalo Bill's Wild West Show as well." Ephraim can see the crowd is uncomfortable with the proposition he has accepted from his old enemy's partner. "This is for the best."

"The 1896 season will open under the guise of Adam Forepaugh and Sells Combined Shows," Lewis announces as he joins his brother in front of the large group. "Major, you and Jennie will be displayed under a new billing."

"What's that?" Major asks from within the crowd. Everyone laughs because no one sees him, but they can hear his high-pitched voice loud and clear.

"From now on you will be billed as the "King and Queen of the Lilliputians," Lewis tells him. Silence. "Major?"

"Yeah, I heard you," he answers, frustrated because he cannot see. Major pokes Captain in the leg and motions for him to lift him above the crowd. "What in the world is a Lilliputian?"

The laughter dies, and Lewis explains, "Didn't you ever read Jonathan Swift's, *Guliver's Travels*?"

"No, I don't think I have."

"Oh, you would remember if you had." Lewis tells the story and everyone listens attentively. "Guliver was a sailor whose ship wrecked off a tiny island called Lilliput in the middle of the ocean. The tiny inhabitants living on this island were called Lilliputians."

"Hey that's you and Jennie all right," shouts a man within the group.

"I understand," Major says. "That's fine with me."

Captain lowers him to the floor and the meeting adjourns. Major overhears Lewis, Ephraim, and Peter speaking as they leave.

"I can't believe you actually let Bailey team up with us," Lewis gripes at Ephraim. "And then you give Forepaugh first billing."

"I don't want to discuss it, Lewis," Ephraim orders. "It was all I could do. We are outta business if we don't join him."

Chapter Twenty-Three

Sickness Strikes

1898. Major and Jennie wait anxiously in their bungalow at the Columbus headquarters for their friends to join them after a long winter and many letters. Ephraim, now sixty-three, knocks at the door.

"I thought I'd come by and make sure you were settled in all right," he says, fumbling with a letter in his hand.

"Come in and rest." Jennie invites him to sit for awhile and offers him a cool glass of lemonade.   "We were just sitting here waiting for Annie and Captain to arrive, but it seems they're running late this year."

"That's what I wanted to talk to you about."   Handing them the letter, he continues, "Seems that Mrs. Shields is expecting another child about the middle of the season, and Captain doesn't think it wise to travel with her in such a delicate condition, so they won't be joining us this year."

Disappointed, but anxious, Jennie opens the envelope and reads the letter aloud:

Greenville, Texas
April 15, 1898
Dear Jennie and Major,

I hope this letter finds you in good health.
Captain and I will not be able to join you this
year. We are truly disappointed, but bad
news is never without good. We are expecting
another child around September. Shade does
not think it wise for us to travel; therefore, we
will remain here in Greenville this year, but
we will be joining you again next year with a
new addition to the circus.
We miss you and hope you have a safe and
prosperous year.
Your loving friends,
Annie and Captain

"I wonder why Annie didn't tell us sooner?" Jennie
walks to the window and, looking out, observes several
children playing. "I'm going to miss Annie terribly this
year," she says sadly.

"I don't think she knew until recently," Ephraim replies.
"We were only told a few weeks ago ourselves, and we had
to work hard to find someone to replace them."

"Did you find someone?" Major asks, curious to know
who is replacing his friend. "Did Captain say anything
else?"

"Yes," Ephraim answers. "Captain said they will be back
next season for sure, so don't worry." He knows what the
little man is thinking because he has watched Major's
friends come and go, and each time Major takes it harder.

"I'll come out to meet the newcomer in a few minutes,"
Major tells Ephraim.

"All right," Ephraim says. "I'll be down by the train.
We'll be packin' up to leave on Monday." He dodges the
children who are congregating near Major's door. A ball

stops at Ephraim's feet. He picks it up, throws it back to the children, and walks on to the train.

"Things are changing so quickly," Jennie says, staring out the window.

"Are you feeling all right?"

"Yes." She turns to face him, casually wiping away a tear before he sees it. "I'm just tired. That's all."

"Are you sure?"

"Yes, I'm sure."

"I'm goin' down to the train to meet this newcomer. You wanna come with me?"

"No, I don't think so. I think I'll just lie down for a bit."

"I'll be back later." Major lightly kisses Jennie's cheek, then grabs his hat and cane as he leaves.

Jennie watches Major stroll out of sight. Suddenly the urge to cough overpowers her. The pain in her chest is almost unbearable, and the ability to breathe grows difficult. The coughing stops. She lowers the white handkerchief from her mouth and sees blood.

"Oh, dear God!" she cries. "I can't tell Major about this." Quickly rinsing the cloth, she pins it to a makeshift clothes line on the porch.

MAJOR APPROACHES THE TRAIN. SEVERAL KINKERS, loading tents and supplies, recognize him. "Hey, Major, ready for another season?" Major waves back and continues searching for Ephraim.

Near the elephant's shelter the smell of straw and manure is strong. The warm sun feels good against Major's back, but the sun disappears and a cold chill replaces it as a huge shadow covers him. Slowly turning, Major finds himself looking head on into the knees of the largest man he has ever seen. He steps back and gazes up into the face of a true giant who stares down at him.

"My word!" Major exclaims, swallowing a huge lump in his throat.

"Major," Ephraim laughs. "I want you to meet Colonel Henry Cooper."

Major is speechless.

"Hello, Little Man." The loud deep voice of Colonel Cooper carries like the low chord on a bass fiddle. His hands are extremely thin, but huge. His body, head and feet look like someone stretched them out of proportion. His face is long, and he wears a thin, dark brown mustache over thick lips. Cooper's extremely high cheekbones cause his gray eyes and jaws to seem even deeper, almost skeletal.

"Watch this," he says, removing a gold ring from his third finger. He takes a large silver dollar from his pocket.

"What's he fixin' to do?" Major asks Ephraim, who just shrugs his shoulders.

Slowly, Cooper passes the silver dollar through the center of the ring. The coin does not touch the sides. It slides through easily. Cooper hands Major the coin, and it covers the palm of his hand.

"Did you see that?" Major exclaims. "I've never seen anything like that in all my life as a sideshow performer. That's great. I guess you perform that trick on stage."

"Yes," Cooper replies. "It gets a big response from the audience."

"By the way, Cooper," Major says, rubbing the back of his neck which is stiff from looking up so long. "I can call you Cooper, can't I?"

"Yeah, sure," Cooper responds. "I don't mind."

"How tall are you?"

Illustration 9:

Little People, Major and Jennie Ray, along with Giant, Colonel Cooper stand among the group of performers in the 1898 Forepaugh-Sells Sideshow.

Photograph courtesy of Circus World Museum, Baraboo, Wisconsin

"I'm eight-feet-six-inches tall, and I weight four hundred pounds."

"Did you hear that?" Major yells to Ephraim. "He's a foot taller than Captain and probably outweighs him by a hundred pounds. Wow!"

"I have some things that need to be done before the circus hits the rails for the season," Ephraim tells Major and Cooper, who are busy swapping measurements, "so, I'll leave you two alone."

"Wow!" exclaims Major again. "Jennie has gotta get a look at you."

"Who?" Cooper asks.

"Jennie, my wife. She'll be surprised when she catches sight of you. I've been in this business for thirteen years, and I don't recollect ever seeing anyone even near as big as you."

The two men, opposites in size, walk to the housing section of the lot. By the time they reach the tiny bungalow, Major is exhausted from running four steps to Cooper's one.

"Jennie!" Major yells from the front step. His voice cracks as he breathes heavily. "Hurry up. I want you to meet someone."

"Major, what do you wan . . . " Her voice trails. She stands at the door, staring at Cooper—speechless.

"Yeah," Major laughs. "That was my reaction, too. This is Colonel Cooper. He's takin' Captain's place this season."

"Excuse my manners," she apologizes and carefully wiping her hands on her apron, Jennie offers her right hand. "I'm Jennie. Won't you please come in and sit for a while?"

"I'm sorry," Cooper says. "I would, Ma'am, but I'm sure my wife is looking for me. Maybe some other time."

"Yes," she answers politely. "And maybe you can bring Mrs. Cooper."

"Is your wife as big as you?" Major asks curiously. "The biggest woman I know is Annie Shields. Of course, I thought I'd seen the largest man too, and I was wrong."

"No," he laughs. "She's tall, but not tall enough to make her a giantess or anything. She's just a beautiful woman to me." Coming from such a large man, his sincerity is touching, and Major knows exactly how he feels.

"We'll be seeing more of you, I'm sure." Jennie excuses herself and goes quickly back to her work. After entering the house, she tries with all her might to suppress the cough that escapes her lips.

When Cooper leaves, Major enters the house. The smell of beans cooking on the stove reminds him of the meals his mother made when he was young. Major watches Jennie busying herself between the sink and the stove. The healthy glow that was once there has faded and her breathing is heavy.

"Jennie," he says concerned. "Are you feeling well?"

"How many times do I have to tell you? I'm fine," she lies, not wanting to worry her husband. "When do we leave and where do we open this time?" she asks, anxious to change the subject.

"We start Monday. Here in town."

"Good. I'm sure that once we're back on the road and active again I'll be fine. You'll see," she assures her husband, but she senses that he knows there is more, much more than either of them can comprehend.

IT IS JULY, AND THE RENOWNED ADAM FOREPAUGH and Sells Brothers Combined moves on to Parsons, Kansas. It is the hottest day of the year.

Jennie stands on the sideshow platform waving a small decorative hand fan, trying to keep cool. She tastes salt as perspiration trickles down her face and meets her lips. Pulling the small white lace handkerchief from her skirt pocket, she gently wipes the sweat from her brow.

Major has noticed Jennie becoming more and more uncomfortable the longer she stands on the long stage. Several times she tries to conceal a cough by placing the handkerchief over her mouth. The heat is unbearable. The rank smell of sweat and perspiration from the crowd of people filing continuously through the large sideshow tent is overwhelming.

"Hey, little guy," shouts a young man in the crowd. "Can you and your little lady do anything besides stand there and look pretty?"

"It's too hot to do much, Sir," Major replies, hoping to receive some kind of sympathy from the rude young man. "And my wife is not feeling well. As a matter of fact, I'm surprised we're not all sick."

"I think she should sing for us. Don't you think she should sing for us or somethin'?" His rugged clothes and poor mannerisms offer the impression of a drunk cowhand out for a good time and trouble. He jabs another man dressed in the same rugged clothing, but sober. "Come on Jim, don't you think they should do somethin' for us?"

"I think maybe you've had too much to drink," Jim says, pulling on his rude friend's arm. "Leave them alone. It's too hot to make trouble."

"Awh, don't touch me."

"I'm sorry for my friend's behavior, Ma'am" Jim apologizes. "He's had a little bit too much fun today."

Jennie smiles and nods, accepting the young man's apology.

"Major, is Jennie sick?" Cooper asks. "She looks awful pale to me."

"I don't know. It may be the heat. It has to be 110 degrees in the shade."

Standing near Jennie, Major questions her about her health, "Are you sure you're feeling well?"

"Yes," she says, irritated and coughing. "I told you it's just the heat." The sporadic coughing grows worse, and Jennie gasps for her next breath, then panics.

"Jennie!" Major cries. He attempts to support her as she falls to the platform floor, gasping for air between coughs.

"Cooper, help me!" Major screams. "Somethin's wrong! Someone get a doctor!"

The coughing stops. Jennie slips into unconsciousness. Blood trickles from the corners of her mouth. Major helplessly sits holding her in his arms, as memories flood his mind from another time when someone he loved slipped from this world.

"NO!" he screams, looking into the air. "Not Jennie! God, not Jennie!" He begins to sob. Clutching his loving wife in his arms, he waits for the doctor to appear. He prays. "Hang on, honey. You're gonna be fine. I promise."

In his mind, he no longer holds Jennie in his arms. It is his father who lies motionless. He sees the light from the sun as it slips away into the darkness behind the vast horizon. He hears the voice of his father once more as he asks for the final time, "Did you hear it?"

"Yeah, Pa. I hear it," Major repeats to himself.

"What did you say?" asks Cooper, returning with the doctor.

The doctor examines her. "Major, I can't be sure what's wrong with Jennie, but I do know she needs the care of a stable physician who has more than a black bag and a few medical tools."

"Doc, there's a wagon waitin' outside!" Lewis yells, peering through the sideshow tent. "Quick, let's get her loaded up and to the town physician!"

Cooper lifts Jennie's lifeless body and places her into the padded wagon. Major joins her, taking her hand in his. "Do you need me to go with you?" Cooper asks.

"Thank you, but no," Major answers solemnly, still looking at his silent wife. "Lewis is driving, and we can handle things just fine."

SITTING HELPLESS ON THE HARD WOOD CHAIR IN THE waiting room of Dr. Daniel Cross, Major's legs hang loosely from the side of the chair. They start to cramp as the pressure from the edge of the chair slows the circulation.

"She'll be fine," Lewis says. "You'll see."

The two sit silently—waiting.

Minutes seem like hours, and hours are an eternity for Major. He sits staring at a crack in the floor. He follows its crooked line across the floor and up the plastered wall in front of him. He wonders what caused it to go in the direction it did."

Dr. Cross appears in the doorway of the examining room. Sitting in another chair nearby, he motions for Major to stand in front of him.

"Mr. Ray, your wife is very ill. Now, I can't be sure about the diagnosis, but I believe you need to take her to the hospital in Wichita." Dr. Cross feels sorry for the man standing before him. "I'm only a small town doctor, and I can't run the types of tests needed to make a definite diagnosis, but I will tell you, it's not good."

"What do you think it is?" Major asks.

"Jennie has some early signs of tuberculosis."

"Tuberculosis? How can she have tuberculosis?"

"Have you been out of the country lately?" Dr. Cross knows that most circuses travel a lot, and many travel out of the country.

"Yes, we traveled to Australia, Hawaii, and Samoa this past year," Lewis interrupts, answering for Major.

"More than likely that's where she contacted it—if, indeed, it is tuberculosis."

"Is there anything we can do?" Major asks sadly.

"Well, sometimes with rest the disease can be suppressed." Dr. Cross explains the results and the possibilities, but also goes on to say, "I can't be positive about my diagnosis. That's why I want you to take Jennie to Wichita for further testing. They have the proper facilities there."

"All right, doctor," Major agrees. "I'll make arrangements to be on the first train to Wichita."

"Good. And I'll send a telegram to the hospital alerting them to your arrival." Dr. Cross rises from the chair. Shaking Major's hand, he points to the examining room. "You can go in now. Your wife is waiting for you."

"I'll make the arrangements for travel," Lewis tells Major. "You just get Jennie and your things together. Don't worry about anything but helping Jennie."

Standing next to his pale, delicate wife who is lying on a narrow bed, he says jokingly, "You trying to get outta work or somethin'?" He forces a smile across his worried face.

"I'm sorry, Major."

"Sorry for what? You haven't done anything." His voice is gentle and consoling. "You're ill and we're going to make you better. You'll see."

"I know you will." Jennie's voice is tired and weak. Slowly, she clasps her hand around Major's and squeezes it reassuringly. "I love you."

Chapter Twenty-Four

The End of a Great Era

Sitting on the bright, lush lawn of the Wichita Sanitarium grounds, Jennie runs her hand over its velvety blades. A soft breeze blows through the large oak tree next to her. She can hear its leaves rustling in the air above.

She lies back and looks into the deep blue sky where billowy white clouds dance about, forming shapes she can clearly see.   A large white rabbit dances across, then slowly turns into a dog and runs away.

"Jennie?"

A familiar voice interrupts her wandering thoughts, and she smiles. Turning on her stomach, she leans on her elbows and sees Major running, not too fast, across the beautifully groomed lawn toward her. He waves a letter high in the air. She waves back.

"It's a letter from Lewis," he says, anxious to read it, but first he makes sure Jennie is comfortable. "Do you need anything?"

"I'm just fine, Major. Open it and read it, please."

Opening the letter, he reads:

Columbus, Ohio
August 15, 1898

Dear Major and Jennie,

    I hope this letter finds both of you well. I was sorry to hear of Jennie's diagnosis, I know you were hoping for better results.

    I regret to inform you that upon returning to Columbus with his wife last month my brother, Ephraim, passed away. He died on August 1, at the age of 64.

    We believe between financial stress and age, the burden finally became too much for him to bear. We will all miss him terribly.

    I hope to see you next season. God bless you both.

Sincerely,
Lewis Sells

A tear slips from the corner of Jennie's eye. Major lowers his head and lays the letter in his lap.

"I want to go home," Jennie says sadly.

"What?"

"Major, I want to go home."

"Are you sure you're well enough to make the trip?" Major, too, misses the comfortable surroundings of their Cardwell farm.

"Yes. I know I'm well enough now."

"I'll talk to the doctor and see if we can leave within the next day or two."

Major remembers the conversation between the Sells brothers several years ago. The anguish and disappointment in Ephraim's voice was a sign that he knew the end was near. The end of a great era—more than a generation of mystical entertainment.

Chapter Twenty-Five

Princess Anna's Prediction

March 25, 1900, a new century begins and times are in-deed, changing. Jennie, Major, Captain, and Annie stand beside three long lines of trains outside New York's Madison Square Garden. They watch as workers unload cars. The trains, each representing a separate circus, form the largest and best circus menagerie in North America.

"I've never seen anything like it!" Captain exclaims. "Look there!" he exclaims pointing at a group of Indians walking toward them.

"I wonder what they're doin' here," Major says. "Jennie, you see 'em?"

Jennie doesn't answer. Her eyes are fixed on a man sitting heroically in the saddle of a beautiful white Arabian. The man's white hair, long and flowing, falls free from beneath a white cowboy hat sitting majestically on his head like a king's jeweled crown. A well-groomed, white goatee and mustache accentuate his strong chin and sharp nose.

"Jennie?" Major notices her spellbound stare and tries to break it. "Jennie!"

Taken by her beauty and intrigued by her size, the powerful image of white moves closer. He addresses the miniature doll by a tip of his hat and the wink of an eye. "Ma'am," he greets, his voice soft and deep.

Her heart pounds within her well developed chest. "Good day, Sir," she giggles slightly. The red in her cheeks grows brighter as she notices his almost seductive stare.

"Buffalo Bill's the name," he announces, riding by. A number of Indians follow him to Madison Square Garden where the tents are erected.

"Did you see that?" Jennie asks Annie, who holds a squirming two-year-old Paul in her arms.

"Yes, I've always heard about him, but this is the first time I've ever seen the famous Buffalo Bill." Annie is almost as mesmerized as Jennie.

"Ah, I didn't see anything that great about him," Major says. "Did you?" he asks Captain.

"Hey, I'm staying out of this," Captain tells him, grabbing eight-year-old Shade by the hand.

Jennie detects a note of jealousy in Major's voice, and smiles at Annie. "Oh, he's too old for me anyway," she teases, "even though he does sit on a horse like a king."

"Let's go," Major squawks, and grabs the small bag at her feet. Jennie laughs out loud.

"Come on handsome," Annie throws her bag at Captain. "Let's go."

"Umph." Captain takes the bag and mutters, "Yes, Ma'am."

THOUSANDS UPON THOUSANDS OF PEOPLE SWARM the railway station and streets to watch the parade of performers march to Madison Square Garden. They will perform to a packed crowd for sixteen days. Some nights hundreds are turned away for lack of space.

Since the death of Ephraim and Allen, the Sells Brothers Circus is gradually losing its ability to hold quality curiosities. Most of the old gang has left to join the better shows.

It is early morning on the sixteenth day. Jennie and Annie walk along the midway before the circus opens for business.

"Annie?" Jennie speaks to the woman walking slowly next to her. "You are the only true friend I've ever had."

"Jennie, thank you." Annie bends down and picks up Paul, who is walking next to Jennie and is almost as tall as she. He sees the horses and is desperately trying to pull Jennie toward them. "I also consider you a true friend and friends in this business are hard to find—even harder to keep."

As they walk along they pass Princess Anna's tent. She is the circus mind reader, fortune teller, and palmist. Jennie often thinks about going in, but usually changes her mind before she enters the small, gaudy tent.

"You ever had your fortune told?" Jennie asks Annie.

"Naw, I never believed in that kind of thing."

"I've thought about it, but I was too scared."

"It's just a lot of hawg-wash anyway."

"How do you know?"

"They tell you the same thing they tell everyone else: 'You're going to meet a tall, handsome stranger.'" Annie speaks with a distinct and exaggerated gypsy accent. "Or they say, 'You're going on a long journey to a faraway place.'"

Jennie laughs as Annie continues. "Where am I going to meet a tall, handsome, stranger?" she asks incredulously, her accent thickening with each word. "Shade's about the tallest I could find, and he's not as tall as I am."

"I guess you're right, but I think I'm going to do it this time." Jennie walks to the entrance of the tent. "Wait for me, all right?"

"Sure, but you're going to meet a tall, handsome stranger. For you everyone's tall, if *not* handsome." Annie laughs and watches Jennie enter the gypsy's tent.

Jennie hesitates, then enters. Her eyes slowly grow accustomed to the dimly lit interior.

"Hello?" she calls in almost a whisper. "Anyone here?"

"Yes, come. Come in." A figure appears from the darkness. "Jennie Ray, how good of you to come and see me."

"How . . . how do you know my name?"

"Everyone here knows you and Major," she answers, in a deep, soft, and mysterious voice. She is from Romania, and her accent is thick. "Besides, Princess Anna knows all."

A beautiful woman steps from the darkness. Her deep olive skin reflects the candlelight. Her thick, long, black hair curls naturally under a colorful scarf that fits snugly on top of her head and ties neatly at the side.

Princess Anna's petite figure fills a peasant dress with scarves attached to the waist. Several necklaces drape her neck, while large hoop earrings accentuate her long lobes. Bracelets jingle from her arms as she walks.

Jennie follows the gypsy to a small table set in the center of the room. Scarves and spangled gold jewelry decorate the tent's interior. Smoke drifts upward from a small dish that sits behind the table. Inside it, something burns. It emits an aroma pleasing to Jennies senses, relaxing her.

"Sit here," Princess Anna says, pointing to a chair at the table. She sits on the opposite side.

"Thank you," Jennie scoots up and sits in the chair, her nose even with the table top. Her eyes watch the gypsy woman in front of her.

"Let me see your left hand."

Jennie slowly extends her hand, palm down.

Princess Anna takes it, turns it over, strokes it, and softly says, "What a tiny hand. Ohh, but what a great past you have had!"

"What?" Jennie asks. She is curious as to what the woman sees.

"I see here you have traveled across a great ocean." Princess Anna looks closer. "You are very ill. You hold on to a deep, dark secret. Not about you but about someone close to you."

Jennie jerks her hand from the gypsy's, afraid the woman will also read the secret she promised Major she would never tell. She is amazed at what Princess Anna can see, but she is also curious about what is to be.

"Please. Please, what I see I do not tell anyone," she assures Jennie. "Let me tell you what I see ahead. Give me your right hand, and I will unravel the truths of your future."

Jennie hesitates, then extends her right hand, palm up.

"I see a tall, handsome stranger coming into your life."

Jennie giggles, then apologizes, "I'm sorry. I was just thinking about something a friend of mine said. Please, continue."

"I see a little boy and a dog. A little blond boy. But wait. He has the face of an old man."

"What else do you see, Princess Anna?"

"I see great sadness. Someone close to you will soon die."

"Who? Can you see who it is?" Jennie begs.

"No, I cannot see a face." She shakes her head and continues, "I do not understand. I see you through glass."

"What do you mean? Is it glass windows?"

"I do not know. Just glass. I also see a great white statue, but I cannot see what it is." She tries harder to concentrate on Jennie's future. "I am sorry. I cannot see any more."

Jennie hands her fifty-cents and says, "Thank you."

Outside, Annie waits with a fussy Paul in her arms. "Well, what did she say?"

"She said I would meet a tall, handsome stranger." They both laugh and continue their walk down the midway.

MAY 10. THE CIRCUS MOVES INTO SCRANTON, Pennsylvania. The group is tired, but the weather is cool and business is great. Annie and Captain are exhibits in the outside show today.

"I suppose we had better get inside," Major tells Jennie, who is busy talking to Annie near the outside platform. "You two will have plenty of time to talk after the show."

"I'm coming," Jennie says. "Meet me in the backyard for lunch." Annie nods in agreement.

Over the past several years, Major and Jennie have developed an act that includes singing and dancing for the people who file through the sideshow tent. Major plays a fiddle, made especially for him by an old man they met years ago, while Jennie dances an Irish jig.

Major's stomach tells him it's almost time for lunch. The last group of sightseers are on their way out. Suddenly, a loud crash echoes through the tent. People scream.

"What was that?" Jennie asks. Her stomach turns. A sick feeling floods her.

"I don't know! Listen!"

They can hear people screaming and running outside the tent. Jennie hears the Captain's voice as he yells for Annie.

"It's Annie and Captain!" a voice yells into the sideshow tent. "The platform collapsed!"

Before Major can say a word, Jennie is off the stage and out the tent door. Her heart races. She sees only a pile of broken wood. The words of Princess Anna cloud Jennie's mind, *"Someone close to you will die."*

"Annie!" Jennie runs to the pile of rubble and begins digging frantically. Pulling boards away with fantastic strength, she continues to cry out, "Annie! Annie!"

"I got her!" yells a worker. Several others struggle to pick Annie up and carry her to a nearby bench. Captain—unhurt but stunned—stumbles over to join her.

"Everything is fine, but we need a buckboard to get her to the hospital!" Lewis yells as he tries to disperse the crowd that quickly gathered about the scene.

"Annie!" Jennie rushes to her friend's side, tears streaming down her face. "Annie, I was so afraid something awful happened to you!"

Annie flinches from the pain in her ankle. Putting an arm around Jennie, she tells her, "When I heard that little voice screaming my name, I knew I was going to be fine."

"I don't know what I'd do without my best friend," Jennie whispers.

"Don't worry, because your best friend doesn't plan on going anywhere." The buckboard arrives quickly, and the men lift the heavy giantess into it. "It feels like my ankle is broken, but other than that, I'm fine."

Captain stays behind with Annie, even though the train is loaded to continue to another place.

IT IS LATE JUNE WHEN THE TRAIN ROLLS INTO TIFFIN, Ohio. The tents are unloaded. Within minutes the great circus city is again ready for business. It is hot, and again, Jennie is feeling poorly.

Inside, the tent is stifling. Jennie dances a little and coughs a lot. Major worries. The crowd that enters is kind and compassionate.

"Excuse me." Jennie hears the voice of a woman calling. "Here, I thought you might like a drink of cool lemonade."

"Thank you." Jennie takes the glass. A young boy, about fourteen stands near the woman, watching and smiling. "You look so familiar. Do I know you?" she asks the woman.

"I didn't know if you would remember us or not, but my son and I met you nearly ten years ago in this same town."

Jennie is suddenly flooded with memories of a terrible storm, collapsed tents, a child's toy, and a man being saved from a horrible death in an abandoned well. "Johnny," she says, recognizing the little boy. "And you are his mother. I remember. I often thought about you and wondered if you were safe. I never saw you after the storm, so I didn't know. I did, however, say a prayer for you. I remember that."

"We made it to a deep ditch just outside the fairgrounds and lay there until the storm passed."

The young boy who was so small then now stands as tall as his mother. "You have grown into a handsome young man," Jennie says.

"Thank you," he says, blushing.

"We don't want to keep you from your work, but we saw the billboard outside and wanted to say hello." Noticing Jennie's pale complexion and aggravating cough, the woman continues, "I hope you get to feeling better."

"Thank you for stopping by," Jennie says with a smile. "Oh, and thanks for the lemonade, too."

Illustration 10: An autographed picture from Buffalo Bill Cody to Major and Mrs. Ray.

Photograph courtesy of Mrs. Imogene Young

The woman replies, "Thank you for the prayer!"

Playing his fiddle, Major is entertaining people who stop to look at them. Jennie, when she can, sings beautifully for her admirers. Several people file through, talking and laughing.

At the end of the line appears another familiar face— one that Jennie sees often, but only from afar.

"Hello, Major and Mrs. Ray. I see you are pleasing the customers considerably." The voice is soft and low.

"Thank you . . . " Major is surprised to see the great Buffalo Bill standing in front of them, but doesn't know what to call him. He waits for the man to finish the sentence.

"Oh, Cody. Bill Cody."

"Mr. Cody, can we help you with something?" Major asks, curious about his presence.

"I would like to talk to you and the Missus about something."

"We should be done here in a few minutes. Maybe you can meet us in the backyard for some lunch."

"That would be nice, I'll meet you then." He tips his hat to Jennie and moves on through the line.

MAJOR AND JENNIE SIT WAITING FOR CODY TO MEET with them. Major wipes his forehead with a handkerchief. He holds to the apple he eats with both hands, its cool juice running down his chin. Jennie wipes it away with a cloth napkin.

Jennie pulls a small hand fan from her pocket and waves it, creating a slight breeze to cool herself. The glass of lemonade she holds in her hand is refreshing. She puts the cold glass against her forehead and closes her eyes.

"Major and Mrs. Ray."

Jennie doesn't have to open her eyes to recognize the person behind the seductive voice of the man who stands in front of her.

"Mr. Cody," Major answers, extending his hand. "Now what did you want to see us about?" Major is always forward and straight to the point. Jennie is embarrassed by his manners, but remains silent.

"I'll tell you, Major, I've watched you and your wife for many years. During that time, I have seen a variety of newspaper articles about Sells Brothers and their great sideshow, especially the two Midgets."

"What do you want from us?" Major asks.

"I want you to come to work for me in my sideshow."

Chapter Twenty-Six

Buffalo Bill

It is the middle of the 1901 season, and part of Princess Anna's prediction comes to pass.   A tall, handsome stranger walks into Jennie's life in the backyard of Sells Brothers and, now, she finds herself walking in the backyard of the famous Buffalo Bill Cody.

The hot July sun filters between the large canvas tents, and feeling the heat, Jennie wipes her forehead with her handkerchief. Sweat from the cold glass of lemonade she holds drips onto her hand.

"Jennie." Annie appears from the sideshow tent. She is pale, and she quickly sits down on a nearby bench.

"Annie, are you all right?" Jennie asks, concerned. "You look awfully pale. You're not getting sick, are you?"

"No. I'm not sick." She places her head between her knees to ward off the pressing darkness that comes like a wave. "I know what it is."

Jennie is confused as Annie speaks in riddles.

"Captain is going to die when I tell him. We need the money so bad. For the past few years, we haven't made a full season because of babies and broken ankles," she babbles. "He is not going to believe this! Should I tell him or wait until he notices?"

"What are you talking about, Annie?" Jennie listens for Annie to answer her questions. "Why would Captain make you leave for the season?"

Annie, raising her head for a brief moment, looks into Jennie's eyes and mentally speaks to her. Jennie understands.

"Oh," Jennie sighs. "OH! You have to tell him, Annie."

"No, I don't."

"Yes, you do. Besides, how are you going to keep it from him?"

"I'll just wait until he asks," Annie replies, confident of her ability to hide her pregnancy from her husband. "And you can't tell him. Understand? This is our secret."

"All right, but if you get too sick, I'm going to have to break my vow of silence," Jennie warns, worried about her best friend. "Meanwhile, my lips are sealed."

"What are you two girls doing back here? Telling secrets?" Major quips as he and Captain join their wives. Major holds onto Paul's hand while Shade Junior runs behind, kicking a rock.

"No, we're just sitting back here trying to get cool." Annie answers.

"Honey, you feeling all right?" Captain asks Annie. "You look awful pale, and what were you doing with your head between your knees?"

"Nothing. I dropped my wedding band on the ground, and I was looking for it." Quickly, she pretends to retrieve it from the dirt and places it on her finger. "Here it is."

She rises quickly, desperately fighting the nauseous feeling that overtakes her. She looks at Jennie with eyes that demand her silence.

Jennie nods. She can hear the whooping of Indians in the background as the Roughriders interrupt the mock

Illustration 11:

Major, Jennie, Annie, and Captain pose with Buffalo Bill's Wild West Sideshow.

Photograph courtesy Circus World Museum, Baraboo, Wisconsin

raid made on the Deadwood Mail Coach. The sideshow tent sits on the outskirts of the huge eleven-acre arena wich is used for the Wild West Show, and they can clearly hear the exciting performance.

"Anybody for watching the show for a few minutes?" Captain asks, watching Shade Junior hollering, whooping, and running in circles, imitating the Indians in the show. "I believe Shade Junior needs something to keep him occupied."

BUFFALO BILL'S WILD WEST SHOW IS NOT WHAT Major and Jennie have been accustomed to. Instead of acrobats and high wire acts, there are cowboys and Indians, Pony Express riders, simulated army artillery drills, and more.

Major holds Jennie's hand as they watch the show in the huge arena. Her clothes stick to her. Her palms sweat. She wishes Major would turn loose, but she does not want to hurt his feelings by pulling away. Her mind wanders as she thinks about Annie and her third child. Jennie is slightly jealous of her friend because Annie has two children.

Ashamed of her thoughts, Jennie shakes her head and gazes into the arena. She sees several Indians circling a settler's cabin. She recognizes many of them and can call them by name.

"Look Major, there's Sitting Bull's son, William." She points at the large Indian straddling his strong, black stallion. William's hair hangs in braids, falling to his waist where it touches the deerskin breeches he wears. His hair is so dark that it reflects as blue in the sun, like the wings of a raven .

"And there is Kills Both Sides." Major points to a brave whose battlescars set an even more impressive scene. He holds a tomahawk high in the air as he hollers, frightening the paying crowd.

Suddenly, from the edge of the arena Buffalo Bill emerges astride his white horse, Isham. He leads a band of cowboys, scouts, and frontiersmen to save the day. Jennie jumps as gunshots ring out and the Indians are either slain or chased away. The crowd cheers. Buffalo Bill holds his white hat in the air and circles the arena triumphantly, saluting the crowd. The show is over. The crowd disperses and Major, Jennie, Captain, and Annie slip unnoticed to their tents. The train is loaded, and once more they travel by rail to their next stop.

OCTOBER. THE WEATHER IS TURNING COOL, AND THE season is quickly coming to an end. Buffalo Bill's Wild West Show is en route to Coolidge, Kansas.

The bunk in the sleeping car is small, but large enough for Major and Jennie to lie together. It is not the bright, full moon shining through the small window that keeps Major awake, but Jennie's constant hacking cough.

"I need to stand up," she says, struggling to climb from the high bunk. "I need some air."

"Are you sure you don't need the doctor?" Major asks. He helps her down and watches as she once more coughs into the small white handkerchief she keeps with her.

"No, I don't need the doctor." She coughs again. The pain in her lungs is unbearable. She bends at the waist for relief, but none is forthcoming. "I'm fine."

The bright moon allows Major enough light to see the handkerchief when she lowers it. It is bloodstained. Jennie's condition is rapidly worsening.

Not wanting to worry Major, Jennie quickly places the cloth behind her back. "I need a drink, that's all. My throat's a little dry. That's why I'm coughing." She struggles to pour a glass of water from a nearby pitcher, and overfills it. The wet substance hits her feet. She takes a drink and climbs back into the bunk next to Major.

"I knew it," Captain roars from the next berth. "Why didn't you tell me earlier?"

"What in the world?" Major asks, stunned.

"Oh, I believe the cat's out of the bag." Jennie answers. "And he's not taking it well at all."

"What are you talking about?" Major asks, trying to listen in on the conversation next door. "Shhh, listen . . ."

"Now, Captain, calm down." Annie's voice filters through the curtain-thin walls. "I'm fine."

"You remember what the doctor said when you had Paul!" he yells. "What could make you go and do a thing like this?"

"Well, I had help you know," she screams back.

"What are they talkin' about?" Major looks at Jennie.

"Annie is going to have another baby."

"How do you know?"

"She told me several months ago."

"You knew it and never said anything?"

"Annie made me promise not to say anything unless she got very ill."

"Captain sounds awful mad. I wonder why? I'd be happy if you were havin' a baby. I wouldn't care how many we already had."

"I think there's more to it than just having the baby. Listen."

Major and Jennie lie quietly in their bunk listening to the battle raging next door. The yelling stops, and all is quiet again. Major hears only the clattering of the train's wheels and Jennie's heavy breathing.

"She's so pale," he says to himself. "Jennie, I promise you, we will stop this life, soon."

She sleeps soundly, never hearing Major's words.

Chapter Twenty-Seven

Death

January 1902, Cardwell, Missouri. The winter wind
whistles through the huge, leafless oak tree outside
Major's and Jennie's bungalow. Everything is dead except
for the animals that remain warm and cozy in their shel-
ters.

John, Major's brother, farmed the land and stored grain
and potatoes for the two little people while they traveled.
Mother Ray canned vegetables and fruits throughout the
summer and stored them in the root cellar for winter.

It is late in the afternoon. The steam from a pot of
boiling beans on the old wood stove fills the cramped but
tidy kitchen with a steamy heat. Jennie is stirring meal for
cornbread. She gently pushes a strand of hair away from
her eyes with her wrist. The aroma of sizzling bacon frying
on the stove permeates the air, making her hungry. She
hums a religious song.

Jennie hears a wagon approaching the house and
knows Major is home. She removes her stained apron and
places it on the kitchen table before meeting him.

"Jennie!" Major yells as he bursts through the door.
"It's a telegram from Captain." His face is red from the cold

air, and his eyes are bloodshot. He hands her the telegram. "Sit down and read it."

She knows by the sound of his voice it is bad news. She reads:

> *Greenville, Texas*
> *January 15, 1902*
> *Major William Ray*
> *Major, Annie had baby. She is very ill. Need*
> *your help. Please come. Quick.*
> *Captain Shadrack Shields*

THE TRAIN IS COLD, BUT THE WEATHER IS WARMER the closer Major and Jennie get to Texas. Jennie sits quietly next to Major. The telegram was a shock, but since the railroad now goes through Hornersville, they waste no time catching the first train headed for Texas. Major made arrangements for Thomas to take care of the animals while they are away.

"Major," Jennie's voice is soft and broken as she cries quietly. "What is going to happen? Annie can't die. She's my best friend."

"Nothin's gonna happen to Annie." He tries to assure her. "You'll see. Why, I bet when we get there, she'll be chasing Shade Junior with that new baby in one arm and Paul in the other."

"She's the only true friend I have ever had." Sobbing, Jennie lays her head on Major's shoulder. "What will I do? What will I do?"

"Now, stop that. You have faith to face what comes straight on. We have to be strong for Captain and the children if, . . . and I said, '*if*'. . . . something should happen to Annie."

"Greenville, Texas!" yells the conductor, an old man with gray hair and a stubble beard. His voice is very Southern and slow. "All out for Greenville!"

Major helps Jennie from the train. Several yards away and directly in front of them stands Captain. His face looks worn and worried. He does not approach them, but waits patiently by a wagon.

"Hello, Jennie," he says. "Thank you for coming." He breaks down and cries. He slides his large body down the wagon wheel and sits on the cool, damp ground.

"Come on, Captain. She'll be fine. You'll see." Jennie places an arm around the great man trying to console him. "Major and I are here now. We're going to make sure you are all cared for."

"How is Annie, Captain?" Major asks softly, almost in a whisper. "And the children?"

"The baby is fine," Captain answers, wiping the tears from his eyes and holding to Jennie's hand. "But, Annie isn't . . ."

"Annie is going to be fine," Jennie demands. "She is just weak from bearing the baby. Let's get going. I want to see her."

THE HOUSE IS DARK. THE CURTAINS ARE PULLED. Jennie can hear a baby crying in the other room. A strange woman appears with the small bundle in her arms. She sits down with her back to them. The baby stops crying. Only the sound of suckling is heard.

Captain sits in a nearby chair. His elbows rest on his knees while his head is in his hands. Looking at the woman who suckles his child, he says, "We had to get a wet nurse, because Annie is too weak."

Jennie's eyes adjust to the darkness, and she sees a large room finely decorated. A photograph of seven men hangs high over the mantel.

"That's me and my brothers," Captain tells her.

"The Texas Giants" is inscribed underneath. Jennie hears voices in the other room. Paul and Shade Junior run to her. Shade Junior is taller than Jennie and Major, but he is still a child who needs a lot of consolation. Jennie holds him in her arms.

"There, there, Shade. Aunt Jennie is here and everything is going to be fine." He sits next to her, and she rocks him in her arms.

"Shh, shh. We have to be strong. Come on, baby Paul. There is plenty of room in Aunt Jennie's arms."

Major stands watching her soothe and mother the children. A tear escapes his eye, and he quickly reaches to wipe it away.

Major places a loving hand on his best friend's shoulder. "Maybe Jennie should go in and see Annie now. It might cheer her somewhat."

Quietly, Captain rises and motions for Jennie to follow him. He opens the door from which the young wet nurse emerged. A large bed is in the center of the room. The curtains are drawn, and very little light filters through from a nearby window.

"Jennie?" Annie's voice is shallow and weak.

"Annie, I'm here," Jennie tells her, trying to see over the high bed. The room smells musty like the interior of an old house that has been shut up for months. Major quickly grabs a nearby stool and helps Jennie onto it.

"Jennie, thank you for coming," Annie says in a near whisper. "I want you to do something for me."

"What, Annie. Anything. It's yours."

"Take care of Captain and the children." She gasps for breath as she tries to fill her lungs. "Promise me you will take care of them."

"Now you quit talking like that, Annie. You are going to be up and taking care of this bustling crew real soon. You know what the problem is? There is absolutely no light in this place," Jennie babbles trying to make herself, as well as Annie, feel better. Quickly, she jumps from the small stool, grabs the drapes, and jerks them open. Light fills the room.

Jennie turns. She sees that Annie is as white as the sheets upon which she lies. Her eyes are dark and sunken.

Annie motions for Jennie to sit by her side. Struggling, she speaks, "Jennie, I need you to be strong. I know I'm not long for this life, but I'll have a good home in Heaven with my Lord. My only regret is I won't have my babies and Captain with me."

"Shh, Annie, stop talking like that!" Jennie orders. "I won't listen to this!" She covers her ears.

"Jennie, please. I need you to make sure that Captain takes the children and moves to Missouri with you and Major." Annie breathes deeply, trying to pull air into her lungs, a job that is virtually impossible. "I want you to make sure that my children have a mother to raise them. I don't want Captain living alone. Do you understand?"

"Yes, I promise." Jennie lowers her head.

Annie takes her hand, and struggling for life, continues, "You are my best friend. I love y . . ." Annie's hand grows limp and falls from Jennie's.

"Someone close to you will soon die." Jennie says softly as the words of the Romanian fortune teller ring in her ears. She places her head on the side of the bed, and still grasping Annie's lifeless hand, begins to wail.

Chapter Twenty-Eight

Another Season

1902. The October air is cool. People file through the musty tent, hoping to see something they have never seen. Major hears Nat Davis outside selling tickets to the crowd.

"Come one! Come all!" he shouts. "See Kathrine the Great Snake Enchantress wrap her body with the world's most deadly snakes! See her tease and please each slithering reptile with ease!"

Major looks at Kathrine, a big-boned woman with black hair and mysterious dark eyes. She stands in the booth across from him. Large snakes rub against her like gentle kittens. Kathrine never worries about getting bitten. "They know who's afraid of them and who's not," she swears.

Major is afraid of them. He doesn't like snakes. Even the sight of the simplest garden snake sends cold chills up his spine.

"See the famous Midget Couple who travel across the world performing for royalty from England to Hawaii. Newspapers around the world describe them as the most intelligent and perfect Little Couple on earth. Come one.

Come all!" Davis exaggerates the extent of Major's and Jennie's travels.

"See the Largest Man in the world!" Davis continues lying and sells a twenty-five-cent ticket to a young couple. "See Captain Shields, one of the famous Texas Giants. See him here with Buffalo Bill's Wild West Show."

People gather, pushing and shoving to purchase their way into a rather odd, but intriguing world. The crowd "oohs" and "ahhs" over the sights they know await inside.

Captain stands alone on the platform next to Major and Jennie. Since Annie's death in January, Captain is not the same. Before, he would talk to the crowd, make jokes, and entertain them with a few dance steps. With a little coaxing from Annie, he might even treat the crowd to a chorus or two of "My Wild Irish Rose."

Now he only stands with a sad look on his face, filled with guilt over Annie's death. He nods or shakes his head when he is asked a question that requires a yes or no. He speaks to no one but Major, and only at night outside the tent.

Jennie's coughing catches Major's attention, and he focuses on her. "Can I get you something?" he asks. He places a loving hand on her shaking shoulder. "Jennie, maybe you should lie down."

"No, I'm fine." Jennie coughs. Blood appears in the corner of her mouth. She can taste it. Quickly, she wipes it away with the back of her hand. The evidence is gone.

"Major? Jennie?" Cody calls. Appearing behind them, he motions for them to join him at the back of the platform.

Buffalo Bill Cody's great white buckskin suit with leather fringe hangs majestically on him. Although he is aging and fine lines appear at his temples, he is still a handsome man.

"I need to speak with you and the rest of the crew during the next break," Cody tells them.

"Okay, I'll tell the others," Major says. "Is there something wrong?" He knows the only reason for a meeting is usually to break bad news.

"No, but I have an announcement to make." Cody can see Jennie is getting worse. He respectfully questions her about her health, "How are you feeling today, Mrs. Ray?"

"I've been better," she answers. Her high voice rattles when she speaks. She clears her throat and continues, "But thank you for your concern, Colonel Cody."

He leaves the tent. The crowd outside cheers as they recognize him.

A slight breeze blows between the tents as sideshow performers wait in the backyard for a brief announcement by their popular employer. Jennie feels better in the fresh air. She can breathe easier.

"I'm glad you're all here," Cody's deep voice rings out across the large lot. "The season is almost over, and you need to be aware of the show's future plans."

"What do you mean, future plans?" yells Vanoran, the Sword Swallower. He holds several swords in his hand. Victoria, his wife and co-worker, stands next to him. "Are we closing down?"

"No, it's nothing like that," Cody answers, reassuring the curious group. "We have made some changes in plans, and you need to be aware of them."

"Uh-oh, sounds like bad news to me!" squawks Professor German, the One Man Orchestra. He wears a pair of symbols between his knees, a large bass drum on his back, a harmonica sits on a wire frame in front of his mouth, and a large oversized accordion is strapped to his chest. He looks funny, but plays each instrument—one at a time—remarkably well.

"Come on, just tell us the bad news and get it over with!" Captain shouts.

"All right," Cody says. Raising his arms in the air, he calms the fretting crowd. "We have made arrangements to travel through Europe."

"Hey, that's great," some performers yell.

"What's the catch?" Major asks. He and Jennie stand near the front where they are easily seen.

"The tour will last three years, starting next season."

Major looks at Jennie. They both know the answer without asking the question.

Chapter Twenty-Nine

Partners

Major sits in front of a large fireplace and listens to the old dried wood crack like firecrackers at a street celebration. The winter wind howls outside the farmhouse door in Cardwell.

Large snowflakes fall and collect along the window ledge. A cold draft blowing between the cracks of the walls gives him a chill.

"Major!" Jennie calls from the kitchen. "Would you please set the table? Captain and the children will be here any minute."

"Yes, Ma'am." He quickly rises and collects the dishes that are sitting on the edge of the cabinet. He deals the glass plates recklessly across the table like a deck of cards in a poker game. He pitches silverware in the middle of each plate. It clangs loudly.

"Major, that's no way to set a table," Jennie scolds and rushes in to set the silverware properly by the side of a plate. "Now that's how it should be."

"I don't see why we have to be so dad-burn formal about it. It's only Captain comin'." He goes around the high table placing each piece of silverware in its proper position on the right and left side of the plate.

He hears a wagon circle in front. Footsteps stomping across the porch vibrate the floor under Major's feet. He hears the boards creak as little feet hit each one. "They're here!" he shouts, opening the door.

Shade Junior runs past Major, and Paul follows. "Aunt Jennie!" they shout, and throw their arms around her.

"My word! You two get taller every time I see you," Jennie says as the boys surround her. Thirteen-year-old Shade Junior is twice as tall as Jennie. Five-year-old Paul looks her in the eye. "Where is the birthday boy?" she asks.

"Here he is." Captain sets one-year-old Adair on the worn, wooden floor. "Let's get these clothes off." Slowly, Captain unwraps the heavy material, and the over-clad child quickly becomes smaller. His strawberry blond hair and light complexion reveal the Irish in him. Jennie sees Annie in his emerald green eyes.

"There he is," she teases the small child, who stands awkwardly at his father's feet. "Now that we're all here, it's time to eat."

AFTER SUPPER IS OVER, CAPTAIN CASUALLY LEANS back in his chair. Patting his full stomach, he praises Jennie's cooking. "As usual, Jennie, that was a wonderful meal."

"I'm glad you enjoyed it, Captain. It's always nice to see healthy appetites," Jennie says, getting up to clear the table.

While the boys play with a toy top in the middle of the floor, Major and Captain discuss business.

"I talked to Mr. Smith in town yesterday," Major tells Captain. He sits at the table, turning his fork over and over in his hands.

Mr. Thomas Smith is an old man who owns the mercantile store in Hornersville. Major has known Mr. Smith and his wife, Evelyn since he was ten.

"Yeah," Captain says, standing to place another log on the fire.

"He's sellin' the store, and I offered to buy it. I thought maybe you and me could be partners."

Captain says nothing. He stands near the fire and stirs it with an iron poker. He watches as a great cluster of bright sparks, like giant fireflies near a thicket of tall grass, travels up the chimney and escapes its cramped domain.

"Well, what do you think? Are we partners?" Major asks, trying to coax an answer from his tall friend. "We have to do somethin' since we're no longer in the circus business."

After thinking a moment, Captain holds out his large hand. With a firm handshake—as binding to the two old friends as a written contract—he says, "Partners."

Major replies, "Partners." With a simple handshake the business agreement is made.

Jennie appears in the doorway holding a round birthday cake with one lit candle stuck in the center. Singing "Happy birthday to you . . . . " she places the cake on the table.

Major notices the sad but proud look on Captain's face and knows what he must be thinking. The guilt for Annie's death has faded somewhat, but the heartache remains.

Adair screams with delight at the pretty candle. After placing a piece of cake on each plate, Jennie sits in a small rocker near the fire, and Adair toddles to her. She places him in her lap and rocks him gently. She thinks about the day he was born and the promise she made to his dying mother. Jennie squeezes him affectionately. A tear rolls down her cheek.

Chapter Thirty

Major's Gift

It is May and the flowers are in bloom. The sweet aroma of honeysuckle permeates the air as Major and Jennie ride to Hornersville. Major is mysterious about the trip, and Jennie is nervous.

"You still haven't told me why you came home during the middle of the day," Jennie says. "Are you going to tell me?"

"Nope."

"Isn't Captain going to be upset with you leaving him alone to mind the store?"

"Nope."

"Won't you tell me what you're up to?"

"Nope."

"Oh." Curious, Jennie sits back in the buggy seat while Tige, a Boston Bulldog, sits at her feet.

Major purchased the dog for Jennie after he bought the store because he didn't want her sitting all alone in the house at night. He named the animal after the dog in his favorite newspaper comic strip, Buster Brown.

"Why would he come home during the day?" Jennie ponders to herself.

For months Major has acted strangely. He just smiles broadly. The trip to Hornersville from Cardwell is a long ride to make each day, especially in the winter. The Mercantile is thriving and people from all across the county come to see the odd proprietors.

Stopping in front of the store on Main Street, Major calls out to Captain, "Everything still goin' all right?"

"Yeah. We're all doin' fine. I've got Shade sweepin' the store. Paul is countin' the stock, and Adair is playing in the beans." Captain stands tall on the porch, his head almost touching the rafters of the overhang. "Here. I thought you might want this." He hands Major a large, new handkerchief.

"Thanks. Here, turn around." Major orders Jennie.

"What for?"

"Because I want it to be a surprise." He ties the handkerchief around her head, covering her eyes. "Now, can you see anything?"

"No. I want to know what you're up to, William Ray," Jennie grumbles. "Is this really necessary?"

Captain points quietly down the street and mouths the words, "I'll meet you down there."

Major nods and tells Jennie, "Yes, it is. Now be quiet." The buggy jerks, and Major guides Colonel, the old bay, down Main Street, and turns right.

Jennie can hear voices ahead. The buggy stops. Major unties the blindfold around her head.

"Taa-daa!" he shouts.

The bright light hurts Jennie's eyes. Slowly they adjust, and focusing, Jennie gazes upon the most beautiful house she has ever seen.

She can smell the fresh white paint covering the outside walls of the two-story, L-shaped structure. A large front porch and miniature upstairs veranda adorn the oversized doll-like house. Beautifully designed lattice accents the overhangs along the roof and porch, like lace on a dress.

"Oh, my!" she cries. "Captain, you knew about this the whole time, didn't you?"

"Yeah, and the boys knew about it too. It was hard as the dickens to keep Paul and Adair from sayin' anything." Picking her up from the wagon, Captain gently sets her on the ground. "Go on inside."

Gingerly, Jennie climbs the shallow steps onto the porch and runs her hand across the banister. She can smell freshly tilled dirt where new flowers have been planted along the base of the house. "The porch doesn't squeak," she laughs. "How will I know when you're home, Major?"

"That's the idea," he teases.

The door knob is lower than most, perfect for her to reach. Slowly, she opens the wooden door adorned with a decorative oblong window.

The sun's rays shine through the lace curtains covering the large beautiful windows on the first floor. Particles of dust dance on the beams of light leading to the parlor with its hardwood floor.

Jennie gently runs her fingers along the wooden trim of an elegant floral love seat. Standing next to it, she places her nose to the material that covers the large piece of furniture. It smells new. The furniture in the room is much too large for her to sit in comfortably.

"I know what you're thinkin'," Major says. "But, your rocker will sit here." He points to a spacious area near the fireplace. "I thought if we entertained much we would need the larger furniture to accommodate our guests."

She smiles and nods in agreement.

Illustration 12:

Jennie stands
on the upstairs
veranda of the
house Major
built for her.

Photograph
courtesy Mrs.
Pat Fraser

The mantel on the fireplace is of cherry wood, polished lavishly, and reflects the light shining through the windows. Above it hangs a painting of Jennie and Major, created from the photograph they had made while in Australia.

Her heart races with excitement as she continues walking through the parlor to the dining room. "Everything is *so large*," she whispers. Jennie sees a vast dining table in the center of the room. An exquisite crystal chandelier hangs overhead.

Quickly, Major takes her by the elbow. "Sit here," he says and helps her up to the platform upon which the table sits.

"Thank you," she whispers softly. Her feet have no trouble following the small, half steps leading to the chairs on the strange platform. Carefully, she sits, positioning herself comfortably.

"Now, Captain, you come over and sit down at the end," Major orders.

Captain sits comfortably at the opposite end of the table. "All right, now, when do we eat?" he quips.

Surprised, Jennie sits evenly with her guest. Her feet are on the floor comfortably, but she sits high enough to speak with her guest on his level. "How did you do that?" she asks excitedly.

"You will notice this end is higher than the other. The chairs are also up on a platform; therefore, it brings the floor closer to the table. So we can sit at the same table as our guests without getting corn up our noses." He laughs, and Captain laughs too.

Even off stage Major is an entertainer. Jennie giggles at his amusing explanation.

Carefully, she steps from the platform and goes into the extremely large kitchen. Jennie notices the indoor kitchen plumbing located on the high cabinet. "Just like Mama's," she says smiling, and points to the new iron pump. "It's beautiful, Major."

She looks around the room, admiring the finely mastered woodwork. Noticing the stairs leading to the second floor, she walks toward them.

"No. That's not your staircase to the second floor," Major announces and pulls her back toward the living room.

"Then pray tell, whose is it?" she asks.

"That's for the housekeeper."

"Housekeeper? Now, what do I need with a housekeeper?"

"I've hired a young lady to help. We can afford it, and I want only the best for you. Besides, Mama is getting too old and unable to care for herself, so I thought you wouldn't mind if she lived with us. You're gonna need help if she does."

"I think that's a wonderful idea! I would love for Mother Ray to live with us!" Jennie stops and lovingly places her hand on Major's shoulder. "You have done so much for me. You moved my family here so they could be near me. You opened the store in Ettawa and let Harding Joel run it. Papa is farming the land. Thank you and . . . "

"Come on, I want to show you something else." Major interrupts, smiling he takes her by the hand. "You're gonna love this."

Practically dragging her back through the kitchen and dining room, Major, before reaching the parlor, stops in front of a tiny stairwell hidden within the walls. Standing in front of it, Jennie looks up toward the top floor.

"Oh, my word!" is all she can say. Jennie places each hand on the banisters that run up both sides of the stairwell. Slowly and easily, she ascends. She notices each step is built for her—no stress, no strain, no work.

Light at the top of the staircase filters down from a small round stained glass window. The reflections on the wall are red, blue, and yellow, a kaleidoscope of colors that dance to the ground floor.

"Well, what do you think?" Major anxiously awaits her reaction. "Do you like it?"

"Like it? I love it!" She turns, and throwing her arms around him, almost knocks him down the stairs.

"If you like this part, wait till you see the rest of it!" Quickly, he urges her onward.

The second floor resembles a child's playhouse. Every piece of furniture and every window is scaled to fit the needs of a person thirty-seven-inches tall. To the right, Jennie walks into a parlor filled with furniture only a child could sit in without breaking.

Looking ahead, Jennie sees a small door leading outside and opens it. A miniature wicker table and chairs sit on the wee veranda which her adoring husband had styled especially for her. The banister railing is at her waist.

Jennie notices another door leading into a room on the other side of the house. She opens it and steps into a beautiful bedroom. Although it is missing the furniture, Jennie knows whose room it is. The fireplace against the wall is also sized according to its future residents.

Major stands on the veranda, waiting for Jennie to join him. Their guests—half the town—stand outside, also waiting.

He holds out his hand to her and says loudly for everyone to hear, "This house, built for a Lilliputian queen, is my gift to you. You are my angel, my queen, and my only love. As long as it stands, or some portion of its foundation remains, I will love you and only you."

Chapter Thirty-One

Fond Memories

1904. Winter is over and the flowers of spring are popping out of their sleep to enjoy the warm sun. Jennie sits on the veranda drinking a warm cup of tea. Although she is only thirty-two years old, she looks fifty. Her chest hurts, but the fresh air feels good after a restless night.

She clutches a lace handkerchief in her hand. Thoughts of the day she received it wander through her mind: Major standing proudly next to her brother, Harding Joel. Her papa finally accepting the marriage and escorting her down the isle. She can still hear the wedding waltz, sung by Reverend McDole at the reception, and she hums the tune.

"Do you need anything, Mrs. Ray?" Tenny interrupts Jennie's journey down memory lane. "Mrs. Ray, are you all right?"

Tenny, short for Tennessee, takes care of Jennie. Her dress is plain, and her hair is tightly pulled back into a bun at the back of her head. She is young, but not interested in finding a husband. She cooks, cleans, helps with Mother Ray, and waits on Jennie day and night.

Illustration 13: Jennie stands next to her housekeeper.
Photograph courtesy of Mrs. Imogene Young

"Tenny. You startled me."

"I'm sorry. You were so still I didn't know . . . "

"That's all right. If you need to do something go on ahead. I'll be fine for a little while."

"I'm only going to the store. I'll be right back," Tenny assures her. "Mrs. Baker is in her garden, so if you need anything, you holler down to her and she'll be right up."

"I'll be fine. You go on." Jennie stares at the paper and pen lying on the table in front of her. She knows she needs to write her mama and papa, but she hates to tell them the news.

She picks up the pen and writes:

April 28, 1904

My Dear, Dear Papa and Mama and Maggie,

I seat myself to write you a few lines this morning as I sit on the veranda enjoying the new life spring has sent. I can smell the honeysuckle from Mrs. Baker's yard as it climbs the old oak tree that stands tall. I wonder how long it has been there?

I hope this letter finds you all well, because I am sorry to say, I am not. My illness is worse, and I believe the Good Lord may see fit to receive me sooner than I had expected. But if He does, it is His will, not mine, that shall be done.

Papa, I still worry about you and your soul. I pray you will one day see the glorious light of our Lord and turn to Him.

As you know, Major and Captain are still partners in the general store here in town. Last month Major accepted a job offer from the

Brown Shoe Company in St. Louis to pose as their new spokesman for their latest line of Buster Brown Shoes.

He hesitated to take the job at first, but there is a sanitarium in St. Louis that may be able to help me. He says he will do anything to make me well.

Good-bye my dearly loved parents, and God be with you till we meet again.

From your loving Jennie and Major

"Jennie?" Major calls from below the veranda. "Look what just arrived!"

Hearing Major's voice, Jennie rises from her chair and looks over the edge. Below she sees him and Tige standing at the foot of the porch. Major has a large object tucked under his arm.

"What do you have there?" she asks.

"Just a box. I decided to make Tige my new business partner," he says. "I told Captain, Tige will make a better partner because he takes orders without talkin' back." He laughs and runs into the house.

She can hear him running up the steps. He goes to the bedroom and stops. She waits for him to come out and join her.

"What are you doing in there?" Jennie can hear him rummaging around in the other room. She stands and starts into the bedroom. "What are you doing?" she asks again.

"Don't come in. I'll be right out," he hollers.

She waits a few more minutes. He appears in the doorway dressed in a little dark blue suit, blue hat, and blond wig. The dog, Tige, sits obediently at his feet. "Taa-daaa!" he shouts. "Well, what do you think?"

Illustration 14: Major Ray poses as Buster Brown with his dog Tige.

Photograph courtesy of Imogene Young

Jennie is stunned. The room spins as she looks at the little blond boy and his dog standing in front of her. The little boy has the face of an old man. The room grows dark.

IT IS THE MIDDLE OF AUGUST. MAJOR AND JENNIE, along with their dog, Tige, arrive in St. Louis on the afternoon train. It has been a long time since Major has seen this many people in one place. His heart races with excitement.

Before he accepted Brown Shoe Company's proposal to play Buster Brown, Major turned it down because of Jennie's failing health and his promise to leave the traveling life alone, but as Jennie's health grew worse, he knew he had to do something. St. Louis, a large city with many doctors and new treatments, may hold a miracle for his darling Jennie.

"Excuse me, Mr. and Mrs. Ray?" a young nurse asks. She stands next to a child's wheel chair. "I'm from the Missouri Baptist Sanitarium here in St. Louis. Dr. Cadwallader asked me to meet you and escort you to the sanitarium."

Weak from the trip, Jennie welcomes the opportunity to rest. Major helps her into the chair.

"Thank you," Jennie says, leaning back. Her feet still dangle uncomfortably in mid-air, but at least she doesn't have to walk. "How did you recognize us?" she asks.

"Oh, that was easy. Dr. Cadwallader said you would be the smallest couple off the train. When I saw you, I knew there couldn't be anyone smaller." She smiles pleasantly at Jennie and pushes the chair toward the coach which is waiting in front of the station.

"How far is it to the sanitarium?" Major asks. "I'm gonna be stayin' here in town near the Brown Shoe

Company durin' the fair. I just wondered how far it is from there."

"Oh, it's not far," she assures him. "In fact, it's about a fifteen or twenty minute walk."

Tige walks dutifully behind Major. During the past several months Major and Jennie have taught Tige to do several tricks. They have also grown closer to the dog, and treat him as their child.

MAJOR SITS NEXT TO JENNIE'S BED WAITING FOR Dr. Cadwallader to enter with news of her condition. Jennie is pale. She cannot talk for any length of time without tiring and gasping for her next breath. She has aged overnight and lost much weight. Major is very worried.

He hears the moans of other patients in the ward. Beds, separated only by yellowed white curtains, line both sides of the room. Nurses come in and out. Major peers into the cloth cubicle next to Jennie's. An old man coughs uncontrollably. Major hands him a small metal pan.

"Can I help you, Mr. Ray?" asks a nurse, politely shoving him aside. She helps the man sit up as he spits into the pan.

"No. I just heard the old man coughin' and thought I'd try and help if I could."

Quickly she stands next to Major and whispers, "Mr. Ray, this old man is only twenty-six years old."

Stunned at the aging process caused by the disease that also attacks his sweet wife, Major returns to Jennie's side in a daze.

"Good-morning," says Dr. I. H. Cadwallader as he enters the room. His soft voice and gentle mannerisms offset the fear and intimidation of his white medical coat. He is tall and in his mid-thirties. His premature gray hair reveals the stress of his occupation. Jennie likes him. "How are you doing today, Jennie?"

"I'm always better when you visit, Doctor." Her voice is shallow. The crease in the doctor's brow tells Major there are reasons to worry.

"You just rest here, Jennie, while I take this husband of yours out in the hall for a chat."

Major follows him. Dr. Cadwallader shuts the door. Major is almost nauseaus from the harsh smell of alcohol and disinfectant. An older woman is on her hands and knees scrubbing the hall floor.

The doctor sits on a bench several feet away from Jennie's door. "Major," he says, and pauses for a moment. "I'm not going to lie to you. Jennie is very ill."

"What do you mean, 'very ill'?"

"What I mean is, she is going to die soon if we can't do something for her."

"No!" he shouts. Then, lowering his voice, he says, "You have to make her better. You don't understand, she is all I have in this world. That woman is my life. If she dies, I die with her." Tears fall from his face as the boy-like man pleads for his wife's life.

Dr. Cadwallader thinks a moment and gives Major time to calm himself. "Major, there is a chance—only a slim chance—that we can save her."

"Anything. I don't care what it is. Just do it."

"It means surgery for Jennie. I can't promise you anything. In fact, she could die on the operating table, but without the surgery she will surely die."

"Do it!" Major orders. "Anything is better than nothin'. I was once a big gambler, and now I'm bettin' on you."

Major shakes the doctor's hand and walks slowly down the hall. He cannot see Jennie now because he knows she will see the fear in his eyes right away. After strolling through the halls, not noticing where he has wandered, Major finds himself standing in front of the hospital chapel.

Slowly he enters and closes the door behind him. Several chairs are scattered around the small, quiet room. Ahead he sees a picture of Christ holding several children in his lap. It is illuminated by many candles that have been lit by others who have also ventured into the holy haven to pray.

He kneels in front of the magnificent altar and stares at the painting above him. He prays, "God in heaven. I know it's been a long time since we have had a good, long talk, but I know you speak to my Jennie often because she talks about you all the time.

"God, I don't ask for much, and Jennie, she never asks for anything, but I'm coming to you now to beg you— please don't take my angel now. I know her beauty would bless your most holiest house, but God, you'll have her forever, and I just want her for a while longer.

"God, I'll make a promise to you right now. If you will only spare her life to me for a short while longer, I'll give up everything I possess. Just please, *please* leave her with me. Let her live.

"I know I don't deserve it, but she's a good woman, and she's so young. I'll try to be better for her and for you. I will keep this promise to you. "

The candles flicker in the room. Major rises, wipes the tears from his face, and returns to Jennie's bedside.

THE BRIGHT MORNING SUN SHINES THROUGH THE ward's high windows. Jennie is nervous as the date for surgery nears. Major comes in and out often, but she

Illustration 15: Jennie stands next to one of several nurses who attended to Jennie's needs during her illness.
Photograph courtesy of Mrs. Imogene Young

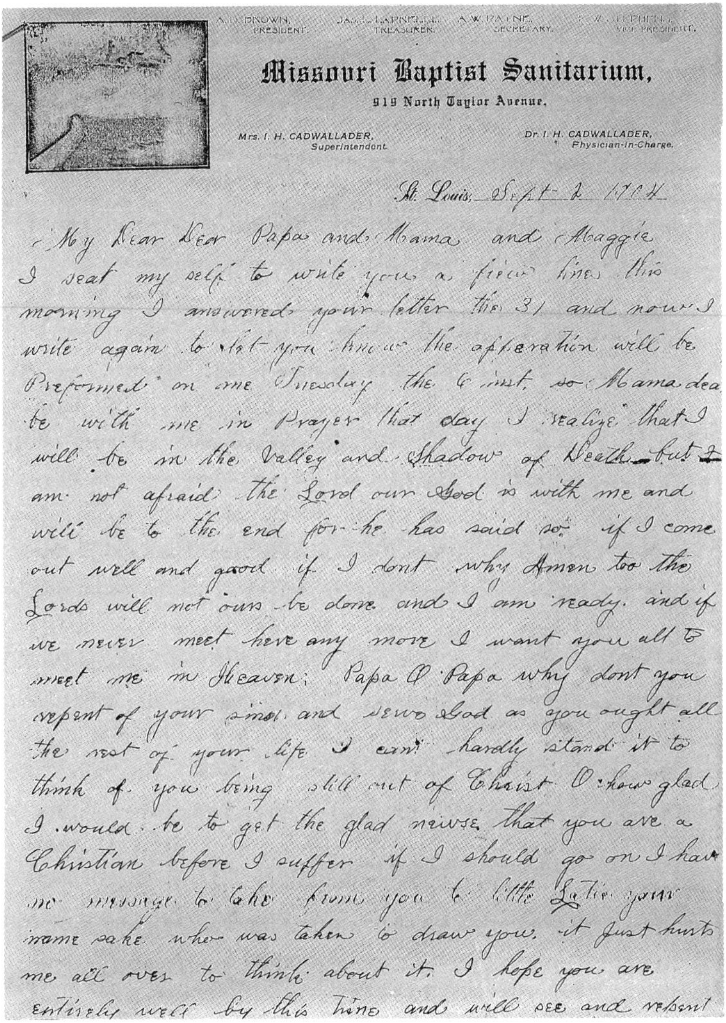

Illustration 16: A copy of the original letter written by Jennie to her family during her stay at the Missouri Baptist Sanitarium, September 2, 1904.

Courtesy of Imogene Young

worries about him continually because of his concern for her.

She can hear the sounds from the street as they filter through the large windows overhead. Bands play and songs such as "Meet Me in St. Louis" echo through the streets. Jennie wishes she could see the World's Fair and Major on stage as Buster Brown, R. F. Outcault's comic strip character, comes to life for the first time.

"Excuse me, Renee´?" she calls to a young woman standing nearby. "Could you help me, please."

"Jennie, what can I do for you?"

Jennie has been in the hospital so long that she and the nurses are now on a first name basis. "Renee´, could you please get me some paper. I need to write my family, and I seem to have run out of stationery."

"Yes, I'll get to some from the front desk." Quickly, Renee´ walks out, returning in a few minutes with several pieces of paper. "Missouri Baptist Sanitarium" is stamped at the top. "I hope you don't mind hospital stationery. That's all I could find."

"No. This is wonderful, thank you." Jennie graciously accepts the paper, picks up a pen, and writes:

> St. Louis, Sept. 2, 1904
> My Dear, Dear Papa and Mama and Maggie,
>   I seat myself to write you a few lines this morning. I answered your letter of the 31st, and now I write again to let you know the operation will be performed on me Tuesday the 6th. So, Mama dear, I will be in the valley of the shadow of death, but I am not afraid because the Lord our God is with me, and will be to the end, for He has said so. If I come out well, good. If I don't why, Amen, too. The

Lord's will, not ours, be done, and I am ready. If we never meet here anymore I want you all to meet me in Heaven.

Papa, oh, Papa. Why don't you repent of your sins and serve God as you ought all the rest of your life? I can hardly stand to think of you being still out of Christ. Oh, how glad I would be to get the glad news that you are a Christian before I suffer. If I should go on, I have no message to take from you to little Latie, your namesake who was taken to draw you. It just hurts me all over to think about it. I hope you will see and repent the error of your ways before it is too late.

Mama, I want you to pray for us both. Pray earnestly for poor little Major. He is worried nearly to death. He told me it made his heart ache to think of an operation, but if that was the only hope of saving my life, it would have to be done.

He said he promised God he would do anything in the world He wanted him to do and would be willing to give up everything we possess if He would only spare me to him a while longer. I want you to pray for him that he will have the grace not to promise to do anything 'till he asks God's guidance in the matter, and to be always led of the Spirit of God whether I live or die.

Major is a great deal better Christian in the last year than I ever have seen him. I don't have to coax him to go to church anymore. He is more than anxious to go without coaxing.

> *I want you to pray and tell all the good*
> *Christian people to pray that our lives will be*
> *used to the entire glory of God from this time*
> *on.*
> *Well, good-bye my dearly loved Parents.*
> *God be with you both till we meet again.*
> *Kisses from your loving Jennie and Major*
> *Be a good girl, Maggie, and be a good*
> *Christian woman.*
> *Major Ray & Wife*
> *Manufacturers Building*
> *Brown Shoe Exhibit, World's Fair*
> *St. Louis, Mo.*

Jennie carefully folds the letter, places it in the envelope and seals it tenderly with a kiss.

TUESDAY, SEPTEMBER 6. MAJOR WAITS IN THE HALL as Jennie prepares for surgery. The door opens, and she lies on a gurney. It stops just outside the door and Major stands on a nearby bench.

"Everything is gonna be fine, Angel," Major assures her. "You'll see. The doctors here know what their doin', and I'll be waitin' right here when you get back."

"Major, I want you to promise one thing," she whispers in a raspy voice. "Promise me that you will be a good Christian man so that if it's God's will and I am taken to Him today, I want you to meet me in heaven later."

"Oh, Jennie, you're not goin' anywhere."

"Promise me Major."

"I promise. Now, I also promise you that I'll be right here when you come back."

"And I promise you if I don't, I'll wait for you up there."
Jennie looks up for a moment. Gazing into his eyes she says, "I love you."

"I love you too!" he replies as they slowly roll her away.

Jennie disappears through the double doors at the end of the hall.

Major sits alone.

Illustration 17:

Major Ray as Buster Brown poses with his dog, Tige during their debut at the 1904 St. Louis World's Fair.

Photograph courtesy Johnny and Lavada Jones.

Chapter Thirty-Two

Jennie's Love

1915. Jennie rarely ventures from the second floor of the beautiful home Major built for her years ago. She sits in a small wheelchair near the upstairs fireplace and holds a worn Bible in her hands. A few lines of *Amazing Grace* escape her lips.

The wild March wind beats against the door leading to the veranda. Jennie will be glad when spring arrives. The fragrance of honeysuckle rides the soft breeze of the early morning, while she sits outside sipping her tea.

Today, March 16, is her birthday. Major is on the road, but promises they will celebrate when he returns. Jennie is only forty-four, but she looks seventy-four. The tuberculosis is gone. Now it is cancer that sucks the life from her withered body. She sits by the fire trying to keep warm.

Jennie opens her Bible to the Twenty-third Psalm and removes a small key. Rolling her chair into the bedroom, she stares at the old worn trunk at the end of the bed.

"You were a beauty at one time," she says, as if the trunk can talk back to her. "I guess time has been rough on both of us."

Slowly, she turns the key and unlocks not only the trunk, but memories of a wonderful life full of people, places, and things—especially love. She stands, and after a slight struggle with the heavy lid, opens it. A musty odor fills her nostrils, and visions of the past fill her mind.

Jennie spies the brooch her mother gave her the day Jennie and Major married. She misses her mother now more then ever. Mary died in 1906, and Mother Ray in 1907—two years filled with sad memories.

Carefully she lifts an old white hat and pulls a bundle of letters from beneath it—letters from Major written years ago.

"If I could do it over again," she whispers, clutching the letters to her chest. "I wouldn't change a thing."

Jennie sifts through old photographs of circus days and good friends. She misses them, too.

Jennie hears the front gate squeak as it opens. There is a knock at the front door.

"Miss Jennie?" Tenny says, standing in the doorway. "Walter Perry is here to see you."

"Thank you, Tenny. Send him up and seat him in the parlor. I'll be right there."

"Yes Ma'am." Tenny quickly turns and leaves.

Jennie returns the photographs to the trunk and closes the lid. She again locks it and places the key in her Bible.

Walter Perry is a young man in his late twenties with a six-foot physique that turns the ladies' heads, including Jennie's. His black hair is short and well groomed. His clean shaven face reveals a strong chin. His big brown eyes sparkle when he speaks.

"Hello, Walter," she says, extending a frail hand. "Thank you for coming so quickly."

"There's no reason to thank me, Miss Jennie," he says, still standing. "I'm always happy to visit with you."

"Please, sit down," she says, pointing to a large chair nearby. "I need to speak with you about a most delicate and private matter. I must also ask you not to speak of this to anyone."

"All right. Whatever you say." Walter is curious and leans forward to hear every word she says. "I'm listening."

"You made furniture special for me, at Major's request. Now I want to do something special for him." Jennie hands Walter a blueprint. "Can you do it?"

He studies the paper carefully and replies, "Are you sure this is what you want?"

"I know it's an odd request, but it's for Major."

"When do you want it delivered?"

"I knew you could do it. Now, this is what I want you to do . . . "

A WEEK LATER, THE WHISTLE FROM THE MORNING train blows, and Jennie knows Major will soon be home. She sits by the window and stares down into the empty flower garden below. She loves to sit in the garden during the spring, when the perfume of the flowers is intoxicating.

The trunk is open and items, like memories, are scattered about the room. Jennie's Bible lies in her lap open to her favorite passage. In her hands, she holds the handkerchief that brought her and Major together. She places it close to her nose.

Jennie feels the coolness from the window pane and leans near it. Softly, she fogs the pane with her breath. Carefully, she sketches a heart and writes, 'J.M loves W.R'. "William Ray, you will always be in my heart."

"What are you doin'?" Major asks. He stands in the doorway with a large suitcase in his hand. Tige runs to greet her. "Who are you talkin' to?"

"Memories. That's all." She smiles and welcomes him with open arms. "How was your trip?"

"Too long," he says, kissing her gently on the forehead. "I missed you."

"Tomorrow's your birthday. What do you want?"

"No, it's not. My birthday was over a week ago," she teases, "and you missed it."

"As far as I'm concerned, tomorrow is the sixteenth and not the twenty-fifth. So, what do you want for your birthday?"

"Just a quiet day with you," she says, holding his hand tightly. "I just want time with you."

"Well, I believe I can fill that birthday wish. There has to be something special you want."

"Nothing. Nothing, but you." She flinches with pain from the disease that eats away at her body. "Major, I'm tired. I think I'll lie down for a while."

"All right. Let me help you." He places the letters in the trunk, closes the lid, and locks it.

"Thank you," she says, taking the key and placing it in her Bible. "Will you be here when I wake?"

"Don't worry, I'll be here." He helps her to the bed and covers her tightly with a beautiful hand-stitched quilt. "Is this new?"

"I made it myself while you were away," she answers as she runs her hand across the perfect cloth squares. "I had to do something. It's probably the only thing I have ever finished in my whole life. Maggie will be impressed."

"It's beautiful. Now, you rest," he tells her, and kisses her forehead. "Come on, Tige. Come on boy."

Tige lies at the foot of the bed. He refuses to leave his mistress.

"All right, boy. You stay with Mama and watch her." He quietly closes the door behind him.

LATER, MAJOR STANDS NEAR THE DOOR IN THE bedroom that leads to the veranda. The sun is setting, casting a yellow hue throughout the room. Jennie is still sleeping when Tenny knocks on the door.

"Major, I have dinner here for you and Miss Jennie," she says before entering the room.

"Come on in and set it down near the fire. I'll wake her. She has been asleep all day." He walks to the bed and places a hand on Jennie's shoulder. "Jennie, Angel, it's time to get up. Tenny has supper ready."

Her body is cold. He steps back and screams orders to Tenny. "Run get Captain Shields! Quick, Tenny! Now!"

Tenny runs from the room. Major hears the front door slam. "Jennie! Jennie!" he screams, shaking her again. "Jennie, don't leave me now! I'm not ready! Oh, God, I know I asked you to spare her life and you did. But, please, I'm not ready yet," he prays.

Major slides to the floor and on his knees, he moans, "Jennie." The last rays of the sun fall across the bed. Once again, the sun hits the horizon.

"Oh, God. I don't want to hear it hit the ground again! Please, not again!"

Major cries into his hands. The room darkens as the sun disappears. Again, he is alone.

"Major!" Captain yells as he runs up the steps. He enters the room and finds Major in a heap near the bed. Quickly, he runs to Jennie and places a large finger beneath her nose. He feels her breath—faintly—against his hand. "Major, she's alive. C'mon. We have to get her to the hospital." Captain wraps Jennie's frail frame in the quilt and carries her down the stairs to the wagon.

JENNIE LIES IN A BED IN THE SANITARIUM IN Paragould, Arkansas. Major stands by her side. For hours doctors and nurses work with her. She is alive, but weak.

Captain stands near the doorway. He can hear his friend babbling relentlessly.

Layton Meadows enters the hospital, approaches Captain, and says, "I got your message. I came as fast as I could. How is she?"

"It's bad. You'd better go on in."

Layton sees Major standing near the bed, holding Jennie's hand. Whispering, he asks, "How is she?"

With tears in his eyes, Major looks at his father-in-law and says, "She'll be fine, you'll see. She's just resting. She'll wake up soon. I know she will."

Layton looks at the doctors standing on the opposite side of the bed. One of them shakes his head slowly.

"Jennie, you have to wake up. Wake up and talk to me," Major begs, shaking her gently. "Look at me!"

Slowly, Jennie's eyes open. She looks at him. Her eyelids flutter, then close.

"Somebody!" he screams. "Quick, do something!"

Unable to cope with the loss of his daughter, and knowing his son-in-law's in shock, Layton runs from the room, tears streaming down his face. Doctors and nurses push Major aside as they once more attempt to revive her. A few minutes—seeming like hours—pass.

Pulling the sheet over Jennie's face, the doctor shakes his head and says, "I'm sorry."

Chapter Thirty-Three

Alone

Major sits quietly in the upstairs parlor. There is a knock at the door. He hears Tenny speaking with someone. Slowly she walks up the stairs and appears at Major's door. Her eyes are swollen. She wipes several tears away and says softly, "Major, Walter Perry is here. He says he needs to speak with you. It's urgent. Somethin' about a letter from Jennie."

Major raises his head and looks at her. There is no expression on his pale and bitter face. He nods. She leaves.

"Major." Walter stands slightly bent over in the doorway. Under his arm he holds an oblong wooden box. "Major?" he says again.

"Yes, come in. What is it that you need to tell me?" His voice cracks as he fights back the tears. "Tenny said something about a letter."

"Yes, Sir. About a week ago, Miss Jennie asked me here. She just told me that I wasn't to speak with anyone about the matter we discussed." Walter is still standing, holding the large box under his arm.

"I'm sorry. Won't you put down your parcel. Sit down and continue."

Walter sets the box behind his chair and continues, "Miss Jennie told me she wanted me to make something special for you. I thought she meant a new cabinet or something. She handed me this piece of paper." Walter hands the rough blueprint to Major.

"Walter, this is a coffin," Major says surprised.

"I know. I was just as surprised as you are when I saw it."

"Did she say why she wanted it?"

"No, but she did tell me to deliver it upon her death and to give you this letter." Walter pulls a white envelope from his pocket and hands it to Major. "I'm sorry, Major. That's all I know."

"Thank you, Walter. I know Jennie loved your work, and I'm sure she's lookin' at it now. If she could, she would say thank you."

"I'll just leave it right here for you," Walter says as he walks quietly toward the door. "If you need anything, you let me or Maudie know."

"Thank you, again," Major says, and watches him leave by the back stairs leading to the kitchen.

Major stands to look at the small handcrafted, walnut casket. Its top is made of glass. It is trimmed in walnut. Delicate roses are etched in the wood frame of the lid. He opens it. He runs his hand along the satin lining inside. It is padded with cotton to make it soft for Jennie.

A tear slips from his chin and lands on the pale pink material. He watches the tiny circle it leaves grow large. He averts his attention to the letter in his hand and sits in Jennie's favorite rocker. He reads:

March 16, 1915

My Dearest Little Major,

I seat myself to write this letter to you, my most kind and loving husband. I know you have many questions, and I hope to answer them in this letter.

While you have been traveling these past few years, I have always tried to be in good health on your return. Nonetheless, the Lord, our God, has seen fit to bring me to him soon.

I have just returned from the hospital in Paragould where doctors there say surgery will not help this time. My days are numbered. I have called for our dear friend, Walter Perry, to join me tonight to ask a favor from him.

By now, you have seen my special gift to you. I do not want you worrying about burying me, so I have made the arrangements for you.

The box I have designed so you may close the lid and see me through glass. I do this for you, sweet Major.

I love you with all my heart. Be a good and righteous man, Major. Follow God's word and always be in keeping with His laws. I go before you to prepare a place for us to share when the day comes for you to "meet me in heaven."

As I look through my trunk of many memories, the sweetest is the day we met. I still hold that small white handkerchief to my lips and can catch the aroma of your skin. I can

still see your shining face as you looked up at
me that day and said, "It's you."

Yes, Major, it was me, but what you didn't
know is that I thought the same of you. I
knew the moment we met that I would be
with you for the rest of my life. Besides the
quilt, that, too, is one thing I finished—my life
with you.

Please do not mourn for me for I am with my
Heavenly Father and am happy. I join my
friend Annie, and we both wait patiently for
you and Captain. I love you forever and always.

Kisses from your loving Jennie until we meet
again.

Turning to the window, Major sees the sun shining
brightly on the dew covered panes. A faint image of something drawn on the window appears. Tears flow as he
reads the message inside the heart: "J.M. loves W.R."

Chapter Thirty-Four

Meet Me in Heaven

An angel sculpted from the finest Italian white marble is standing on a pedestal, staring across Hornersville Cemetery over the fields of sprouting cotton toward the distant Western horizon. One hand holds a Bible while the other points to heaven. Her gown flows as if blown by a light spring breeze, and the detailing of the feathers on her wings is so fine they could flutter if not made of stone. Her tiny feet are bare so that she can walk through green clover. Underneath them is inscribed the words, "Meet me in heaven."

"Isn't she beautiful, Captain?" Major asks.

"She sure is."

"I told you she had wings," Major tells him sincerely. "Now, she'll always stand on a pedestal where she belongs."

"I can't get over how much it looks like Jennie." Captain is amazed by the marble statue. "It's incredible."

"That's because it *is* Jennie, and now I can look at her every day for the rest of my life," Major says wistfully. He runs his hands gently over the cold, gray marble base. "She's still my angel."

"I just don't understand how the statue was made. I mean, if people didn't know better they would think Jennie was turned to stone by some evil sorceress."

"No evil sorceress, just an Italian sculptor Jennie and I once met in our travels. It was a brief meeting, but he told us where he lived in Italy." Major stands gazing up into the eyes of the white figure above him. "I sent him a picture along with her measurements and asked him to sculpt my angel from the finest stone. "

"I'm sorry she can't see it."

"Oh, I think she sees it." Major says, smiling.

"You know we were all worried about you. For the past several months all you did was sit by her open grave and stare at her through the glass lid of the coffin." Captain speaks sincerely to Major and places a heavy hand on his friend's shoulder. "Tenny kept tellin' me that it just isn't right for a body to keep a grave open like that, much less sit by it every day."

"I know, and I'm sorry for the worry I caused you, but I just couldn't turn loose of her," he says, looking up into the angel's eyes.

"I'm relieved you finally decided to fill the grave and place the monument here."

"The monument took many a month to get, but it was well worth the wait. Besides, it couldn't have come at a better time."

"Why do you say that?" Captain asks curiously.

"She always liked spring, and we've placed her out here in time to watch the flowers bloom and the cotton sprout." He smiles at the tiny white statue. "She will like it here."

"Are you ready to go?" Captain places a bouquet of flowers at the base of the monument.

"You go on. I'll be with you in a minute," Major answers.

"I'll wait for you in the wagon." Captain leaves him alone.

Once more, Major reads the inscription on the monument. "Jennie, wife of Major Ray. Born March 16, 1871. Died March 24, 1915. Age 44 years and 8 days."

"When my work here on earth is done, I'll meet you in heaven," he whispers. Placing his lips against the cold stone, he kisses it. "Wait for me, my angel. Wait for me."

Illustration 18: The burial sites and monuments of Jennie and Major Ray. Hornersville, Missouri. The Hornersville Cemetery.

Illustrations

1. Page 45. A copy of the original letter Major wrote to Jennie from Trenton, Missouri, on July 25, 1890. The original letter is fourteen pages long and is currently owned by Mr. and Mrs. Charles Miller. (Parts of the letter have been omitted from this publication; however, it will be recorded in its complete form in the bilography.)

2. Page 89. This photograph is believed to be a wedding photograph of Jennie. The dress appears to have the same floral pattern as described in the February 13, 1891, *Yates Center Newspaper.* The photograph was obtained from Mrs. Imogene Young.

3. Page 105. Photograph of Major Ray standing between his mother, and his wife, Jennie. This photograph was obtained from the Monday, June 15,1959, *Daily Dunklin Democrat.* The newspaper was a gift from Johnny and Lavada Jones.

4. Page 150. Photograph of Hawaiian Queen Liliuokalani was obtained from the Sunday, January 10, 1993, *Jonesboro Sun.*

5. Page 174. Photograph of Major Ray and Jennie taken at the Adelaide Photo Company in Sydney, Australia. The photograph was taken during the first two weeks of May, 1892.

6. Page 191. A photograph from the June, 15, 1959, *Daily Dunklin Democrat.* Jennie Ray sits on a jenny.

7. Page 199. Annie Shields, Major, Jennie, and Captain Shields. Photograph courtesy Mrs. Edna Allen.

8. Page 205. Major Ray poses with his custom-made rifle, while Tige sits at his side. Photograph obtained from the June, 15, 1959, *Daily Dunklin Democrat*. Newspaper was a gift from Johnny and Lavada Jones.

9. Page 226. Little People, Major and Jennie Ray, along with Giant, Colonel Cooper stand among the group of sideshow performers in the 1898 Forepaugh-Sells Sideshow. Photograph courtesy Circus World Museum, Baraboo, Wisconsin.

10. Page 245. Autographed picture from Buffalo Bill to Major and Jennie. Photograph courtesy Mrs. Imogene Young.

11. Page 250. Photograph of Buffalo Bill's Wild West Sideshow. Major and Jennie are standing on the platform in the center. Captain Shields and Annie stand to the right in back row. Photograph courtesy Circus World Museum, Baraboo, Wisconsin.

12. Page 270. Photograph of the house Major build for Jennie in Hornersville. Today, only a small concrete slab remains where the porch once stood. Photograph courtesy Mrs. Pat Fraser.

13. Page 276. Jennie stands next to her housekeeper who has been identified as Tennessee (Tenny). Photograph courtesy Mrs. Imogene Young.

14. Page 279. Major poses as Buster Brown with his dog, Tige. The date of this photograph is between 1905-1914. Photograph courtesy Mrs. Imogene Young.

15. Page 284. Jennie stands next to one of several nurses who cared for her during her illness. Photograph courtesy Mrs. Imogene Young.

16. Page 285. A copy of the original letter Jennie sent to her parents while she stayed at the Missouri Baptist Sanitarium in Saint Louis. Letter courtesy Mrs. Imogene Young.

17. Page 290. Major Ray as Buster Brown poses on stage with his dog, Tige during his debut at the 1904 World's Fair. This was when Buster Brown was first introduced to the public as a real character. Photograph came from 1959 *Daily Dunklin Democrat.* The newspaper courtesy Johnny and Lavada Jones.

18. Page 304. Photograph of Jennie's monument sculpted by an Italian sculptor. The monument is her exact size and is sculpted in her image as an angel. Major's monument stands beside it with a picture of Buster Brown and Tige carved into the marble. Both monuments are located in the Hornersville Cemetery. Photograph by the author.